Foundation and Endowment Investing

Founded in 1807, John Wiley & Sons is the oldest independent publishing company in the United States. With offices in North America, Europe, Australia, and Asia, Wiley is globally committed to developing and marketing print and electronic products and services for our customers' professional and personal knowledge and understanding.

The Wiley Finance series contains books written specifically for finance and investment professionals as well as sophisticated individual investors and their financial advisors. Book topics range from portfolio management to e-commerce, risk management, financial engineering, valuation, and financial instrument analysis, as well as much more.

For a list of available titles, visit our Web site at www.WileyFinance.com.

Foundation and Endowment Investing

Philosophies and Strategies of Top Investors and Institutions

LAWRENCE E. KOCHARD, PhD, CFA
CATHLEEN M. RITTEREISER

John Wiley & Sons, Inc.

Published by John Wiley & Sons, Inc., Hoboken, New Jersey.
Published simultaneously in Canada.

Wiley Bicentennial logo: Richard J. Pacifico.

For general information on our other products and services or for technical support, please contact our Customer Care Department within the United States at (800) 762-2974, outside the United States at (317) 572-3993 or fax (317) 572-4002.

Wiley also publishes its books in a variety of electronic formats. Some content that appears in print may not be available in electronic books. For more information about Wiley products, visit our Web site at www.wiley.com.

Library of Congress Cataloging-in-Publication Data:

Kochard, Lawrence E., 1956-
Foundation and endowment investing : philosophies and strategies of
top investors and institutions / Lawrence E. Kochard, Cathleen M. Rittereiser.
p. cm.—(Wiley finance series)
Includes index.
ISBN 978-0-470-12233-4 (cloth)
1. Institutional investments. 2. Endowments—Finance. I. Rittereiser,
Cathleen M., 1960- II. Title.
HG4521.K5763 2008
332. 67′253—dc22

2007025168

Printed in the United States of America

10 9 8 7 6 5 4 3 2 1

Contents

For

*Firewalkers everywhere and the prudent men
standing by watching and laughing at them*

Our families and friends

Tug McGraw because "You Gotta Believe!"

Preface

I t has been nearly three years since I had the privilege of joining George-town University to help create an investment office at the country's oldest Catholic and Jesuit university. After joining Georgetown, I realized that our success would be helped by learning from the best practices of well-established investment offices at other institutions. We made an effort to reach out to colleagues in the endowment and foundation investment community to learn about the governance and investment processes that contributed to the success of their investment programs.

Additionally, for the last several years I have been lucky enough to teach undergraduate and graduate investment courses at the University of Virginia and Georgetown University. I currently teach a graduate course, Investment Management for Endowments and Pensions, at Georgetown University, which exposes students to the investment approach of large institutional investors. Topics covered include the purpose of the endowment and pension, portfolio choice, manager selection, asset allocation, risk management, and alternative asset class investing.

The text for the course has been *Pioneering Portfolio Management* by David Swensen, the chief investment officer of the Yale University endowment. David Swensen is the best-known and one of the most successful endowment CIOs, having achieved 16.3 percent per annum returns since he started at Yale, 21 years ago. Swensen's books (he wrote a second book aimed more to individual investors), a Harvard Business School case about the Yale investment office, and increasing attention by the business media (e.g., a February 18, 2007, *New York Times* article, "For Yale's Money Man, a Higher Calling") have exposed other investors to his approach to investing Yale's endowment.

Swensen's success over many market cycles clearly warrants the amount of attention he has garnered over the past few years. Other investors have become interested in learning about his "secret sauce." I have received suggestions from many Georgetown alumni that we should be "just like Yale." My response has always been that we should strive to achieve the process, philosophy, and discipline that contributed to Swensen's success, but shouldn't imitate the investments of Yale's that worked in the past. This "rearview mirror" approach to investing inevitably leads to disappointing results.

Reaching out to peers in the endowment and foundation community made me realize that other CIOs have had investment success similar to Swensen's. Having enjoyed reading books like *Market Wizards*, written by Jack Schwager, and *Investment Gurus*, by Peter Tanous, in which the authors interview portfolio managers to learn from their experiences, I tried to find a similar book about foundation and endowment CIOs. None existed. The world was familiar with David Swensen and, to a lesser extent, Harvard University's Jack Meyer, but it ended there.

I wanted my students and other investors to learn about the experiences of these other accomplished endowment and foundation CIOs. They have influenced me as much as Swensen, and I felt strongly that other investors, both institutional and individual, could benefit from hearing about the approaches and philosophies of endowment and foundation investors who deserve similar credit for the investment programs and offices they helped build.

I first met Cathleen Rittereiser from Alternative Asset Managers, LP, at a hedge fund conference in July 2002, and we became friends when I joined Georgetown in 2004, communicating primarily by e-mail. We attended the same conferences and shared similar opinions about the growing power and unsung talents of foundation and endowment CIOs. In 2005, we recognized that the combination of my vision for the book and endowment investing experience, Cathleen's writing skills and investment marketing experience, our network of industry contacts, and a great working relationship made us the right team to bring these investors together and write this book.

Having now interviewed these accomplished investors, I know readers will learn from their experiences, philosophies, and strategies and will be well positioned to make more informed and thoughtful investment decisions. It will give greater insight into how to approach asset allocation and investing for the long term, and a greater understanding of the mind-set and knowledge required to succeed in the current challenging investment environment.

We hope that their experiences and approaches will help guide other investors, including smaller institutions, family offices, and individual investors, just as my informal survey of other CIOs helped me establish "best practices" at Georgetown from an investment policy or "road-map" standpoint.

Taking a step back, we provide background on the foundation and investment community and will describe how and why this group has become a bigger and more influential investment force.

Successful people in any field don't stick their heads in the sand—they are always hoping to learn new ideas from other innovators and leaders in any field. As investors, we all want to do a better job establishing a disciplined and successful investment process and generate better returns on our portfolio whether it benefits an institution or our families.

Cathleen Rittereiser and I feel privileged to learn from these leading endowment and foundation investors and want to express our gratitude for their participation in the book. Our goal was to capture their thought processes, so that we and our readers would understand their philosophies and gain investment insight. We believe we have achieved our goal.

LAWRENCE E. KOCHARD
Georgetown University
June 2, 2007

Acknowledgments

When Larry Kochard first told me about his idea for this book and suggested we work together to write it, it seemed like a great idea, but...how would we do it? When could we do it? It seemed impossible. Yet just over two years later, we have written a book investors should find interesting and valuable, and we take great pride in having written it.

We could not have done it without each other and we could not have done it without the people we thank here.

Starting off, we must thank our employers and colleagues.

Randy Yanker and Rodney Yanker, the founders of Alternative Asset Managers, LP, and my other colleagues in the firm provided resources, support, lunch, and proofreading. I really appreciate their help. Also, we thank Ken Grant, who tested the concept with editors and helped us contact publishers.

From the Georgetown University investment office, we want to thank Justin Toumey for research assistance, analysis, and support; Meghan Woodhouse for coordination and logistics; and Christine Kelleher for editorial feedback and advice. Larry appreciates the support of his entire staff at the investment office and the members of the Georgetown investment committee. Because his students, past and present, inspired him to write this book, he thanks them as well.

Sandra Urie and Celia Dallas of Cambridge Associates spoke to us on background and graciously allowed us to use their original research in the text; Both Tim Barron from Rogers Casey and Dennis Hammond from Hammond Associates had helpful insights as well.

Andrea Szigethy of Morgan Creek Capital Management approached certain investors to ask for their participation and read early chapters, giving us valuable feedback.

Jason DeSena Trennert, managing partner and chief investment strategist, Strategas Research Partners, introduced us to Vinny Catalano, CFA president and global investment strategist with Blue Marble Research and author of *Sectors and Styles: A New Approach to Outperforming the Market*. Vinny introduced us to Wiley.

We especially want to thank Kevin Commins, the acquisitions editor at Wiley. He decided to publish the book, has supported our ideas, and has worked with us to make it happen.

Elden Mayer and Sam Kirschner gave me a copy of their book, *The Investor's Guide to Hedge Funds*, and Sam advised us on how to put together a book like this. Next time, I will do it his way.

My dear friends and fellow authors, Dave Singleton and Johanna Skilling, gave me advice and assistance preparing the proposal, interviewing, writing tips, and managing workflow. Dave also helped introduce the proposal to agents. I paid him back by being "The Spoiler."

Stephen R. Quazzo of Transwestern Investment Company, LLC, an old friend from Merrill Lynch, had several good ideas and contacts and made an important introduction for us.

Jeff Skelton and Michael Henman at Symphony Asset Management put the wheels in motion. Thanks.

Emilie Herman has been patient, helpful, and supportive and deserves a prize for working with first-time authors with full-time jobs.

Finally, we thank family, friends, and anyone we forgot.

On behalf of Larry Kochard and myself, with great appreciation,

CATHLEEN M. RITTEREISER
June 8, 2007

About the Authors

Lawrence E. Kochard was appointed chief investment officer at Georgetown University in June 2004. In addition to serving as CIO, he teaches investment courses for the McDonough School of Business at Georgetown. Previously, Larry was managing director of equity and hedge fund investments for the Virginia Retirement System (VRS) and adjunct professor of finance for the McIntire School of Commerce at the University of Virginia. Prior to joining VRS, he was a full-time faculty member at UVA. Before his return to academia, Larry accumulated over 10 years of experience in corporate finance and capital markets. He currently serves on the investment committee of St. Louis University and chairs the investment committee of the College of William & Mary.

Larry holds a BA in economics from the College of William & Mary, an MBA in finance and accounting from the University of Rochester, an MA and PhD in economics from the University of Virginia, and is a CFA charter holder. He is married and has four children.

Cathleen M. Rittereiser is an alternative investment sales and marketing executive focused on the institutional investor market, particularly foundations and endowments. Cathleen has held sales, marketing, and client relationship management positions at leading asset management firms, investment banks, and research firms. Her experience includes serving as Vice President, Marketing for Alternative Asset Managers, LP (AAM) an independent investment boutique specializing in emerging hedge fund managers. Before joining AAM, she handled business development for Symphony Asset Management, a Nuveen Investments company, and began her career at Merrill Lynch.

An accomplished public speaker, Cathleen has participated in investment industry conference panels on topics ranging from securities valuation to the impact of technology and has extensive knowledge of digital media, social networking and Web 2.0 technology. Cathleen leads 100 Mets Fans in Hedge Funds, an organization she co-founded with Larry Kochard, and writes and performs comedy material. Cathleen received an AB from Franklin and Marshall College and an MBA from New York University's Stern School of Business. She lives in New York City and at www.cathleenrittereiser.com.

Foundations and Endowments Rise as Powerful Institutional Investors

CHAPTER 1

The Evolution of Foundation and Endowment Investment Management

From Poorhouses to Powerhouses

Foundations and endowments have become investment powerhouses, managed by sophisticated investors using advanced investment techniques. Despite a smaller asset base than pension funds, they have become increasingly influential institutional investors because their long-term perspective gives them the latitude to take more investment risks and the impetus to adopt new asset classes and strategies long before other investors. While the number of foundations and endowments is not necessarily growing, the numbers that have chosen to dedicate professionals to their investments has grown. There are more organizations with in-house investment staffs or new chief investment officers (CIOs) than ever.

It could have turned out differently. Until 1969 most endowment funds had conservative portfolios, which underperformed other investors. If McGeorge Bundy at the Ford Foundation had not intervened, foundations and endowments might have become investment poorhouses today.

This chapter chronicles the evolution of foundation and endowment investment management from the first gifts to Harvard to the important changes set in motion by McGeorge Bundy and the Ford Foundation, the global economic and market conditions driving investment performance, and the rise to prominence of foundation and endowment CIOs.

It will give an overview of how these institutions became so powerful and a rationale for profiling the talented CIOs who got them there.

ORIGINS OF ENDOWMENT MANAGEMENT

Endowments can be traced back to the fifteenth century, when donors in England made gifts to churches, schools, and universities to support them in perpetuity. Usually, these gifts carried the restriction that the principal (the donated amount) needed to be preserved, although the income from the endowment could be spent. Donors frequently restrict the use of an endowment for a specific purpose, such as professorships or scholarships. Endowments are intended to be a permanent source of income for institutions that traditionally did not have income.[1]

The core pool of assets managed by either foundations or educational institutions is known as its endowment, although in the investing community, *endowment* has become shorthand for describing the investments of educational institutions. Throughout the text, *endowment* will generally be used to describe the assets of educational institutions or a specific institution. In this chapter and occasionally throughout the book, the word will refer to the assets of nonprofit organizations in general.

Harvard University traces its endowment back to 1649 when two members of the class of 1642 who also were the school's first teaching fellows, John Bulkeley and George Downing, and two from the class of 1646, Samuel Winthrop and John Alcock, gave the college a real estate parcel. The one-time cow yard was planted with apple trees and became known as the "Fellow's Orchard." The land remains part of the Harvard campus; the school's Widener Library occupies part of the site. In 1669, lumber merchants guaranteed the school a payment of 60 pounds per year for seven years and met the obligation by providing lumber products that the school then sold. Today, close to 11,000 separate funds constitute the Harvard endowment, the majority restricted to supporting specific programs such as scholarships, building maintenance, teaching, research and student activities and designated to support that purpose in perpetuity.[2]

In 1890, Trinity College, a Methodist institution in North Carolina, had chosen the city of Raleigh over Durham for its new location. Behind-the-scenes maneuvers by Durham community leaders and family members led Washington Duke to pledge $85,000 for an endowment to locate the school in Durham. With that pledge in hand, Trinity's president, John F. Crowell, secured a donation of land on the western edge of the city. When Duke made the formal offer to the board of trustees on March 20, citizens of Durham had raised an additional $9,361 to support the school. Trinity College is now known as Duke University.[3]

Those anecdotes exemplify the origins of modern endowment funds and foreshadow how endowment assets have been acquired, managed, and manipulated for over three centuries. Harvard's cow-yard gift displays several factors that have characterized endowment management, including the generosity and corresponding influence of powerful alumni, handling gifts of property or goods, and the "naming gift" and "matching gift." The prospect of a large financial gift appears to have resulted in the trustees of Trinity College backing out of a commitment to Raleigh, although one could argue that they met their fiduciary responsibility and followed the "prudent man rule." Traditionally, committees of wealthy, powerful men donated and managed the assets, volunteering their services even when lacking expertise, until 1969, 300 years after the lumber merchants donated their products to Harvard.

Powerful, wealthy alumni of institutions or benefactors of foundations can still exert enormous influence over an organization and its investments, but the shift to a more structured, modern, and professional form of investment management began to take shape in 1969. Academic research—namely, Markowitz's modern portfolio theory—and evidence that excessively restrictive endowment management policies thwarted asset preservation came to the forefront with two groundbreaking and influential studies commissioned by the Ford Foundation. The changes in fiduciary law and investment policy changed endowment management, creating this formidable investor base.

Unbeknownst to John Bulkeley and George Downing, their cow-yard donation would form the cornerstone not only of the Widener Library, but also of a powerful, influential institutional investment community led by prestigious, professional, talented, and accomplished CIOs.

CATALYSTS OF CHANGE

Toward the end of the 1960s, McGeorge Bundy, then the head of the Ford Foundation (a leading donor to education), became concerned about the rising costs of higher education. He began to study the management of endowment assets to determine if they could be managed more productively and, if so, to assist in alleviating the problem.

At the time, these assets tended to be managed by wealthy trustees guided by personal trust law. Funds were not commingled in investment vehicles, trustees were forbidden to delegate investment decisions, and rules limited the endowments to spending only dividend and interest payments. The funds were managed to generate current yield and to maintain principal over time and invested in bonds and other fixed-income vehicles rather than equities. The use of cost accounting, recording the price of a security when purchased and adjusting the value only when sold, obscured the fact that bonds actually had been declining in value and that equities generally delivered superior returns over the long term.

A narrow interpretation of the famous original prudent man rule ruling of *Harvard College v. Amory* in 1830 also limited the investment approach. In the original case, Harvard and Massachusetts General Hospital would each receive half the estate of John McLean when his widow died. The executors, the Amories, had invested the assets in stocks. Fearing the loss of their eventual principal, the two institutions sued because they believed stocks were too risky. In ruling against Harvard and Mass General, and in favor of the Amories' right to invest the assets, Justice J. Putnam wrote:

> *All that can be required of a trustee to invest, is, that he shall conduct himself faithfully and exercise a sound discretion. He is to observe how men of prudence, discretion and intelligence manage their own affairs, not in regard to speculation, but in regard to the permanent disposition of their funds, considering the probable income, as well as the probable safety of the capital to be invested.*

Thus, the prudent man rule became the standard for managing trustlike assets. The rule became more narrowly interpreted over time, primarily due to the influential works of Professor Austin Wakeman Scott, "Restatements of Trusts" (1935) and "Scott on Trusts" (1939). He restated the rule in such a way that modern academics and legal scholars agree that it lost its flexibility and led fiduciaries to evaluate investments individually, rather than as part of a portfolio.[4]

Before Bundy addressed this issue, there had been signs that the approach to investing these assets needed to change. The birth of modern portfolio theory in Harry Markowitz's 1952 paper, "Portfolio Selection," reinvented investment thinking and eventually earned him the Nobel Prize in economics.[5] In a less seismic, yet still important change, the College Retirement Equities Fund (CREF) had introduced total return and market value accounting to the community in 1952. In 1966, the book *Pension Funds: Measuring Investment Performance* (The Graduate School of Business) by Peter Dietz also made the case for measuring total return and implementing market value accounting. Since many trustees also had leadership roles in companies and familiarity with these concepts, they started to consider applying them to endowment management. Investment books and academic papers, including research by Yale University's treasurer, John Ecklund, shifted thinking by persuasively advocating for investing in growth company equities.

But it took the leadership of McGeorge Bundy and the resources of the Ford Foundation to cause change. In the Ford Foundation annual report published in 1967, writing on endowments Bundy said:

We believe there may be room for great improvement here. It is far from clear that trustees have reason to be proud of their performance in making money for their colleges. We recognize the risks of unconventional investing, but the true test of performance in the handling of money is the record of achievement, not the opinion of the respectable. We have the impression that over the long run caution has cost our colleges and universities much more than imprudence or excessive risk taking. The Foundation intends to make a careful study of this whole field.

The Foundation commissioned two studies, released in 1969 as "Reports to the Ford Foundation." The first, "The Law and Lore of Endowment Funds" by William L. Cary and Craig B. Bright, addressed legal principles that had governed endowment investing and recommended changes in thinking and policies. The second, "Managing Educational Endowments," by Robert R. Barker, analyzed investment performance and recommended changes to investment processes and procedures.

The Law and Lore of Endowment Funds

Bundy realized the mistaken belief that personal trust laws applied to endowments impeded change. He charged William L. Cary and Craig B. Bright, lawyers with the firm Patterson, Belknap & Webb in New York City with reviewing and reporting on these legal constraints. Mr. Cary had been the chairman of the Securities and Exchange Commission and was the Dwight Professor of Law at Columbia University.

The report made several conclusions that essentially released trustees from their self-imposed investment prisons and cleared the path for permanent changes in managing endowment assets. They included the following:

- Endowments are corporations with one beneficiary and were not subject to the laws governing personal trusts with many beneficiaries.
- Trustees represent the institution and have responsibility for establishing spending and investment policy.
- Trustees could delegate the execution of investment policies to qualified, outside investment advisers but retained responsibility for supervising and monitoring advisers.

The authors also recommended establishing a new uniform state law that would allow trustees to consider the total returns of the portfolio from realized and unrealized gains along with dividend and interest income when determining the spending policy. This directly led to the formulation in 1972 of the Uniform Management of Institutional Funds Act.[6]

Managing Educational Endowments

Bundy was not just concerned about the management of educational endowments; he was also concerned about the Ford Foundation's ability to manage its assets and meet its commitments to supporting higher education. In the 1966 Ford Foundation annual report, he noted that an incremental 1 percent improvement in performance of the Foundation's assets would double the amount of money it could grant. The second report, also released in 1969, "Managing Educational Endowments," by Robert R. Barker (not the famed television game show host, but an academic and member of the Smith College Investment Committee), studied the ossified investment techniques hindering endowment growth and performance.

The report compared the performance of the endowments at "fifteen important educational institutions" from 1959 to 1968 to balanced and growth-oriented mutual funds and the University of Rochester's professional investment office. The 8.7 percent average annual performance of the endowments lagged all the others. The balanced funds beat endowments by only 0.5 percent, but the growth funds and Rochester delivered 14.6 percent and 14.4 percent, respectively, almost a 6 percent per year difference.

The report blamed the poor performance of endowments on the management of trustee committees, stating that their focus on avoiding losses and maximizing current income had led them to choose bonds at the expense of better-performing growth-oriented equities because the latter provided virtually no dividend yield. It predicted that this approach would result in "highly adverse consequences for long-term endowment values" and recommended that "endowment managers must be able to select securities on the basis of total return over the long term rather than on the basis of maximizing dividends and interest to help in balancing the operating budget." The report also proclaimed that "delegation to an able professional portfolio manager who has a capable organization around him is essential for successful investment management." The report advocated a spending rule based on a percentage of the three-year moving average of the assets' market value.[7] In fact, the Smith College board of trustees implemented the total return and market value accounting approach in 1969 as a result of the research.[8]

Also in 1969, Section 4944 of the Internal Revenue Code established the "no jeopardizing investment" rule for foundations and contained language that allowed an investment to be considered as part of a portfolio.

Many historians consider 1969 a seminal year in U.S. history. Neil Armstrong walked on the moon, Woodstock happened in upstate New York, and the New York Mets won the World Series. It also became a seminal year in investment history. Barker's investment thinking, Cary and Bright's legal thinking, and even the IRS's policy thinking converged and enabled permanent, substantial changes in the approach to investing endowment and foundation assets that led to their investment prominence today.

Transition

Since few institutions had the capacity to manage their endowments under this new investment approach, one of the first outcomes of the Ford Foundation work was the establishment of the Commonfund, an investment company that pooled assets of its members, initially educational endowments, to manage the investments professionally. The Ford Foundation seeded the Commonfund with a $2.8 million grant. The firm launched its funds on July 1, 1971, with a total of $72 million from 63 endowments.[9] The firm remains a leading asset manager and thought leader for the endowments of colleges, universities, foundations, and health care systems and has helped lead changes in asset allocation and asset class selection—such as forays into private capital and alternatives—that have influenced the management of endowments. In 1991, the Investment Fund for Foundations was formed to serve foundation investment officers.

In 1972, the work of Cary and Bright directly led to the passage of the Uniform Management of Institutional Funds Act Building on the prudent man precedent, it codified their recommendations and set a new standard for managing foundation and endowment assets. Following is a summary of the act from the National Conference of Commissioners of Uniform State Laws:

> *The Uniform Management of Institutional Funds Act was promulgated by the Uniform Law Commissioners in 1972, and since has been adopted in 46 states. This act clarifies the right of governing boards to invest funds of such institutions as hospitals and colleges for total return. This means governing boards could, for example, invest in growth stocks paying low or no dividends but having a high potential for appreciation in long-term value, rather than concentrate entirely on investments with immediate high income yields.*

> *The act also sets a standard of conduct for governing boards of institutions. This would require members to exercise ordinary business care and prudence under the facts and circumstances prevailing at the time of the action or decision and . . . consider long and short term needs of the institution in carrying out its . . . purposes, its present and anticipated financial requirements, expected total return on its investments, price level trends, and general economic conditions.*
>
> *Under this act, governing boards would be allowed to retain professional investment counsel and managers, and to seek removal of restrictions on gifts which have become obsolete, inappropriate, or impracticable.*
>
> *The act also defines an institution as an incorporated or unincorporated organization organized and operated exclusively for educational, religious, charitable, or other eleemosynary purposes, or a governmental organization to the extent that it holds funds exclusively for any of these purposes.*[10]

Although it took almost 300 years for endowment asset management to experience any substantive change, once it began it spurred more change. Between 1972 and 2006, these institutions transformed from a group of risk-averse, rule-driven, volunteer investors to respected investment organizations, overseen by talented professionals managing increasingly complex and sophisticated portfolios. Today, the Harvard endowment would probably not sue the Amories—it might even encourage them to take more risk. A review of that period shows the significant developments that created this transformation.

TRANSFORMATION

Despite the progress that had been made to allow for more sophisticated investment decisions, up until the late 1980s, for most foundations and endowments that meant adjusting their percentage allocations to stocks and bonds, in favor of more stocks. A study of endowment growth conducted by the Commonfund in 1990 showed the need for more progress. The funds had grown substantially while the level of investment sophistication had grown imperceptibly.

Still Lagging in 1990

Even though the research team had fragmented and limited data, it had enough evidence to conclude that the investment process needed to evolve further. Using a 1962 Department of Health, Education and Welfare survey of 105 endowments as a base, the researchers collected enough usable data from 35 organizations and information on asset allocation "from only a handful" of institutions. The study showed that the bulk of asset growth came from investment performance, primarily attributed to the bull market in equities that began in 1982, yet that return percentage lagged major benchmarks. The spending rate had averaged 4.4 percent of market value, a rate that has remained historically consistent. Because they had such little relevant historical asset allocation data, yet recognized the importance of the allocation policy, they analyzed the most recent (1989) asset allocation mix of the participating institutions.

The analysis showed that endowments continued to follow more conservative investment policies—for example, weighting equities 53.7 percent when the recommended level was 60 percent—that resulted in continued underperformance. The majority of the equity allocations invested only in the U.S. equity market even though it represented only 40 percent of global market capitalization. In fact, in presenting the results authors referred to foreign stock as an "alternative asset." Although the Commonfund was recommending a 10 percent allocation to nonmarketable alternatives—primarily private equity assets—the average endowment in the study had a 3.5 percent allocation. The authors presented asset allocation guidelines, reiterating that diversification into perceived "riskier" investments could increase return while reducing the overall risk of the portfolio, and cautioned overseers that performance would most likely remain subpar if they remained risk averse and would hamper their ability to achieve their long-term objectives.[11]

Global Developments Bring Growth, Challenges

Since the release of the Commonfund survey in 1990, important developments in global financial markets, government, and industry have spurred asset growth but have made the investment environment more challenging. Foundations and endowments have become investment powers because they responded to these conditions by adding sophisticated investment talent and building increasingly diversified and complex portfolios. Those developments include the following.

Financial Markets The bull market in equities that began in 1982 persisted with some troughs through the 1990s, culminating with the technology and dot-com boom. Endowments and foundations still had significant U.S. equity exposure—the total annual compound return of the Standard and Poor's (S&P) 500 including the reinvestment of dividend from September 1,

1982, to March 31, 2000, was 19.75 percent—and benefited from this performance. By the late 1980s, endowments and foundations had started to invest more heavily in private assets, such as venture capital, and the tech investment boom drove performance in those investments as well. Then came the bust. By September 30, 2002, the equity markets had lost $6 trillion in market cap.[12]

In both fiscal year 2001 and 2002, foundations and endowments lost market value. While most of the largest foundations and endowments had invested in hedge funds for many years, market conditions from 2000 to 2003 led more investors into them because of their risk/reward characteristics and diversification benefits. Driven by the demand and attractive compensation structure, more hedge funds offering a variety of portfolio construction approaches across an increasing number of asset classes have formed. Hedge fund manager selection requires more thorough due diligence and specialized knowledge. Additionally, investors contend with innovative new derivative securities such as credit default swaps, hard assets such as timber, or less familiar international markets.

Technology   The advances in technology products that fueled the bull market in technology stocks in the late 1990s and led to outstanding investment returns impacted institutions in other ways. Technology has helped investors become more sophisticated by making better analytic tools more widely available at a much lower cost. It has also forced investors to become more sophisticated by providing faster, more efficient information delivery systems that have leveled the playing field and reduced the ability of investors to gain an information edge. The rapid, instantaneous distribution of information has increased the pace of the markets. Software analytic packages make sophisticated analysis more available and affordable and enable investors to analyze and measure risk more efficiently and effectively.

Mass ability to access and analyze information, while making certain investment functions easier, has made navigating the markets and finding opportunities much more difficult. Advanced technology has helped grow endowment and foundation assets, by enabling efficient processes and earning substantial returns in the tech boom, but has created a need for more qualified, talented people to make investment choices based on what that technology has wrought.

Asset Allocation   For foundations and endowments, the thorough and rigorous approach to asset allocation policy has been a major driver of growth and professionalism since they were liberated by the Ford Foundation and the Uniform Management of Institutional Funds Act. Research published in 1986 by a team led by Gary Brinson concluded that most of the variation in portfolio returns stemmed from differences in asset allocation. This finding became investment management gospel and remains so, since researchers have failed to disprove it in any meaningful way. Larger funds began moving away from the generic 70/30, 60/40 equity/bond mixes into new asset classes and toward customized policies, and others have followed. The commitment to devising and implementing institution-specific asset allocation policies and expanding into new asset classes has made these institutions influential investors, but has increased the need for skilled CIOs.

Manager Selection   The explosion of new asset classes and derivative securities and the ability to employ technology to construct portfolios and manage risk has resulted in investment managers with increasingly narrow or complicated specialties. Finding managers with an edge among such proliferation adds another layer of complexity to managing the endowment. Muted returns throughout traditional asset classes have forced CIOs to seek opportunities in new strategies or less liquid asset classes. Pursuing a new asset class requires them to learn it, find specialized managers, and then evaluate whether those managers actually have the proper skills. The growth in the breadth and depth of hedge fund strategies and the need for specialized expertise to evaluate them provides a good example of the challenge.

Globalization   Since the Commonfund study in 1990, endowments and foundations have broadened their allocations to international securities markets including emerging markets such as India, China, and Russia. Besides the diversification and investment return opportunities available in other markets, globalization has influenced foundation and endowment investing in other ways.

Global investing not only adds investment risk to the portfolio; it also adds more managerial, oversight, and operational risks. Certain systems and communications technologies are less developed. Securities regulations may be weak and insufficiently protect investors. Differences in government policies or human rights violations can adversely impact investment performance and raise concerns about socially responsible investing. Even time zone differences and expending time and money to travel to monitor the manager create more external risks. None of those risks should preclude an investment in global markets, but they must be controlled. Information technology has fostered globalization by allowing efficient information flow 24 hours a day and 7 days a week but speeds information dissemination and devaluation. Despite the complications, a well-managed endowment almost has no choice but to invest in international markets.

Government   The government has had some influence on the foundation and endowment investment community because Employee Retirement Income Security Act of 1974 (ERISA) pension laws have influenced all institutions.[13] In the case of foundations, government influences the management of the assets because of its stricter tax policies. In the case of educational endowments, government has withdrawn much financial support and forced them to deal with painful financial realities.[14] Costs, including student aid, continue to increase while federal and state aid packages have decreased. Universities depend on endowment income more than ever, increasing the need to preserve and grow assets and achieve investment performance. Alice Handy, the former president of the University of Virginia Investment Company, said at an industry conference, "State support had declined to less than 10 percent of the University of Virginia's operating budget, increasing the reliance on the endowment."[15] Even private schools have lost research funding. "Trustees no longer have a choice about managing their endowments."[16]

These developments have made asset management more complex. To keep pace, organizations need sophisticated knowledge and expertise in asset allocation, markets, and securities. Decisions take more time because of the need to analyze more data and choose among more investments. Investment committee members can no longer substitute for full-time investment talent, because the task requires too much labor and specialized skill. Institutions need their assets to produce returns in a more complicated and challenging environment and need talented professionals to manage them.

THE RISE OF THE CHIEF INVESTMENT OFFICER

Today, endowments and foundations represent substantial pools of assets that support and sustain the mission of the institutions. As of fiscal 2005, an estimated 746 educational endowments in Canada and the United States held assets worth $299 billion, as measured by the National Association of College and University Business Officers (NACUBO) survey.[17] The Foundation Center counted over 60,000 foundations of all types with approximately $480 billion in assets. The top 100 foundations manage over a third of all foundation assets.[18]

The actions of McGeorge Bundy and the Ford Foundation not only set the stage for the growth of the assets—between 1980 and 2005, Harvard's endowment grew 1,508 percent, Yale grew 2,176 percent, and University of Texas 821 percent—but also freed these organizations from stultified and misinformed investment policies and enabled them to develop into sophisticated investment organizations and influential leaders of the institutional investment community.

Despite their leadership, or maybe because of it, foundations and endowments face an increasingly murky and complex investment landscape. This excerpt from a Foundation Center report explains the market conditions CIOs face:

> *In the latter half of the 1990s, the soaring stock market and robust economy and the amount of new gifts and bequests from donors to their existing foundations were the key drivers for the increased value of foundation assets. The rapid rise in personal wealth during this period also led many individuals to create foundations. Between 2000 and 2002, however, the stock market decline and a sluggish economy caused a 10.5 percent drop in the value of foundation assets overall. (Many of the largest foundations experienced a much larger decrease in their assets.) The return of positive stock market performance in 2003 helped to reverse this trend. However, the 9.5 percent rise in foundation assets in 2003 was followed by slower 7.1 percent growth in 2004 and an estimated 2 to 4 percent increase in 2005. This slowing rate of growth in assets, combined with the unprecedented two-year decrease in the value of their assets between 2000 and 2002, appears to have made foundations more cautious about increasing their levels of giving. In both 2004 and 2005, the rate of growth in foundations' giving has lagged a couple of points behind the rate of growth in their prior years' assets.*[19]

Today, foundations and endowments find more complexity throughout their investment process, including asset allocation, markets, securities, and manager selection. Cambridge Associates compared various asset allocation policies and produced the efficient frontier graph seen in (Figure 1.1).

The graph shows that the most optimal risk-adjusted return portfolio, *85%/15% Diversified*, is the most complex, highly diversified portfolio with the most specific exposure to alternative investments. Complexity does not just exist because of global trends and proliferating asset classes; it exists because it provides the best chance to achieve outstanding performance.

The complexity has driven the need for professional management of the assets and prompted foundation and endowment trustees to hire full-time investment professionals as CIOs. "Before 2000, the title 'chief investment officer' didn't even register on the database of the College and University Professional Association for Human Resources," said Michael Sullivan of the University of St. Thomas at a 2005 event. As of 2004, there were 100.

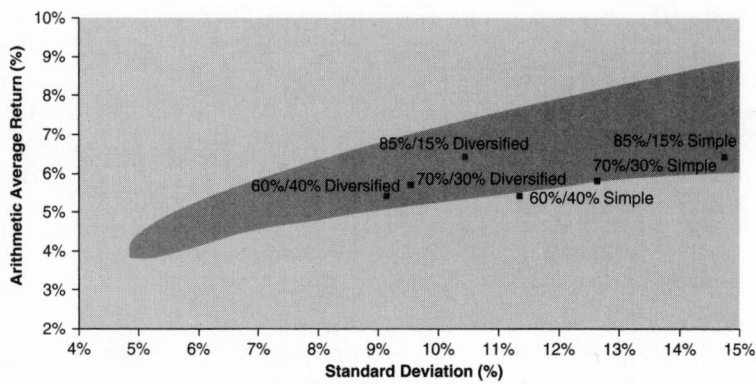

	Simple	Diversified	Simple	Diversified	Simple	Diversified
	60%/40%	60%/40%	70%/30%	70%/30%	85%/15%	85%/15%
U.S. Equity	60.0%	30.0%	70.0%	30.0%	85.0%	20.0%
Global ex U.S. Equity	- - -	12.5	- - -	12.5	- - -	15.0
Absolute Return	- - -	2.5	- - -	5.0	- - -	10.0
Hedge Funds	- - -	2.5	- - -	5.0	- - -	10.0
Venture Capital	- - -	2.5	- - -	4.0	- - -	7.5
Private Equity	- - -	2.5	- - -	3.5	- - -	7.5
REITs	- - -	- - -	- - -	1.0	- - -	5.0
Real Estate	- - -	5.0	- - -	4.0	- - -	2.5
Commodities	- - -	2.5	- - -	5.0	- - -	7.5
U.S. Fixed Income	40.0	40.0	30.0	30.0	15.0	15.0
Real Arithmetic Return	5.4%	5.4%	5.8%	5.7%	6.4%	6.4%
Standard Deviation	11.4%	9.2%	12.7%	9.6%	14.8%	10.5%
Real CompoundReturn	4.8%	5.0%	5.0%	5.3%	5.4%	5.9%
Arithmetic Return/Risk	0.47	0.59	0.46	0.59	0.43	0.61
Sharpe Ratio	0.39	0.48	0.38	0.49	0.36	0.51

C | A
CAMBRIDGE ASSOCIATES LLC

FIGURE 1.1 Comparative Asset Allocation Policies
Note: Unconstrained frontier assumptions.
Source: Exhibit reprinted with permission from Cambridge Associates LLC. This exhibit cannot be reproduced without written permission from Cambridge Associates.

That same year, executive search firm Heidrick and Struggles counted 20 CIO searches with 8 representing newly created positions.[20]

While some of this shift grew out of the need for professional investment management, it also grew out of the fact that the foundations and the universities themselves have become more complex enterprises. Treasurers and chief financial officers now have too many challenges in their primary responsibilities to manage assets on the side.

Andrew Golden, president of Princeton University Investment Company (PRINCO), speaking at the Goldman Sachs Institute Conference, stated that a CIO is needed for a number of reasons. When he started, the trustees had so much involvement in all decisions that they could focus only on getting the most important items accomplished. He thought the organization had missed opportunities to add value by implementing more effectively with more focus on the details. By transferring responsibility to the investment staff and establishing policies that allowed trustees to focus on the long term, PRINCO was better positioned.[21] The CIO can also reinforce fiduciary responsibility. The CIO can take full-time ownership of the process, make sound financial decisions, and stave off investment decisions that previously might have been made for social reasons.

In *The Paradox of Choice: Why More is Less* (Ecco, 2004), Barry Schwartz studied complexity created by too much choice. The complexity of choice will challenge foundation and endowment CIOs in the years ahead. There are more opportunities, more risks, more asset classes, more products, more intellectual capital, more technological advances, and more competition for good information, ideas, and investments.

LEARNING FROM HISTORY

In 1969, foundation and endowment trustees faced the paradox of *no* choice. Constrained by erroneous views of the "law and the lore of endowments," the assets languished and could have dwindled away if Bundy had not acted.

Foundations and endowments have always needed talented CIOs—they just did not know it in 1669 or 1969. Institutions that recognized the need early have benefited from the expertise of a number of the CIOs profiled in this book. Most foundations and endowments will continue to need capable, knowledgeable, decisive CIOs or equivalents because the income from investment returns has become more important while the ability to generate the returns has become more difficult.

The CIOs chronicled in this book represent the best of the last 35 years of foundation and endowment investing. We have profiled experienced CIOs who participated in making the foundation and endowment investment community the powerful base it is today and those who will lead the community over the next 30 years. These smart, creative, insightful, and successful investors have gone unheralded until now. They will become even more influential in the years ahead as more organizations add CIOs. Reading their stories and sharing their knowledge, experience, and advice will benefit investors and demonstrate why endowment and foundation CIOs have become and will remain forces in the investment world.

CHAPTER 2

Foundation and Endowment Investing 101

Essential Practices of a Successful CIO

F oundations and endowments represent substantial pools of capital dedicated to supporting the mission and operations of their organizations in perpetuity. They have similar investment profiles and approaches, characterized by the much longer-term investment time horizon compared to other investors. Since the assets are managed on behalf of a beneficiary, the chief investment officer (CIO) serves as a fiduciary and usually reports to an investment committee comprised of the organization's board members, trustees and outside advisors. Those individuals also function as fiduciaries. As fiduciaries, foundation and endowment CIOs and committees employ a standard, structured investment process to ensure thorough analysis and prudent decisions.

It is important for any institutional investor to establish a governance and investment process that is consistent with the people involved and goals of the institution. This chapter outlines the main components of the investment process executed by foundation and endowment CIOs. It will describe certain similarities and differences between the two types of organizations that influence investment policy. It will also cover fiduciary responsibility, regulations, and investment committees.

FIDUCIARY PRINCIPLES

CIOs, investment staff, trustees, board members, and consultants all function as fiduciaries of foundations and endowment investment funds and must consider that responsibility paramount when managing or advising these funds.

Very simply, a *fiduciary* is defined as a person who has legal responsibility for managing money or property on behalf of another person or entity, exercises discretionary control or authority over assets, and/or acts as a trusted professional provider of continuous and comprehensive investment advice. Driven by the tenets of care and loyalty, fiduciaries must manage a prudent investment process that includes defining, implementing, and evaluating an investment plan.

Two pieces of legislation guide the fiduciary process relating to foundation and endowment investing. The Uniform Management of Institutional Funds Act (UMIFA) was enacted in 1972 and gave educational institutions and endowments more latitude to invest under a "prudent-man" rule and to implement spending policies based on the results of total return investing.[1]

The Uniform Prudent Investor Act (UPIA) defines guidelines known as "The Uniform Fiduciary Standards of Care," which state that you must:

1. Know standards, laws, and trust provisions.
2. Diversify assets to the specific risk/return profile of the beneficiary or client.
3. Prepare investment policy statement.
4. Use "prudent experts" (investment managers) and document due diligence.
5. Control and account for investment expenses.
6. Monitor the activities of "prudent experts."
7. Avoid conflicts of interest and prohibited transactions.[2]

Fiduciaries at times have misinterpreted the prudent man rule to mean the "conservative man" rule. The standard does not mean the fiduciary must choose the most conservative investments; it means that the process of choosing those investments must be conducted in a prudent manner. If necessary, a review of the investment analysis and decision process would determine whether a standard of prudence has been met. Thus, aggressive and unconventional investments can be considered prudent, while a conservative investment that does not meet the investment goals of the organization could be considered imprudent if implemented without the appropriate review process.[3]

MISSION STATEMENT

Before we discuss the investment process, we first must understand the purpose of the portfolio and objectives of the investment office. Simply stated, the endowment is the permanent capital of the nonprofit institution, providing funding for its academic or philanthropic mission for current and future students or beneficiaries. Meeting this objective involves designing an investment program that addresses the needs of all generations of students or programs by balancing the risks and returns of different asset allocations and mix of investment managers. David Swensen writes in *Pioneering Portfolio Management*:

> *Understanding the purposes of accumulating assets represents the first step in the investment process. Permanent funds provide institutions with greater independence, increased financial stability, and the means to create a margin of excellence. Focusing on the fundamental purposes of an endowment provides a firm foundation for developing a sensible investment process.*

Merely delivering investment returns is not enough. To successfully define and implement an investment policy and program, the CIO, staff, and fiduciaries must understand the mission and objectives of the organization the funds support.

Mission statement considerations related to the investment process include:

- The expectations for the fund as a source of support near term and long term.
- The organization's image to donors, regulators and recipients.
- Legal requirements (such as foundation excise taxes).
- Characteristics of the organization's programs.
- Specific limitations imposed by donors.

INVESTMENT POLICY

An important first step is establishing the investment policy and documenting it in an investment policy statement. The investment policy statement lays out the investment objectives, governance, and process to be used by the investment staff. Before making any investments, an institution must develop such policies to provide a framework for investing. An investment policy statement defines important functions of the investment office and responsibilities of the CIO and investment committee and describes the decisions and policies regarding each aspect of the policy. The statement includes:

- Objectives
- Spending policy

- Asset allocation objectives and process:
  - Asset-class definitions and objectives
  - Investment risk
  - Rebalancing
- Investment policy implementation
- Benchmarks
- Governance

To assist in writing an investment policy statement for Georgetown, in 2004, Larry Kochard, coauthor of this book, surveyed approaches to decision making and asset allocation at 22 endowments, foundations, and pensions with total assets exceeding $100 billion. This was not a formal survey but rather conversations with investment professionals and CIOs at other institutions who either had an interesting approach to investing or recently wrestled with the challenge of establishing an investment office from scratch using best practices. This experience was one of the catalysts for interviewing the CIOs for this book. This earlier survey helped clarify the range of alternative models used by endowment investment offices, focusing on the interaction between investment committees and investment staffs and the process for making asset allocation changes. The remainder of this chapter discusses the important parts of the investment policy statement and its implementation.

Objectives

In formulating the investment policy, the CIO needs to understand specific income and investment objectives of the organization. This includes:

- Type of organization
- Total return goal
- Expected inflows: gifts, bequests
- Liquidity needed
- Risk tolerance of the board, investment committee, and investment team

Differences between Foundations and Endowments   Whether an organization is a foundation or an endowment influences the investment objectives and policies of the institution. Differences between the two types of institutions include:

- *Time horizon.* Not all foundations aim to exist in perpetuity and may intend to spend down the principal over a set time period. The most prominent foundation as of this writing following that policy is the Atlantic Philanthropies. The foundations profiled in this book aim to exist in perpetuity and will have a similar investment profile to educational endowments. Educational endowments use the concept of "intergenerational equity"—treating the next generation as fairly as this generation, generally by providing an endowment of the same inflation-adjusted value—as a guideline for managing endowment funds. The intergenerational equity doctrine results in funds managed with the objective of perpetuity.

■ *Foundation regulations.* While both types of organization are considered charities, another key difference is the more restrictive Internal Revenue Code regarding the proper practices for managing and distributing foundation assets.

■ *Limited inflow of new assets.* As described in the next section, most institutional foundations have been established by gifts or bequests from wealthy individuals and families that form the core of the assets. Most foundations do not receive additional assets into their funds. If the foundation aims for perpetuity, then it is likely to have a more aggressive investment policy.

The majority of institutional foundations described in this book are classified as private foundations known as family foundations. Individuals or families establish these foundations to distribute money for charitable purposes, usually in the form of grants to other charitable organizations. Educational endowments are considered public charities. Operating foundations conduct their own charitable activities rather than supporting other charitable organizations and are treated more like public charities or educational endowments regarding distribution requirements and tax treatment for donors.

Foundations receive greater scrutiny and regulation due to a presumption that foundations controlled by a family or small group of people could violate laws regulating charitable activity more readily than a public charity funded by a broad group of donors able to hold the charity accountable. The Internal Revenue Code defines certain improper practices and establishes guidelines to ensure that the foundation achieves its stated mission. Violations can result in a foundation's paying excise taxes.[4]

Section 4942 of the tax code most directly affects investment policy in foundations. Known as the payout or distribution requirement, it mandates that foundations distribute a minimum amount of its funds, currently 5 percent of the average fair market value of the foundation's investment assets. Besides grants to independent charitable organizations, administrative expenses such as salaries, rent, travel costs, and buying property qualify as long as they further the foundation's stated exempt purpose.

The foundation can make the required distributions up to 12 months from the end of its tax year.[5] The foundation is subject to a 30 percent tax if it fails to pay out the minimum and a 100 percent tax if not paid in the tax period.[6]

Foundations must pay a 2 percent excise tax annually on net investment income. The code allows that to be reduced to 1 percent if certain conditions are met. Net investment income equals the sum of gross investment income and capital gains net income less the cost of producing investment income (such as investment management and brokerage fees).[7] Because the formulas used to calculate the exemption are so complicated, many foundations do not attempt to reduce the excise tax.

In practice, due to excise taxes, long-term commitments to grantees, and compensating for periods of lower performance, the foundation spending rate tends to be higher than 5 percent, averaging 6 percent in a recent Commonfund benchmark study.[8]

Other regulations that apply to foundations include rules against self-dealing or transactions between the foundation and a "disqualified person" such as a trustee or donor. A foundation cannot make jeopardy investments that could endanger its ability to carry out its mission. Foundations and "disqualified persons" cannot together hold more than 20 percent of the voting stock of an entity. If, however, the foundation is funded with a donation of closely held stock, the foundation has five years to reduce those holdings.[9]

While these regulations do not apply to endowments, their similarity to fiduciary law results in endowments adhering to these standards. Educational endowments can face excise taxes on tax shelter transactions under Internal Revenue Code Section 4956.[10]

Spending Policy

A key objective or parameter that must be considered in forming the investment policy is the spending policy of the institution. As mentioned above, foundations must abide by the rule requiring the distribution of 5 percent of foundation assets every year when establishing investment objectives and policies. Educational endowments have more flexibility regarding the distribution of assets from the endowment. Though not subject to government-mandated distributions, most institutions rely on the endowment as a source of income annually. Since the endowment will need to deliver consistent cash flows over time, a university's investment policy must conform to the demands of the spending policy.

In general, the fund will be managed to provide an income stream that will grow in accordance with the organization's cost structure. Coincidentally, a rate of 5 percent of asset value has shown to maintain steady cash flows while preserving principal for all types of institutions.[11]

The concept of "intergenerational equity" strongly influences an educational endowment's objective to exist in perpetuity and thus influences its spending policy. Intergenerational equity requires the organization to balance its short-term income needs with its long-term needs and to spend the endowment in such a way as to preserve the value of the endowment for future generations.[12] A standard formula in recent years has been 5 percent of a three-year moving average of market value, although many institutions have added a formula to match inflation.

A thorough description of an evolving spending policy is found in the Yale University 2005 Endowment Report:

Yale University Spending Policy

The spending rule is at the heart of fiscal discipline for an endowed institution. Spending policies define an institution's compromise between the conflicting goals of providing substantial support for current operations and preserving purchasing power of Endowment assets. The spending rule must be clearly defined and consistently applied for the concept of budget balance to have meaning.

Yale's policy is designed to meet two competing objectives. The first goal is to release substantial current income to the operating budget in a stable stream, since large fluctuations in revenues are difficult to accommodate through changes in University activities or programs. The second goal is to protect the value of Endowment assets against inflation, allowing programs to be supported at today's level far into the future.

Yale's spending rule attempts to achieve these two objectives by using a long-term spending rate combined with a smoothing rule that adjusts spending gradually to changes in Endowment market value.

The amount released under the spending rule is based on a weighted average of the prior year's spending adjusted for inflation and an amount determined by applying the target rate to the current Endowment market value.

The spending rule has two implications. First, by incorporating the previous year's spending the rule eliminates large fluctuations, enabling the University to plan for its operating budget needs.

Over the last twenty years, annual changes in spending have been less than a third as volatile as annual changes in Endowment value. Second, by adjusting spending toward the long-term target spending level, the rule ensures that spending will be sensitive to fluctuating Endowment market values, providing stability in long-term purchasing power.

ASSET ALLOCATION

A seminal article entitled "Determinants of Portfolio Performance," by Gary P. Brinson, L. Randolph Hood, and Gilbert L. Beebower, published in the July/August 1986 issue of the *Financial Analysts Journal*, concluded that over 93.6 percent of investment returns can be attributed to strategic asset allocation, not security selection and market timing. This finding profoundly impacted investment management policy and fostered the belief that asset allocation is the most important aspect of implementing an investment policy. Despite numerous studies from other investment researchers debunking various elements of the paper's results, notably the wording of the question, research has consistently shown that long-term asset allocation policy drives much of the total return of the portfolio.[13]

Asset allocation—determining the percentage of the portfolio that will be invested in various asset classes based on the investment objectives and risk tolerance of the organization—remains one of the most important decisions a foundation or endowment CIO and investment committee makes. Very few decisions are as difficult in terms of coming up with the "right" answer and the outcome defines the basic risk and return characteristics of the investment portfolio. Given the importance of and the need for efficient interaction between the investment committee and the CIO, it is important to have a clear written statement of the fund's asset allocation philosophy and process. The CIO's and investment committee's views about asset allocation are an important component of the investment policy statement.

The asset allocation process can be determined in accordance with two broad approaches. In the first, a strategic asset allocation is set infrequently, with the endowment religiously hugging the target asset allocation through disciplined rebalancing. The alternative model is much more tactical, where institutions make frequent shifts between asset classes in an attempt to capitalize on ever-changing market opportunities. In practice, most endowments are somewhere in between, incorporating long-term strategic asset allocation while permitting and adding value from shorter-term tactical "tilts."

Many successful endowments and foundations have evolved in their thinking about asset allocation, with the process becoming a mix of bottom-up and top-down. Institutions are being influenced more by themes, and allocations are increasingly driven by where the institutions are finding opportunities as opposed to the old approach of filling a bucket. In addition, distinctions between different asset classes are increasingly blurred, with some of the most interesting opportunities being "tweeners," having characteristics of public-equity, private equity, hedge funds, and real assets.

Asset Classes

The first step in the asset allocation process established in the investment policies is to define and describe the purpose for each asset class included in the total portfolio. There is no single "correct" approach to the number of asset classes. A recent trend with a handful of endowments is moving toward fewer asset classes—one as simple as equities (both U.S. and non-U.S. and public and private), fixed-income, and hedging (low to zero correlations with the other two asset classes) assets. Other institutions have more asset classes, slicing public equities into small, large, value, and growth quadrants and slicing private equity into its components: venture, buyout, mezzanine, and distressed. Each asset class should be adding some unique return or risk (or risk-reducing) characteristic into the portfolio. One alternative is to have U.S. public equity, non-U.S. public equity, investment-grade fixed income, non-investment-grade fixed income, cash, real assets, absolute return, and private equity.

Traditional Asset Classes

U.S. public equity. These investments are liquid opportunities to capitalize on the profit growth of U.S. public corporations. These securities provide a long-term (in the short-term they perform poorly in periods of unexpected increases in inflation) hedge against inflation and have historically outperformed fixed-income investments over long periods of time. However, this risk premium over fixed income is needed to compensate investors for the greater risk or volatility of these assets over short to intermediate periods of time.

Non-U.S. public equity. These investments are liquid opportunities to capitalize on the profit growth of public corporations in developed and emerging markets outside the United States. These securities provide diversification benefits due to the imperfect correlation between U.S. and non-U.S. corporate profits (although sentiment correlations cause the U.S. and non-U.S. public equities to have higher price correlations over short periods of time). These securities also provide foreign currency exposure, which helps provide a hedge against U.S. dollar inflation. These securities can outperform and underperform U.S. public equity over extended periods of time but also historically have outperformed fixed-income assets. Like U.S. public equity, this risk premium over fixed income is needed to compensate investors for the greater risk or volatility of these assets over short to intermediate periods of time.

Fixed income–investment-grade. Intermediate- to long-term investment-grade bonds offer protection against deflation risk by providing more predictable cash flows that hold up better during economic downturns. Historically, the return has been higher than cash, due to the usual upward slope of the yield curve. However, these securities are subject to the risk of unexpected inflation increases and higher interest rates, which reduces the real value of these investments over short periods of time.

Fixed income–non-investment-grade. Fixed-income securities with higher credit risk can provide the opportunity for higher returns than investment-grade fixed-income securities. Historically, the returns and risk for such securities have averaged between that realized for public equity and investment-grade fixed income. This risk premium varies over time.

Cash. Cash and cash equivalents (i.e., high-credit and low-duration fixed-income securities) provide the lowest risk (in terms of both volatility and liquidity), but also offer the lowest return over long periods of time.

Alternative Asset Classes

Real assets. This asset class provides the best hedge against inflation risk. The largest portion of this asset class is real estate, but it also includes other real assets, such as inflation-indexed bonds, commodities, oil and gas, mining, timber/farmland, and any other "hard asset" that would perform well during periods of high inflation. This asset class ranges from very low-risk (in terms of volatility and liquidity) and return inflation-indexed bonds to high-risk-and-return oil and gas exploration, with the latter being more similar to private equity.

Private equity. Private equity investments allow investors to access private companies, providing a liquidity risk premium in terms of higher expected returns over public securities (although with higher risk). Private equity includes venture capital, distressed securities, buyouts, and mezzanine funds. These investments are the least liquid and typically structured as limited partnerships, which return cash flow to investors over a long period of time. The lack of liquidity, higher complexity, and ability for general partners (i.e., private equity fund managers) to add value to their portfolio companies, makes such investments potentially more attractive than public market investments. However, these investments are also characterized by a wider dispersion of possible investment returns across different investment managers, making manager selection the most important of any asset class.

Absolute return. Absolute return strategies offer the ability to invest with talented investment managers that perform a variety of active strategies, including arbitrage, long-short equity, and distressed investing. These investments often have lower volatility relative to other asset classes, but introduce other, harder-to-measure types of "tail risk," liquidity risk, complexity, and lack of transparency that require more careful management than traditional asset classes. Absolute return investments are less liquid than the traditional asset classes, but more liquid than private equity due to the shorter lockup.

Asset Allocation Analysis and Tools

A university or foundation is a long-term, going concern; the portfolio is intended to support the academic or philanthropic mission of the institution for many future generations of students or beneficiaries. Therefore, in the absence of any special insights or knowledge about financial market activity over shorter time frames, the investment-planning horizon should be long term, which often is simplified to 10 years. While focused primarily on the long term, the asset allocation process may allow room for analysis and action on exceptional shorter-term investment opportunities that arise from time to time.

Historical Record and Prospective Returns Any asset allocation process, regardless of the length of the planning horizon, requires assumptions about the expected characteristics of asset-class returns and their interrelationships. Specifically, asset allocation inputs include expected returns, standard deviations, and correlations. Traditionally, many analysts have tended to place a heavy emphasis on the historical record of asset-class returns, with the exception of fixed income, where the return assumption has always been strongly influenced by currently available market yields. However, this backward-looking analysis led many investors to use equity return assumptions that were too high in the late 1990s, causing many large institutions to rely too heavily on large allocations to equities. This excessive reliance on historical averages was used in developing equity return expectations, while fixed-income returns were projected using current market valuations (i.e., if a bond price increases, then the yield—and hence future return—is lower).

Forward-looking returns are based on a reasonable analysis of the potential components of future total return, including income and valuation changes. This building block approach frequently leads to 10-year return assumptions that are significantly different from the returns observed over the entire historical record of an asset class. Expected returns for alternative asset classes are even more difficult to estimate, being more art than science. Using historical averages for alternative assets is a useful starting point, but the numbers should be lowered, given the increasing capital being attracted into all these asset classes.

Frequency of Asset Allocation Studies   Another decision is the frequency of asset allocation studies. Traditionally, the philosophy underlying the management of most large institutions was that market timing doesn't work. Strategic asset allocations were set and not changed. This imposed a discipline that helped committee-led institutions avoid the temptation of chasing returns and following the herd. However, many endowments, foundations and pensions have moved to more frequent reviews of their asset allocations. Most institutions surveyed review their strategic asset allocation annually. Additionally, many institutions allow and often encourage their CIOs to make smaller tactical shifts in asset allocation within ranges that are established at the time of each strategic asset allocation review. The lines between strategic and tactical asset allocation are increasingly blurred. This may seem a bit at odds with the concept that long-term investors should use long-term assumptions. However, a higher frequency is necessary, given the level of volatility that exists in the markets. Financial asset prices can change significantly over short periods of time, and it is unavoidable that these changes will have an impact on future returns. The clearest example of this effect can be seen in the bond market. A bond portfolio purchased at a yield of 3 percent has a lower expected return than the same portfolio purchased later at a 5 percent yield.

This same thought process can and should be applied to equities and other assets. An equity portfolio purchased with a high dividend yield and low price valuation should have a higher expected return than the same portfolio purchased at a low dividend yield and high price valuation unless there is a compelling difference in growth expectations. The essential point here is that the current yield and the price of an asset class matter to the prospective total return, and these are constantly changing.

Much of this debate over the process of asset allocation was fueled by a speech given by Peter Bernstein in early 2003. Responding to the misplaced belief that equities should always be expected to generate their historical average low-double-digit returns, Bernstein made a point that other researchers and investors (Arnott, Asness, Campbell, Grantham, Shiller) had been saying for several years: namely, that price matters. He made a strong case that an asset allocation should not be set and remain unchanged for years to come, because of constant changes in prices and market opportunities. The benefit of long-term thinking is the ability to avoid the behavioral pitfalls that cause many investors to chase the latest fads. However, if everyone operates under the belief that "market timing doesn't work," then there are probably opportunities to be more tactical.

Peer Analysis It is worthwhile to compare a strategic asset allocation with those of other funds that have similar objectives. This analysis is intended to be useful background information and should not constrain the allocation decision. Use of peer analysis for direct performance comparisons must be applied carefully, since each fund has unique investment objectives, liabilities, and risk tolerances. The value of peer analysis is twofold. First, if the objective is to have "above average" performance, then this necessarily will require a different or "above average" asset allocation. Second, since contrarian investing is difficult to maintain over certain periods of time (i.e., when the contrarian position is temporarily not working), it is helpful to know how the allocation compares to that of other institutions, particularly those with which an institution most closely identifies. This may help sustain such contrarian positions during difficult periods.

Asset allocation and asset liability analysis involves sophisticated quantitative techniques, and it is tempting to assume a high degree of accuracy in the output. It is important to understand the weaknesses inherent in these models and the significance and sensitivity of the underlying assumptions. In the end, these models and procedures should be viewed as tools to assist the decision-making process. The final policy mix should be one that makes sense from an intuitive judgment standpoint.

Risk

The asset allocation process should be influenced by an organization's investment mission, the behavior of financial markets, and the structure necessary for effective group decision making under conditions of uncertainty. In a broad sense, an endowment's or foundation's objective is no different than that of any other investor seeking to maximize returns while controlling risk. The benefits of higher returns are clear—the higher the return of the investment fund, the greater the resources that can be provided by the endowment or foundation to fund future academic or philanthropic programs. However, the pursuit of higher returns must be undertaken within a risk management framework. It is impossible to evaluate the attractiveness or success of prospective or realized returns without some measure(s) of the risk of the investments. Perhaps the most important policy decision to be made is the determination of how much risk to take.

There are many different measures of risk that are helpful in the management of a portfolio, including a myriad of statistics such as volatility, tracking error, liquidity risk, complexity risk (i.e., the risk of being uninformed about the "true" downside of an investment) risk of not earning a specific return threshold, and so on. While these measures are all very useful, they deal with risk in the asset portfolio, and do not account for the fact that the nonprofit institution has liabilities as well as goals for funding future initiatives, both of which may be sensitive to some of the same economic factors that drive financial asset returns (e.g., interest rates and inflation). To be complete an asset allocation analysis for an endowment must look at both sides of an institution's balance sheet in order to estimate the potential impact of various alternative portfolio structures on key measures of total risk. An asset/liability (A/L) model would be used to accomplish this. The output of the A/L model describes for each alternative portfolio the probability distribution of outcomes, as measured by key factors such as percentage of the institution's budget provided by the endowment and perhaps the institution's credit rating.

Rebalancing

In addition to an asset allocation approach and process, the investment policy must address an approach toward rebalancing. Rebalancing can be triggered upon the passage of time; by an asset allocation that moves outside an established range; when the risk (either volatility or tracking error) exceeds a given risk budget, based on the qualitative judgment of the investment committee or CIO; or never. An investment process that recognizes the discipline of managing to a strategic or long-term target asset allocation would use one of the first three. The passage-of-time approach requires that the CIO mechanically rebalance back to the target asset allocation after a predetermined period of time, typically monthly, quarterly or annually. Sometimes a qualitative overlay is permitted, in particular during periods of macro events (e.g., terrorist event or market distress). However, the discipline and risk management involved with rebalancing requires that the process be rather mechanistic.

Another rebalancing issue is whether the institution rebalances back to the long-term target or a portion of the way back to the target (e.g., to the edge of the range). Another issue is how to handle illiquid alternatives, which often involve committing capital to a partnership that is drawn down over a period of three to five years. The uncertainty of the cash drawdowns and the ultimate cash distributions create issues with managing these asset classes and subclasses to a target. Often, institutions target an annual commitment amount that will come closest to hitting their long-term target. However, this is based on a number of assumptions and is merely a long-term prediction. Recognizing the difficulties inherent in managing to a target for many of these asset classes, some institutions exclude these asset classes for purposes of rebalancing and instead manage their liquid asset classes to a target allocation.

Rebalancing can involve the sale of investments or redemption from commingled funds. However, sometimes this is not possible in the instance of manager lockups or desirable in the instance where a manager may be closed (i.e., is not willing to manage any additional assets). Partial or full redemption from a closed manager will likely prevent the institution from being able to reinvest with this manager in the future, when the asset class is below its long-term or strategic target. In either instance, the institution can rebalance through the use of an overlay. The institution could use a swap or forwards/futures to maintain the manager exposure, while swapping or converting the asset-class exposure into another asset class, which is underweight in the portfolio. Implementing such an overlay requires active cash-flow management.

INVESTMENT POLICY IMPLEMENTATION

Once the investment policy has been written and responsibilities delegated, the investment process focuses on investment analysis and selection, portfolio management, and risk management. The investment policy should include the institution's policies regarding passive versus active and internal versus external management.

Active Management versus Passive Management

Many endowments and foundations don't explicitly address active management, taking it as a given that active management adds value over low-cost indexed or passive investing. It is more common for large public pensions to employ more passive management. However, active management is expensive, and numerous studies have produced statistics that the majority of active managers fail to outperform a passive approach to investing. By definition, investing is a zero-sum game, so if someone beats an index, another investor must underperform. In fact, high investment management fees imply that it is a negative-sum game and, therefore, a majority of professional managers are unlikely to beat their benchmarks over an extended period of time.

This combined with the widely observed lack of performance persistence (i.e., past performance is not predictive of future performance) implies that successfully selecting active investment manager is what Charlie Ellis refers to as "the loser's game." David Swensen, in his second book, *Unconventional Success: A Fundamental Approach to Personal Investment*, recommends that individual and underresourced institutions should simply index their entire portfolio, not having the ability to source and research managers and investment ideas as thoroughly as the better-endowed institutions with their large and more experienced investment staffs.

External Management versus Internal Management

The majority of endowments and foundations hire external investment managers to select individual securities, with the investment offices and CIOs adding value through asset allocation, selection of themes, and manager selection. However, Harvard Management Company is the largest exception to this norm, having a long track record of successful internal management. Advantages of internal management include lower costs of hiring internal staff relative to external management fees and the greater transparency and hence ease of risk management associated with this approach. The downside to internal management is the difficulty in attracting and retaining staff. It boils down to a build versus buy decision, and usually it is easier to buy the best talent than to hire them inside—it is unlikely that the most talented investment manager will be in-house, and if perchance an institution were able to attract such a person, it would become too expensive (relative to the compensation paid to other members of this nonprofit organization) to retain him or her.

Institutions face the potential for an adverse selection problem where the most talented managers would be more likely to leave for greater compensation managing money for other investors outside the nonprofit constraints, while the less talented managers remain. Some larger institutions introduce some active management by coinvesting alongside their external managers, typically involving investments in private companies originated by the institution's private equity managers. Coinvestment has the benefit of concentrating bets in some of the manager's higher-conviction investments, reducing the total investment management fees paid to external managers and helping maintain a more engaged investment staff. Such coinvesting also has the benefit of helping the investment staff become closer to and hence better at the ongoing monitoring and due diligence of the external manager. One of the interviewees has also managed money internally.

Other versions of internal management can include implementation of passive or enhanced-passive strategies, tactical or hedging overlays, and fixed-income management. Fixed income is the most common internally managed asset class. The spread between top- and bottom-performing active fixed-income managers has the smallest dispersion of any asset class and hence has the smallest payoff for the time and effort involved with staff finding an active fixed-income manager.

External Manager Selection

Since most endowments and foundations use external investment managers to perform the security or company selection, the focus is on manager selection In *Endowment Management: A Practical Guide,* Jay Yoder presents a structured and thoughtful best-practices approach for selecting appropriate investment managers. This approach is paraphrased as follows:

1. Hire managers to fulfill a specific investment objective. (Don't hire the "hot" growth fund when you need a value manager.)
2. Set clear and reasonable objectives for conducting the search. Understand what the institution wants to accomplish. Focus on hiring a good manager, not necessarily "the best" manager.
3. Delegate due-diligence responsibility to investment professionals such as consultants or manager-of-managers when the investment staff lacks expertise or time to conduct a search.
4. Establish criteria for the search and the rationale for those criteria.
5. Choose organizations you know or whom your colleagues know. First, consider managers or organizations where you have an investment or have monitored for an extended period of time. Second, ask respected colleagues, investment committee members, or asset-class specialists for recommendations.
6. Conduct thorough due diligence. Evaluate investment management organizations based on:
   a. People
   b. Philosophy
   c. Process
   d. Performance
   e. Professionalism
   f. Prudent instinctual reaction
7. Follow the prudent man rule. Understand that the guidelines may not help find the absolute best manager for a particular strategy, but they do help investors follow a prudent process to find a suitable manager for their objectives at the time of the search.[14]

Portfolio Management

Portfolio management involves combining investment managers in a portfolio that provides diversification benefits, considering both quantitative (i.e., low correlation of historical returns with other investment managers) and qualitative factors (managers are doing something different—using either different analytical approaches or information sources, or focusing on a different region or sector). Consideration must be given to the appropriate number of investments relative to the resources (e.g., investment staff) of the institution. For example, an institution with limited staff should not have too many manager relationships.

Foundation and endowment CIOs face the aforementioned risks to their investment decisions, the most significant one, of course, being the loss of capital and the inability to meet its payout commitments to the institution. Risks abound at various points throughout the investment process. Besides volatility and risk to principal, specific investment risks include liquidity risk, inflation risk, deflation risk (e.g. credit risk), currency risk, complexity risk (e.g., hedge fund failure), and peer-group risk. Risk also arises from operations, compliance, custodians, and counterparties. With increasingly sophisticated systems and tools available, a CIO absolutely must implement a systematic approach to risk management with clearly defined responsibilities and support from the investment committee.[15]

BENCHMARKING AND PERFORMANCE EVALUATION

The most common method for evaluating performance involves comparing total portfolio performance against a policy benchmark, which is an average of each asset-class benchmark weighted by the target long-term or strategic asset allocation. Common benchmarks for traditional asset classes include Russell 3000 for U.S. public equity, MSCI ACWI for non-U.S. public equity, and the Lehman Aggregate Bond Index for investment-grade fixed income. Each benchmark represents a passive exposure to an asset class. The benchmark should also adequately reflect the risk of the asset class.

For alternative investments, the choice of benchmark is less straightforward. There are two broad approaches for benchmarking alternative assets. One choice is benchmarking the return to a spread over a public benchmark, with the additional spread reflecting the greater risk (both volatility and liquidity). For example, an absolute return benchmark may be three-month Treasury bills plus a spread of 350 basis points (bps). The second approach measures a passive approach to investing in the alternative asset class, namely, the average return of a universe of managers. For example, a private equity benchmark may be a custom benchmark provided by Venture Economics that is a weighted average return of all funds raised in the years in which the institutional investor made private equity commitments.

The first method is better for measuring the risk-adjusted performance of an asset class, while the second approach does a better job of measuring manager selection of the institutional investor. The problem with the first benchmark is that choosing the appropriate risk-adjusting spread is often arbitrary and difficult to justify on theoretical grounds. Why choose 350 bps versus 600 bps? The second approach, while more objective, is also flawed since manager databases and universes are often prone to various biases, such as including managers that are univestible (i.e., closed to new investors).

Institutions often supplement the policy benchmark with several other benchmarks, including inflation plus the institution's spending rate (e.g., inflation plus 5 percent), a passive 70/30 or 60/40 U.S. public-equity/fixed-income benchmark, and a peer comparison. Although total portfolio returns will not track the "inflation plus" spending benchmark over short periods of time (e.g., monthly), it is important that the institution beat this benchmark over the long term to be able to maintain a real level of support for the institution over time. The 70/30 or 60/40 benchmark is often used since most institutions have experience investing in this traditional asset mix.

Most institutions also formally or informally track performance against peer organizations. Every year, the performance of leading institutions such as Yale, Harvard, and Stanford are widely publicized. Their outstanding performance has contributed to a growing interest in duplicating the investment strategies and processes of these institutions. This increasing focus on peers has also contributed to the demand by foundations and endowments to hire CIOs and improve their investment offices to compete against other institutions.

GOVERNANCE

Large foundations and endowments can and do attract extremely talented investment professionals to their investment committees. Responsibilities vary depending on the size of funds, but, in general, investment committee members focus on strategy, oversight, avoiding conflicts of interest, and researching and approving investments. Smaller foundations and endowments tend to rely more heavily on the committee for tactical investment advice and decisions. While the investment committee will be involved throughout the investment process, the role and responsibilities, particularly regarding decision-making authority, of the investment committee and staff must be delineated in the investment policy statement.

Decision Making: The Buck Stops Where?

There are two basic models of decision making: one in which the investment committee makes all investment decisions, and the alternative, in which the CIO makes most decisions. In practice, there is a continuum of approaches between these two extremes involving varying degrees of delegation and communication between the investment committee and staff.

The coauthor's informal survey in 2004 found most institutions reviewing their strategic asset allocation annually and allowing and encouraging tactical asset allocation within prespecified ranges. The strategic asset allocation process was typically driven by staff and approved by the investment committee, while tactical asset allocation was usually delegated to staff. The ultimate authority to hire managers was evenly split between CIOs and investment committees. With only one exception, investment committees did not meet with managers who were candidates for hiring. In all instances, the investment staff controlled the process, and when the investment committee had authority, it rarely overruled the CIO's recommendation. Most CIOs strongly recommended that, if manager changes required investment committee approval, this be accomplished between meetings via e-mail correspondence. Most CIOs had the authority to fire investment managers and rebalance the portfolio. All CIOs emphasized that they err on the side of inclusion, even if they have authority over decisions, communicating all portfolio changes to the investment committee.

The decision-making structure essentially boils down to a trade-off between efficiency and confidence. It is universally acknowledged that investment decision making by consensus or committee can hinder the ability to respond quickly to investment opportunities. However, investment committees must have assurance their fiduciary duty is being fulfilled when delegating decision making to a CIO. This requires a high level of confidence and a close relationship with their CIO and investment staff. This can be cultivated by close cooperation and communication. A model that works well is one in which decision-making authority is delegated, but the investment committee is actively involved in the process—the committee is consulted prior to decisions and is responsible for oversight. Investment committee meetings involve discussions of policy and periodic reviews of asset allocation.

In his book, Jay Yoder strongly contends that the investment committee and board should be actively involved in establishing investment policies and asset allocation, as well as the general oversight of the investment office, but should delegate all other decision making to the investment office/CIO. Yoder quotes several endowment experts on this issue. William Massy, author of *Endowment: Perspectives, Policies and Management*, which discusses Stanford University's governance, writes:

> *The board's investment committee should debate the vision and its underlying assumptions and ... submit to the board for its approval general policies which shall be followed. ... Within the framework of the policies so approved, the committee shall have general supervision of the investment of the trust endowment ... The key terms are "general policies" and "general supervision." The committee and board are supposed to set direction and provide oversight, but they should not become involved in day-to-day portfolio management. The investment committee should ask searching questions*

about policies and proposals . . . but it should not attempt to perform the investment job itself.[16]

Anecdotal experience with a public pension, the Virginia Retirement System, is consistent with the aforementioned observations. The Virginia Retirement System was a typical public fund until the early 1990s, with much of the decision making residing with the investment committee and the board. A governance change occurred in the early 1990s with the assistance of a consultant. Since that time, most decisions have been made by the investment staff, with the exception of setting policy and asset allocation. The benefits have been quite apparent—they have beaten their long-term benchmark, and the investment staff has been empowered to be more opportunistic and more active with alternative assets than with other public funds. The delegated governance allows contrarian investment decisions to be made and maintained for longer periods of time. Although the staff has been empowered to make such timely decisions, members of the investment committee and board are very actively involved and are informed about all investment decisions—their advice is eagerly sought on all large changes to the portfolio.

There are counterarguments to the delegated governance structure. First, this structure works well if the CIO and investment office are known commodities, having established their reputations after years of solid investment performance. Credibility is important for the investment committee to be comfortable delegating this much responsibility. This is becoming a larger issue as more endowments and foundations struggle with higher staff turnover in their investment offices.

A second advantage of requiring investment committee approval on most decisions is that it may help an institution live with large "bets" for longer periods of time. There is an argument that the investment committee should approve manager hire/fire and tactical asset allocation decisions so members have a sense of ownership of the investments. This may enable such decisions (either manager or asset allocation) to be maintained for longer periods of time in instances where short-term performance turns negative. Again, a counterargument to this approach is that without responsibility resting with one individual, the group decision making of a committee may lead to excessive caution and premature abandonment of difficult investment decisions.

Investment Committee Guidelines

Panelists at a University Endowment Summit sponsored by the Goldman Sachs Market Institute[17] listed the ideal investment committee, which included:

- Members who are willing to commit their time.
- Diversity of investment and governance expertise.
- Continuity of the investment team.
- Open-minded thinkers that resist micromanaging the decisions of the staff.
- Investment committee support by the full board of trustees or regents.

Most experts agree that the investment committee should remain small—five to six members at most—and should meet four or five times a year. Others also believe committee membership qualifications and term limits should be defined in the investment policy document. The CIO of a foundation or endowment investment pool should remain wary of group-think and should endeavor to build a strong relationship with the investment committee.

The Yale University Endowment Report provides an excellent example of the definition of an investment committee.

Yale University Investment Committee Description
Since 1975, the Yale Corporation Investment Committee has been responsible for oversight of the Endowment, incorporating senior level investment experience into portfolio policy formulation. The Investment Committee consists of at least three Fellows of the Corporation and other persons who have particular investment expertise. The Committee meets quarterly, at which time members review asset allocation policies, Endowment performance, and strategies proposed by Investments Office staff. The Committee approves guidelines for investment of the Endowment portfolio, specifying investment objectives, spending policy, and approaches for the investment of each asset category. Eleven individuals currently sit on the Committee.

SUMMARY

Factors contributing to the investment success of leading endowments and foundations include strong governance, well-vetted investment philosophies and structured processes. The investment policy statement establishes the investment principles, governance, objectives, and asset allocation process for the institution—a type of road map or rules of the game between the investment staff and the institution, which is *necessary* for investment success. The *sufficient* condition for investment success lies in the philosophy and execution of that philosophy in a repeatable process by the investment staff, working with the investment committee. The interviews will help us better understand both the necessary and sufficient conditions that have led to the success of the CIOs profiled in this book. Before we read these interviews, we want to first review the current market environment in which these CIOs are currently investing.

CHAPTER 3

The Investment Landscape

You Are Here

W hy are investors intrigued with the investment strategies and approaches of the large foundations and endowments? Foundations and endowments are increasingly being recognized as some of the most sophisticated investors, having achieved impressive track records over a number of years by investing in new asset classes long before other institutional investors.

This chapter surveys the current investment landscape, starting with a brief review of the factors that have made foundations and endowments industry leaders and a description of the macro market environment. It studies the significant contribution alternative asset classes have made to their outstanding performance and provides detailed information about the alternative assets that chief investment officers (CIOs) continue to add to their portfolios. Concluding Part One with a look toward the future, it will set the stage for the CIO profiles in Part Two.

HOW DID WE GET HERE?

Sandy Urie is the president and chief executive officer (CEO) of Cambridge Associates, a consulting firm that has been advising endowments and foundations for 34 years, starting as an external resource for predominantly Ivy League schools (initially helping Harvard University). She attributes the success of endowments and foundations to their long-term time horizons.

Although these institutions have increasingly built strong internal investment teams, she believes that a disciplined process has been instrumental for their success: "The key to success is sticking with the policy, not trading in and out of asset classes. . . . Process matters enormously to produce attractive results."

Sandy also believes that endowments and foundations will continue investing globally, noting that this trend is only just starting. Allocation to non-U.S. equities recently surpassed allocations to U.S. equities at large endowments. However, Sandy notes, "It will be increasingly hard for endowments to cover all asset classes globally—you need to be on the ground. ... For example, Asia is a region, not one market."

In addition to Cambridge Associates, a number of other investment consultants have been active providing advice and resources to endowments and foundations, including Hammond Associates and Rogers Casey. Dennis Hammond, founder and CEO of Hammond Associates, which has advised institutional investors for over 22 years, echoed many of Sandy Urie's conclusions for the cause of endowments' investment success: a long-term investment focus, good governance, and a willingness (and ability) to be early adopters of new asset classes and strategies.

Tim Barron, CEO of Rogers Casey, also shares Sandy's views on the success of many endowments, saying, "Endowments and foundation's have forged their own paths ... their governance structures are better than other investors such as pensions—they have tended to make smart moves for intelligent reasons and live with those decisions."

INVESTING BASICS

Investment managers talk much about alpha and beta. Beta is the return generated from the allocation to an asset class or exposure to a risk factor, which could be implemented passively. Alpha is the excess return generated by active investment managers above what could have been generated by investing in a passive exposure to any particular asset class.

Most endowments and foundations seek to add value through asset allocation (i.e., beta) and manager selection (i.e., alpha). David Swensen focuses on strategic asset allocation, expressing his dislike for tactical asset allocation in *Pioneering Portfolio Management*, considering such attempts at market timing unlikely to succeed on a consistent basis.

Tim Barron also notes that people are great at investing in the rearview mirror, so big asset allocation shifts always occur after an asset performs poorly. "Investors tend to add asset classes after they perform well. ... The fear for smaller endowments and foundations is the Swensen factor—they try to imitate what he's done, but they will likely end up buying what he is selling. ... You want to be somewhere where you can see the herd, but not be in the middle of it. ... "

Over time, the attractive performance records of most endowments and foundations can be attributed to their asset allocation process (which may include identifying and capitalizing on themes), rebalancing discipline, and process for identifying and evaluating external investment managers across a variety of asset classes.

The key to successful investing is investing with talented people doing unique and interesting things and this hasn't changed over time—you just need to look in different places—it's getting harder to find.

The next sections will provide an overview of current macro and market conditions and the types of issues and asset-class decisions faced by CIOs today.

Macro Environment

What is the macro investment climate? While good investments are getting hard to find, every investment climate provides opportunities. Macro conditions are the major global economic and market trends impacting investors at any point in time. Macro conditions influence tactical asset allocation decisions.

An investment environment is often influenced by an "issue du jour." It's impossible to forget a former boss obsessively checking oil prices in the early 1980s, at the exclusion of everything else happening in the markets and economy at that time. Other market hot buttons over the years have included government policy, the dollar, the Fed, terrorism, deflation, inflation, and federal elections. In almost every instance, the recent experience or trend, good or bad, is extrapolated and is assumed to continue inexorably into the future.

Recent concerns have included high and rising energy and commodity prices, a housing bubble, credit bubble, and "low-risk premia." A common refrain is "nothing is cheap right now" or "there are no obvious investment bargains." However, investment bargains are always obvious in hindsight, never being quite so clear in the present. Wide credit spreads for bonds or low price-to-earnings ratios (P/Es) for stocks always occur at a time of financial distress, which people assume will continue or become even worse. There is always a concern and conventional wisdom du jour in any market environment, but it invariably borrows too heavily from the recent past.

These analyses tend to be much too simplistic. The global economy is a complex web of relationships and transactions, being very diversified and able to withstand many shocks. Simple analyses fail to predict because, although the direction of the marginal impacts may be correct, the magnitude will usually be wrong because the economy and hence market is influenced be many other factors, which may not be the issues du jour. Behavioral finance research has highlighted a number of weaknesses among investors, which include this extrapolation of recent events as well as herding. In fact, most shocks, both good and bad, are totally unpredictable, not those that garner the attention on CNBC and on the pages of the *Financial Times* and *Wall Street Journal*. These unexpected events, such as terrorist attacks on the downside or technological breakthroughs on the upside, cannot be predicted and will trigger sustained moves in the economy and markets, which in turn, usually trigger a regime change to a new "issue du jour."

An event that still weighs heavily in the minds of investors is the stock market bubble in the late 1990s, which finally burst in 2000. Since that time, investors have been on the lookout for other bubbles (e.g., housing and credit). The stock market (as measured by the S&P 500) declined by 49 percent from its peak on March 24, 2000, to its low on October 9, 2002. This burned many investors that bought into the prior conventional wisdom that stocks outperformed and hence were less risky than other asset classes over the long run. The current conventional wisdom is that yield or current cash flow is safer than the much less certain (witness the 49 percent loss) growth or capital gains from equities.

Investors tend to chase recent returns, although some of the leading endowments have successfully avoided this behavioral weakness. Therefore, to understand the current investment environment and fads it is useful to look at a range of asset-class returns, shown in Table 3.1.

Since the stock market crash in 2000, there has been a demand for value and yield—growth investing is out of favor. This has contributed to the demand for real estate and credit. Current conventional thinking is

TABLE 3.1 Annualized Asset-Class Returns (as of December 31, 2006)

Benchmark	1 year	3 year	5 year	10 year
U.S. Public Equity Russell 3000	15.71%	11.19%	7.17%	8.64%
Non-U.S. Public Equity MSCI ACWI ex-U.S.	26.65%	21.32%	16.42%	8.59%
Fixed-Income Lehman Aggregate	4.33%	3.70%	5.06%	6.24%
High-Yield ML HY Master II	11.77%	8.38%	9.86%	6.61%
Hedge Funds HFR Index	12.91%	10.40%	9.65%	10.60%
Private Equity Buyout*	26.68%	26.47%	18.14%	15.15%
Private Equity Venture Capital*	16.98%	13.35%	−0.39%	16.98%
Real Estate— Public NAREIT	34.35%	23.80%	22.55%	13.75%
Real Estate— Private NCREIF	16.59%	17.02%	13.27%	12.72%
Commodities GSCI	−15.09%	7.73%	14.79%	4.69%
Energy GSCI Energy	−26.79%	6.59%	17.85%	7.15%

*Data from Cambridge Associates.

that global risk premia are low because all credit spreads (e.g., high-yield and emerging market bonds) are at historical lows. Another explanation for the "credit and real estate bubble" (using the term *bubble* very loosely) is possible. Ever since the stock market crash decade and perhaps because of the demographics of an aging population, there has been an increase in the demand for yield or current cash flow. Although people are looking to take more risk than short-term Treasuries in an effort to improve their returns, they are still being risk averse by looking for assets that pay a coupon or dividend over riskier assets that return an uncertain capital gain. Therefore, any asset with a coupon or dividend has been bid up in price, perhaps explaining the strong performance of real estate investment trusts (REITs), high-yield debt, emerging-market debt, and dividend-paying stocks (which tend to be value stocks). Therefore, what appears to be a global reduction in risk premia may actually be increased risk aversion, motivating investors to purchase yield or current cash flow over uncertain capital gains.

The equity crash also increased the demand for other alternative asset classes that held up well during this painful period for equities. Although large-cap U.S. equities (which were most overvalued) declined substantially, other equities, such as small-cap, value stocks, and international stocks held up better or did quite well. In addition, the average hedge fund increased in value in 2000, 2001, and 2002, contributing to a flood of new money into this asset class (some would argue against hedge funds being an asset class, being rather an incentive compensation scheme) over the following years.

Investors who lost money in the equity market selloff responded by allocating money to hedge funds, being fearful of another market trade-off. HedgeFund Intelligence recently estimated that global hedge fund capital reached approximately $2 trillion, growing nearly four times since the beginning of the decade. Other alternative assets, including private equity, real estate, and natural resources have also experienced similar growth in investor interest. In fact, these asset classes, which were once small and truly "alternative" and unconventional, are now large, institutional, and unlikely to generate the same returns going forward that they generated for early adopters such as endowments and hedge funds. I heard one endowment investor recently mention that they now feel compelled to look for alternative "alternatives."

MARKET FOCUS ON ALTERNATIVE ASSETS

Asset classes come in and out of favor and in and out of existence based on performance over time. The current market environment has been favorable to alternative asset classes—hedge funds, private equity and real

TABLE 3.2 Average Asset Allocations from NACUBO Surveys (dollar weighted)

	1996	2006
U.S. Public Equities	44.9%	29.2%
Non-U.S. Public Equities	13.0	18.5
Fixed Income and Cash	26.6	16.3
Private Equity	5.2	7.8
Hedge Funds	4.6	18.0
Real Assets	4.3	9.4
Other	1.1	1.0
Total	100.0%	100.0%
Total Alternative Asset Classes	15.5%	36.0%
Total Traditional Asset Classes	84.5%	64.0%

assets—due to the strong performance over the past 5 to 10 years. In particular, real assets such as real estate, commodities, and energy have been the top performers, attracting increasing fund flows from all investors.

Endowments and foundations have been leaders in finding and moving into new asset classes and the adoption of new investment ideas. Table 3.2 shows the increase in allocation to alternative asset classes by endowments over the past 10 years.

Most striking are the largest endowments and their more active commitments to alternatives than smaller endowments.

Although size is often the enemy of returns, it appears the largest endowments have been the best performers. From the 2006 NACUBO (National Association of College and University Business Officers) survey we find that endowments exceeding $1 billion as of June 30, 2006, generated average returns of 11.4 percent per year over 10 years, outperforming smaller endowment returns (e.g., 9.8 percent for funds between $500 million and $1 billion and 8.8 percent for funds $100 million to $500 million) and the U.S. public equities (Russell 3000 Index) of 8.5 percent. The larger more successful endowments have also allocated the largest percentage of their assets to alternative investments, as seen in Table 3.3.

According to the NACUBO survey, the average $1 billion plus endowment had 60 percent in traditional assets compared to the average endowment of 81 percent allocated to traditional asset classes. Anecdotal evidence from foundations points to the same performance and asset allocation trends seen above with endowments.

As an example, Yale's 2006 annual report shows them having only 30 percent invested in traditional assets, with the remaining 70 percent being allocated to alternatives.

TABLE 3.3 2006 NACUBO Asset Allocation (%) as of June 30, 2006

	U.S. Stocks	Int'l Stocks	Fixed & Cash	Private Equity	Hedge Funds	Real Assets	Other
In Aggregate:							
Equal-Weighted Mean	44.4	13.3	23.6	2.8	9.6	5.0	1.4
Dollar-Weighted Mean	29.2	18.5	16.3	7.8	18.0	9.4	1.0
By Investment Pool Size (Equal-Weighted Mean):							
$25 million or less	50.1	8.8	34.3	0.7	2.6	2.5	0.9
$26 million to $50 million	51.4	10.8	25.4	0.6	6.0	4.5	1.4
$51 million to $100 million	46.9	13.1	24.3	1.4	7.8	4.6	2.1
$101 million to $500 million	41.6	15.3	19.5	3.6	12.3	6.0	1.8
$501 million to $1 billion	33.7	19.2	15.5	7.3	17.4	6.4	0.4
Over $1 billion	26.3	18.6	14.2	9.4	22.4	8.6	0.5

Source: National Association of College and University Business Officers.

The next sections introduce a number of the asset classes and alternative strategies that have become the focus of the successful endowments and foundations.

Absolute Return or Hedge Fund Strategies

Investing in absolute return strategies is no longer unconventional. Most large pensions, endowments, and foundations have allocated an increasing portion of their funds to these strategies and managers. The growing popularity of "hedge funds" creates a more challenging environment for endowments and others investing in this asset class. Providing talented managers with a larger supply of capital helps make all markets more efficient, creating fewer security mispricings and arbitrage opportunities. Accordingly, future returns will likely be lower than they have been in the past.

Why Stop at Hedge Funds? The term *hedge fund* is being used so broadly that it seems to describe any fund with a fee structure of "1 and 20" or more. Traditionally, hedge funds are private investment vehicles structured as limited partnerships with the investment manager as the general partner and the investors as limited partners. "Hedge funds" is not a traditional asset class but rather an amalgam of investment managers and traders who are compensated by a performance fee, have an opportunity to invest in any number of strategies across various asset classes, and use return-enhancing tools such as leverage, derivatives, and short sales. The defining characteristic of hedge funds is their goal: to generate an absolute return over time with little systematic or public-equity market exposure. Similar to asset classes in general, there are many approaches to categorizing hedge fund strategies. Hedge fund managers and investors generally describe strategies in one of three major categories.

1. Arbitrage/Relative Value
2. Event Driven
3. Directional/Tactical

In addition to these individual strategies, an increasing amount of capital is being invested with *multistrategy* hedge funds. These funds are typically large, established hedge fund platforms that employ multiple investment teams within a single organization, each focused on a specialized investment strategy. Capital is allocated among the various underlying strategies on a tactical basis in response to changing market conditions in an effort to enhance returns.

It has become common wisdom that hedge funds can provide investors with low-double-digit returns with low volatility and low correlation to equities and fixed income. Using mean-variance optimization, hedge funds appear to be an attractive addition to an endowment's portfolio and in some instances look better than all other asset classes, causing some endowments to increase their allocations to hedge funds to more than half of their total fund. Too many investors view hedge funds as a free lunch, providing a higher return with lower risk.

The main reason hedge funds have received so much attention in recent years is their performance during the equity market downturn of 2000–2002. Ten-year average returns ending December 2006 beat both U.S. public equity (Russell 3000) and bonds (Lehman Aggregate), by 200 and over 400 basis points (bps) per annum, respectively. Although many individual funds have underperformed, as a whole they truly have provided an absolute return due to a neutral exposure to the equity market.

Where Are We Going with Hedge Funds?   Endowment and foundation investors continue to allocate capital to hedge funds because they continue to present an opportunity to invest with talented investment managers.

- Incentive fee structure typically attracts the most talented analysts and portfolio managers.

- Structure aligns the interest of managers with investors.
- Assets under management tend to be smaller than those of traditional investment managers.
- Hedge fund mandates give managers more flexibility.

As the hedge fund industry grows, it is becoming more institutional—having better-managed institutions that are better at attracting and retaining talent, providing client coverage and managing risk, in addition to being good investors. As the firms mature they become less dependent on one person and more dependent on a culture, process, and philosophy that is repeatable. The key for investors such as endowments and foundations is to ensure that the "institutionalization" retains the attractive features of hedge funds—their incentive structure and nimbleness—and avoids the undesirable aspects of many large traditional managers—a tendency to grow assets to generate higher management fees and become a closet, yet expensive, indexer.

The trend toward larger platform or brand-name funds—the largest being about $30 billion—has benefits as well as costs, and investors will be busy trying to distinguish between the large funds benefiting from any economies of scale and those that are merely asset gatherers. Another trend requiring attention is the monetization or sale of equity interests in hedge fund companies. Given the propensity to imitate successful deals, we could very likely see more of these transactions. While this is a great development for hedge fund managers, as the opportunity for an attractive exit strategy provides another avenue for managers to create wealth for themselves, it is unclear how this will benefit investors.

As markets today become more efficient, successful investors across all asset classes must have some edge in obtaining or processing information. Unfortunately, the attractive compensation has also drawn individuals who are purely seeking such compensation but have little or no skill (i.e., no edge). Given the greater competition and high fees, it is likely that investors will be disappointed with average hedge fund managers.

As in the past, the key to a successful hedge fund program will be manager selection and the identification of markets that have less capital relative to the investment opportunity set. Manager selection will be crucial for success.

Private Equity Strategies

Like hedge funds, private equity is an alternative asset class that has generated attractive returns for a number of the large endowments and foundations (e.g., according to its 2006 annual report, Yale University has generated private equity returns of 34.4 percent per annum over the past 10 years and 30.6 percent per annum since the program's inception in 1973). Like hedge funds, this asset class is also raising substantial amounts of capital, especially the buyout part of the market that has produced the most recent attractive returns.

Private equity as an asset class is comprised of a number of substrategies—including venture capital (early to late stage), growth financing, buyout, mezzanine, and distressed debt—as well as other niche approaches that don't easily fit into one of these categories.

There are several theoretical reasons that private equity should deliver higher returns than public equity. First, private equity is less liquid and should therefore yield a liquidity premium over the public markets. Second, a return premium can be generated by value-added contributions of private equity general partners to the management of their companies. General partners are able to reduce principal-agent inefficiencies where managers make decisions in their own interests at the expense of shareholders. Good private equity managers are active in their portfolio companies, serving on boards, helping management and—when necessary—making changes to the management of companies. Finally, private equity may become the preferred ownership structure for smaller companies. The costs and risk associated with Sarbanes-Oxley compliance for public companies are particularly onerous for those that are small and thus provide financial incentive to "go private." This increases the opportunity set for buyout firms that specialize in small to middle markets. Sarbanes-Oxley has made public companies more conservative.

Institutional investors have recognized the potential for returns that are higher than the public markets. The theoretical justification for investing in private equity combined with attractive returns through the mid-1990s encouraged investors to increase allocations to this asset class. In the early 1980s, total industry-wide private equity commitments averaged less than $10 billion per year. Today, one mega-fund can raise well in excess of that amount, as Carlyle, Goldman Sachs, KKR, and Blackstone have recently proven.

According to an INVESCO (2007) private equity report, venture capital commitments were $100 billion in total from 1980 to 1997, but increased to $231 billion over the four years of 1998 to 2001. Buyout fund raising has continued to increase, with $240 billion raised in 2005–2006, being nearly the same as the $253 billion that was raised between 1980 and 1997 (according to the INVESCO report).

Most private equity funds are structured as limited partnerships: limited partners (endowments and other institutional investors) provide the majority of the capital, and the general partners manage the funds and provide a small percentage of the capital. The limited partners "commit" to providing a fixed amount of capital, which the general partners "draw down" over the life of the investment period as they find investments. The investment period generally ranges from 3 to 7 years, and fund life, from 7 to 12 years. After an investment has been realized (e.g., a company is sold to a strategic buyer), the partnership will make a "distribution" of capital to the partners, comprising the original invested capital plus profit. The long "lockup" allows the general partner sufficient time to hold and add value to investments before they must be sold or exited. In return for management of the fund, the limited partners pay the general partner a management fee and a "carry" or performance fee. Average fees have been increasing over time. Today, the typical management fee is around 2 percent of committed capital per year, up from a rate of 1 percent in the early 1990s, and the current rate of carry for good funds is between 20 percent and 30 percent of profits.

Due to the nature of capital calls and distributions, the net cash flow to investors in a private equity fund is negative in the first few years until reaching profitability and turning positive. These negative cash flows and fees paid on committed capital contribute to negative returns for private equity over the first several years. Returns don't improve until companies are sold for a profit. The initial negative returns and hence lower net asset values (NAVs) create what is referred to as a *J curve*.

Despite the compelling theoretical case for private equity, the historical results are not clear. A comprehensive study by Kaplan and Schoar (2003) finds average private equity returns to be mediocre. They report buyout net returns that are lower than the Standard and Poor's (S&P) 500, and venture returns that slightly exceed the S&P 500 on a capital-weighted basis, but are lower on an equal-weighted basis. In addition, the venture returns are deceiving—the strongest performance is skewed toward a small number of top funds, which are generally closed to new investors. They also find that funds raised during "boom times," when fund raising is high, tend to perform worse.[1]

Why has the history of private equity not lived up to the promised benefits? A contributor to the disappointing private equity returns is high fees. Although the performance fee structure aligns the interests of general partners with limited partners, fees are still large. The primary reason average returns are mediocre is the large amount of capital raised by private equity funds.

Some investors became involved with private equity when funds were smaller and there was less competition between general partners for invest-ments. The spectacular returns produced by top quartile funds and by private equity programs such as Yale's attracted too much attention. Despite the mediocrity of average returns, most investors were confident in their ability to obtain top quartile returns. This helped fuel the large institutional demand for private equity. Future studies most likely will report even lower returns given the rapid ascent of private equity commitments.

What's the Best Way to Experience Private Equity?   Endowment and foundation success in this asset class has been due to early participation and access to some of the best funds, which are inaccessible to new investors. However, access to closed managers is not the sole reason for the endowments' success. Endowments were also better at forecasting the performance of follow-on funds, avoiding poorer funds and reinvesting in the better funds. Endowments have been better at using information they gain as inside investors.

Many small (and some large) institutions get exposure to private equity through fund-of-funds, due to the complexity of sourcing and due diligencing, and the difficulty in accessing the best funds. However, research finds that private equity fund-of-funds have historically been one of the least successful private equity investors. According to a study by Lerner, Schoar, and Wong (2005), the private equity programs of endowments have enjoyed annual returns 14 percent higher than that of the average investor from 1991 to 2001. Endowments have been particularly successful in venture capital, with an average early-stage venture fund internal rate of return (IRR) of 35 percent.[2]

One approach to investing in private equity involves purchasing private equity interests of existing limited partners who are looking to exit a partnership. The secondary market is relatively inefficient due to a lack of liquidity, and secondary interests can be bought at a discount to par value (cost) or at above par for those top-quartile funds that are closed to new investors. Secondaries are sometimes used in a new private equity portfolio to "reach back in time" to achieve a better time diversification to earlier vintage years.

Investors should not seek a passive allocation to private equity—fund selection is crucial for success. The good news is that there is stronger evidence of performance persistence among private equity managers, which helps with manager selection.

Real Estate

The strong performance of real estate over the last decade combined with modest return expectations for public equity and debt have encouraged institutional investors to increase their allocations to this asset class. The flood of institutional money has caused cap rates to decline to record levels in many sectors. Accordingly, future expected returns from real estate will be less attractive. Like other alternatives, the asset class is characterized by high fees, wide cross-sectional dispersion in returns, and illiquidity (except for REITs).

In hindsight, it is clear that the attractive time to invest in real estate was 10 years ago, following the deepest real estate slump since the Great Depression. Cap rates were high and the recent return experience had been poor. Many large institutional investors were burned in the early 1990s, and it was hard for most to justify increasing their allocations at the time. A retired CIO once told me that real estate was the "punk asset class," creating 90 percent of his headaches and not contributing attractive returns. He liked public equity, which was on a tear. That was in the 1990s. Much of this attractive return was generated by "core" exposure to real estate through both the private and the public markets. Core real estate is a more passive approach to the asset class, and in rising markets, a passive exposure is attractive. At this point in the cycle, however, a passive exposure may struggle to deliver the same type of returns.

Real estate was the original "alternative investment." Endowments included real estate in their portfolios long before hedge funds to provide an alternative to public equity and debt. Most endowments use external managers to manage their real estate investments, similar to the approach used with other asset classes. However, a number of endowments have been quite successful making direct investments in real estate, including Stanford's investment in the Stanford Shopping Center. However, there are some endowments that believe they already have sufficient real estate exposure through their campus land and buildings, causing them to have very small allocations within their endowments. In fact, endowments in general were slower to get involved in real estate than public and corporate pension funds, which have been active in real estate for over 20 years.

Institutional investors have allocated money to real estate to generate returns, to provide diversification, and to hedge against inflation risk. Investors, hungry for yield, continue to be attracted to real estate relative to equities and bonds. In an environment where all asset classes seem poised to deliver lower returns, the relative attractiveness of real estate is what continues to contribute to higher allocations. These trends, combined with inexpensive debt financing, have combined to drive property values up and cap rates down to record lows in all property sectors.

What are the Accommodations in Real Estate?   Real estate strategies can be placed in many different style buckets. First, strategies are either private or public, and either debt or equity. Second, strategies can be classified along a risk/return spectrum, core real estate being the most passive and having the lowest return/risk, and opportunity funds requiring more active manager involvement with portfolio properties and producing higher return/risk. Third, real estate managers are either generalists or specialists that focus on a geographic region (within the United States or other countries) or a property sector (e.g., industrial or office). Most strategies are characterized by a lack of liquidity. However, public market alternatives, such as REITs or commercial mortgage-backed securities (CMBSs), allow investors to acquire liquid real estate exposure. Similar to private equity, investors should earn a return premium for private real estate investments over public-market alternatives to compensate for the illiquidity. Endowments and other long-term investors have a comparative advantage over others as they are able to bear the illiquidity necessary to generate the higher returns. However, there is evidence that equity REITs have delivered better risk-adjusted returns than the private alternatives, suggesting that illiquidity may be an uncompensated risk. One of the most important sources of return is the active or value-added contributions of real estate managers to their portfolio properties. This is particularly significant in an environment such as the current one, when the passive returns from the asset class are modest at best.

Direct investing can be an attractive approach to real estate: The investor purchases all or part of a real estate asset directly and controls all decisions, such as purchase, sale, leasing, and management. This strategy has the potential to produce the highest returns, taking advantage of local knowledge and capitalizing on the value created by the university. However, concentration in a single market creates the risk of a downturn in the local economy. In addition, direct investing is labor intensive—real estate deals are highly complex, requiring a significant amount of expertise. Furthermore, much of the return in real estate is created by active management of the properties in terms of development, leasing, and improvements. Therefore, only investors with very large investment pools and the capacity to hire an experienced and dedicated real estate staff will have the ability to consistently add value through a direct real estate strategy.

More commonly, endowments have chosen to invest in the private real estate market through commingled funds. The various legal structures for commingled private funds generally serve the same function—a real estate manager (general partner) raises capital from investors (limited partners) to be invested in a diversified pool of real estate assets. No single investor has outright ownership of any individual property, but rather each limited partner owns a pro rata stake of each property in the pool. While this structure offers investors less control than direct investment, it provides the benefits of professional management, diversification, and economies of scale. This vehicle has been the most common with institutional investors over time. Endowment and foundation investors have actively funded commingled real estate opportunity funds over the past 10 years. These funds are similar to private equity, where talented managers have the ability to generate returns by actively adding value to the portfolio properties. Also like private equity, these funds show a wide dispersion between top- and bottom-performing funds, making manager selection essential for success.

REITs are an increasingly popular way for investors to get core real estate exposure. REITs are corporations that invest in real estate–related assets. A REIT investor can get exposure to different property sectors (e.g., office or residential) and asset classes (e.g., equity REITs or mortgage REITs). By accepting certain restrictions, the REIT structure shields investors from double taxation—the income REITs generate is taxed when received as income by REIT shareholders and not at the corporate level. Historically, institutional investors have been slow to accept REITs into their long-term strategic asset allocations, heavily favoring private, commingled vehicles instead. Although both public and private real estate are driven by the same supply and demand fundamentals, some investors think of them as separate asset classes with different risk and return characteristics. Investors are beginning to view private and public real estate as fungible.

Energy

The increase in energy prices over the past few years has drawn a lot of attention. Investors with exposure to energy-related commodities have done well. After hitting a low in December 1998, prices for crude oil reached $77 per barrel in the summer of 2006. Like real estate and other alternative assets, a lot of institutional money has been attracted by the recent returns. There are other interesting opportunities in the energy sector with little or no commodity risk, which includes a substantial need for infrastructure investment in oil and gas and in power generation and transmission.

The energy industry is classified by stages, from exploration to end user. Upstream refers to the development, extraction, and production of raw materials. Processing, storing, and transporting resources comprise midstream processes. Downstream refers to the refining, generation, marketing, and distribution of energy and power to the end user. Upstream investments tend to be the riskiest (energy price fluctuations, production risk, etc.) but offer the highest potential return. Commodity price risk is particularly high at the moment, but exposure to commodity prices also provides the greatest inflation-hedging and diversification benefits for a portfolio.

Proponents of Hubbert's peak theory claim that world oil production is currently at or near a peak, to be followed by an inexorable decline in future production. In 1956, M. King Hubbert predicted that U.S. oil production would peak in the early 1970s. Although Hubbert was criticized by many energy experts, in 1971 his prediction came true. Professor Kenneth Deffeyes is one of several experts (including Matt Simmons and T. Boone Pickens) who believe that oil will continue to rise in price due to a growing demand from developing nations and declining global supply. Even assuming supply does not decrease but continues to increase at a modest rate, the pace of economic growth in many parts of the developing world will continue to lead to higher energy prices. Energy may be one of the best ways to capitalize on global and in particular emerging market growth.

What If We Run Out of Gas?   The gloomy outlook for energy prices (unless you are long energy, and then it's bullish) is countered by a view that global energy needs will be supplied by a number of sources, which include oil, natural gas, coal, nuclear, renewables, and conservation. In each instance, technology and additional capital investment will play a role—as they have historically—in developing more efficient and effective uses of these resources.

Additional oil production will come from new production in places such as Russia and the tar sands of Canada, the latter of which may have the capacity to produce more oil than Saudi Arabia. At today's higher oil prices and improved technology, the tar sands become a viable source of future oil production. Natural gas is plentiful but requires additional investment for transportation and storage. In addition, gas-to-liquid technology can convert natural gas into a fuel that can power diesel cars. Coal is the United States' most plentiful energy resource but is also the dirtiest-burning fuel. Clean-coal technology will make coal a more attractive power source in the future. Advances in building nuclear plants and storing their waste also make this energy source more viable going forward. Similarly, technological advances in wind, solar, and biomass make investments in these energy sources interesting, especially in light of regulations mandating that a minimum percentage of energy be supplied by renewables. Finally, conservation has the potential to save a tremendous amount of energy, accomplished primarily through technology. The capital required to finance this diverse set of solutions to the world's energy needs is huge, creating opportunities for both public companies and talented private equity managers focused on energy infrastructure and early stage technology investments.

The energy sector is broad and complex, ranging from exploration to distribution. Implementation of an energy strategy can include investing with private equity managers to take advantage of the large capital requirements for developing energy infrastructure and new technology, as well as public equities and commodities. Similar to the other alternative assets, investors must be aware that strong inflows into this asset class may negatively impact future returns.

WHERE ARE WE GOING?

Already, many endowments are pushing well beyond the aforementioned assets into niches strategies such as intellectual property, litigation finance, frontier emerging markets, and farmland. Others are finding all alternatives too crowded, expensive (from a fee standpoint) and difficult to access. Some are advocating a return to simplicity and the S&P 500.

This chapter gave a view of the current investment landscape and asset classes that have been most important to foundation and endowment investment success. Undoubtedly, given the ever-changing investment landscape, a reader of this book in several years will find this description somewhat dated and of less use. However, it is a snapshot of the current investment landscape faced by today's CIOs, which should help the reader appreciate comments from our interviewees over the following 12 chapters.

From different backgrounds and perspectives, the CIOs have much to say about their overall investment experience, including their response to the current environment. The profiles bring together theory and reality as the CIOs discuss how they apply the principles detailed in Chapter 2 under market conditions described in this chapter. We believe investors will learn as much from the actual experiences of the 12 investment leaders as we did.

The CIOs describe the investment experiences and strategies that made them successful and got them to where they are today, and they share lessons and advice that will help investors determine where they are going from here.

Profiles in Capital

Philosophies and Strategies from Leading Foundation and Endowment Chief Investment Officers

CHAPTER 4

Another Sage of Omaha

Laurie Hoagland, CIO, Hewlett Foundation

Having the opportunity to work for philanthropic families, companies, or institutions has been a theme throughout Laurie Hoagland's career. A tall, lean, authoritatively soft-spoken gentleman in his early 70s, in his quiet, matter-of-fact way, he says, "That's not the original plan, but that's how it worked out."

Among the most experienced and modest investors managing endowed assets, Hoagland commands stature and respect throughout the industry. He compares his role to that of an orchestra leader. As such, he has successfully performed at two organizations and mentored several investors that run endowed assets or investment firms today. Many consider him the sage of this investment community.

Laurie Hoagland is the vice president and chief investment officer (CIO) of the Hewlett Foundation. Prior to joining the foundation in January 2001, he served for nine years as president and chief executive officer (CEO) of Stanford Management Company, Stanford University's $14 billion, now $20 billion investment and real estate organization.

For the 11 years prior to joining Stanford in 1991, Mr. Hoagland was a cofounder and partner in the investment management firm of Anderson, Hoagland and Company in St. Louis. He has also held positions as vice president and treasurer of Cummins Engine Company, and vice president and portfolio manager of the Irwin Management Company in Columbus, Indiana.

Laurie currently serves on the board of the Commonfund. He is chairman of the investment advisory committee of the Howard Hughes Medical Institute and serves as an adviser to the investment committees of Caltech, the David and Lucille Packard Foundation, and the Kamehameha Schools. He served on the board of the Lucille Packard Foundation for Children's Health from 1999 to 2005, as a member of the finance committee of the

Rockefeller Foundation from 1995 to 2001, as a director and chairman of the investment committee of the board of pensions of the Presbyterian Church from 1981 to 1992, and as a director of the Louisville Presbyterian Theological Seminary from 1994 to 2006.

Mr. Hoagland graduated from Stanford University with a degree in economics in 1958; as a Marshall scholar received an MA in philosophy, politics, and economics from Oxford University; and earned an MBA from Harvard in 1962.

BACKGROUND

After graduating from business school, Laurie Hoagland went to work for a wealthy family in southern Indiana, in what would now be called a family office. Taking the position because the family had a reputation for giving young people a lot of opportunities, he started out supporting the primary family member, working on projects like the Yale Corporation budget because his employer served on Yale's board. He became fascinated by investments and moved into the investment area as an analyst. A few years later when the family's portfolio manager retired, Hoagland became the portfolio manager at age 28, serving in that role for the next 11 years.

Hoagland then joined Cummins Engine, a multinational diesel engine manufacturing company at the heart of the family's fortune. As a vice president of corporate finance and treasurer, he took responsibility for managing the pension just as the U.S. government enacted the influential Employee Retirement Income Security Act of 1974 (ERISA) pension laws. In the course of four years, he hired a team, brought the investment management in-house, and worked on "a strange new idea at the time" called asset allocation.

After Cummins, Hoagland moved to St. Louis to start a money management firm with Dave Anderson, his colleague from the family office. They provided clients, mostly high-net-worth individuals and a few small endowments, the same sophisticated investment services such as asset allocation programs they had implemented for companies as corporate pension officers.

For the next 11 years, they ran a purposely small, successful investment business. Hoagland says he enjoyed a great partner, loved working directly with clients, and liked picking stocks and bonds. He began thinking about whether "making wealthy people wealthier" was gratifying enough. He tried to "visualize myself working in a soup kitchen without much success." One day, "the phone rang and the headhunter said the magic word, 'Stanford.' Twenty members of my family had gone there. It was as close as you can get to getting 'The Call.' My wife was happy to trade life in Missouri for life in northern California. We met at Stanford, and she was wondering why we were still wandering around the Midwest."

Stanford Management Company

Hoagland joined the newly formed Stanford Management Company as its first CEO in 1991. For him, "the situation was sweet, in the sense that everything was set up for success." However, the Stanford administration needed to overcome tragedy and setbacks before forming the company and creating the CIO role.

According to Hoagland, his predecessor Rodney "Rod" Adams, the treasurer of the university, "one of the real leaders" in endowment management, had died prematurely of cancer. Stanford University administration spent a year seeking a replacement, presumably a person with endowment investing experience that could also serve as treasurer, and could not find a candidate. "They went back to the drawing board. They took a look at Harvard Management Company and Princeton Investment Management Company, and decided to set up Stanford Management Company. They spent two or three months getting it approved by the trustees."

He describes the situation as "loaded" for success, because the university had learned what worked from experience and from other universities and structured the Stanford company accordingly.

"Stanford's old trustee management committee that had been known for micro-management was gone. The trustees had put in place a new Stanford Management board to focus on policy. The investment team had been hired—everything was set up. I did not have to fix things."

He had a turnkey operation.

Hoagland modestly points out that he started at Stanford in 1991 at the beginning of a bull market. Still, he delivered impressive results. Starting with $1.8 billion in assets, over the nine years he was there, the endowment paid out $1.4 to $1.6 billion and took in about half that amount in new gifts. When he left, Stanford Management had $8.6 billion in assets with most of the return coming from bull market equity returns and venture capital distributions.

"I am very proud of the fact that we had added about $1 billion in value over the policy benchmark. I felt very good about that."

Conducting the Symphony   Hoagland's view of the role of the CIO led him to begin planning his 2000 departure from Stanford 2 years before. "I visualize the job of the CIO as being like the conductor of a symphony. The in-house team, assuming you are a large enough organization to have one, are the principals in the orchestra. Your outside investment managers are all the other musicians. For the music to be good everyone has to be performing well. It's not a one man band. It's also true that when the symphony is playing the conductor can walk off the podium for awhile and things will go just fine. So you're not as crucial as you think you are."

Hoagland had four to five major things he wanted to accomplish at Stanford, including building a good potential succession team.

"I felt I had done that. When the stars are right on the team you better move, because if you try to stretch it out too long it can fall apart. I felt like I had been successful in getting the team ready. I was unsuccessful in the fact that my choice didn't get the job."

Meanwhile, Hoagland had been on the investment committee at the Hewlett Foundation for five years. "It was a great move going onto the payroll." He started at the beginning of 2001.

Hewlett Foundation

Two weeks into his new position the foundation dealt with the death of founder Bill Hewlett. At that point 61 percent of the pro forma balance sheet was in Hewlett Packard and Agilent stock, so that spring he implemented a plan to diversify the portfolio over a four-year period. Five percent of foundation assets remain permanently allocated to HP and Agilent stock. His team focuses on the diversified portfolio.

Hoagland did not have to wait until Hewlett passed away to diversify the portfolio—it just happened that way. The subject of diversifying had been broached previously.

"Diversification was already accepted because of Arjay Miller, the former president of Ford, dean of the Stanford business school, a director of the foundation and a leading force in its finance and investment policies. To do a historical re-creation, I imagine that he put his arm around Bill Hewlett's shoulder and said, 'Bill, you need to understand that Hewlett Packard may be a great company, but that doesn't mean it's always a great stock.' For all the classic reasons of diversification, we took a fresh look at it in 2001. You really do need to expect a higher than market return from a single stock to justify the volatility."

BEING CHIEF INVESTMENT OFFICER

Hoagland states that the long-term investment process involved in being the CIO of an endowment has many implications, including some that are behavioral. "We as human beings are wired to think in shorter-term horizons and so we have to counter that and focus on thinking longer term."

HEWLETT-PACKARD PROXY FIGHT

Hoagland had quite an interesting first year on the job. On Labor Day 2001 he landed a minor role in a major corporate and equity-market event, the proxy battle opposing the merger of Compaq Computer and Hewlett Packard. Both the Hewlett and Packard foundations got involved.

In Hoagland's case, Walter Hewlett, the chairman of the foundation and its investment committee, came to him and said, "We should really do an analysis of this merger and determine whether we think it is in the interest of the foundation to vote for or against it." They decided that independent members of the investment committee should make the decision based on the results of the survey.

As a member of that four-person team, he says, "It wasn't about our opinion. We tried to get a cross section of opinion among knowledgeable people that did not have an ax to grind on the deal. We talked to buy side analysts and buyout firms and studied the history of large mergers. Sentiment was that about 80 percent thought it was not a good deal, 20 percent thought it was good, but were kind of lukewarm. We took that result to the committee and they agreed it was not a good deal.

"Then Walter Hewlett personally came out and led the charge against it. The Packard Foundation decided they better figure out what to do, hired Booz Allen to do a similar study, and reached the same conclusion.

"If I had been Carly Fiorina, I would have folded my tent—gone on, forgotten the deal. Carly was incredible, she dug in her heels, conducted a great campaign in favor of it, and finally won 51 percent of the vote versus 49 percent.

"That was a diversion for several months in 2001 and 2002. My formal role was over early on."

Governance Structure

He considers the governance structure of the organization and the stability and longevity of the investment committee and staff crucial for achieving long-term objectives and mitigating short-term thinking.

"Committee members have terms, so people come and go and staff comes and goes over a period of time. The decisions time horizon is really longer than the individuals. Part of the issue is bringing the discipline to the whole governance structure including the staff to try to focus on the time horizon that's really congruent with the organization.

"Closely related to that, long tenures on the staff are generally good. If you did a study on the endowments with the best performance and the length of tenure, I'm sure you would find a strong relationship between the two. In particular, low turnover of the CIO and senior investment staff is very beneficial.

"Corollary to tenure is that one really shouldn't plan to go for work for an endowed institution in a senior role unless one sees that as something they would like to do for a long period of time. Part of that is to be comfortable with the fact that some of the compensation is going to be psychic and the dollar compensation is likely to be below what equally good people could earn working at for-profit institutions. And that doesn't mean one needs to do that for one's whole career, but you have to be comfortable with thinking about it for a long enough period of time that it can really be beneficial to an institution."

Hoagland suggests that not only is the governance structure important to the institution, but also, it is important to the individual serving as the CIO.

"One of the things to really ask about is the governance structure. I sort of presaged this by describing the great situation I walked into at Stanford. You want to see as much of that structure as possible. You want to get the assurance of the key board or committee members involved in the governance structure of the endowment that they are relying on the staff to initiate strategy. The role of those in the governance structure is to help refine ideas and test them. They presumably have other day jobs. The reason you want to have this job, what makes it exciting is that the CIO and his team are leading the charge. I think it's the most successful model because endowment investments really need day-to-day attention."

Asset Allocation

Considering that Hoagland employed asset allocation techniques long before research demonstrated the impact of asset allocation on portfolio performance, his perspective on asset allocation today seems particularly relevant.

When he joined Stanford, he was "religious" about asset allocation. He says, "You tried to pick the best portfolio. If you had to lock it up for 20 years and couldn't touch it, what portfolio would you pick? You would do that with the knowledge that a year later when you took a fresh look, the world might have changed. There might be new asset classes, so what you decide to put in the lockbox for 20 years at that point in time might be different. It was a very top-down, 'what's the best portfolio?' process."

Hoagland has evolved since then. While he still believes you need to look at the allocation from the top down, he says, "You also want to pay a lot of attention to bottom-up opportunities and build parts of your portfolio from the bottom, particularly in areas like private equity, real estate, and natural resources. At Hewlett, we have 12 to 13 percent in real assets. That's not a top-down decision. If we had started earlier and found investment managers we wanted, we probably would be at a higher level at this point. So it's very much an iterative top-down/bottom-up approach."

His approach implies that he does not adhere to rigid policy portfolio targets and would not invest in inferior or less desirable investment managers just to achieve the target allocation percentage in an asset class.

Hoagland goes on to say, "The fact that the borders of asset classes are melting is even more reason not to be sharp about exactly how much you have in each asset class."

Portfolio Construction

Hoagland became CIO of Hewlett in 2001 but had been involved in managing the endowment since 1995, when he joined Hewlett's investment committee. His experiences with Hewlett give an excellent view of his portfolio construction process.

When he first joined the committee in 1995, the foundation had recently established its first allocation to alternative investments representing 20 percent of the portfolio. The committee hired the consulting firm Cambridge Associates to research and select the managers.

"Private equity, real estate, and absolute return—the allocation took several years to build. That program was phenomenally successful. I would have said starting then that they were too late to catch the venture capital curve, but they did."

When he joined Hewlett in 2001, recently harvested venture profits were $1 billion of a $3 billion portfolio. In two of their first three venture investments, they had invested $6.8 million in one fund and $10 million in another. Both firms returned a quarter of a billion dollars a piece. They made those investments in well-known firms that would not normally have taken on a new investor. The Hewlett name gave them access.

The Hewlett portfolio remains a work in progress. Since private equity was already a significant part of portfolio, he has mainly focused on building the allocations to absolute return and real assets. The real assets portfolio primarily consists of private real estate funds and natural resources. When he arrived at Hewlett, real assets made up 4 percent of the portfolio and now make up 12 to 13 percent of the portfolio, as mentioned in his discussion of asset allocation.

When he left Stanford, that portfolio had a 25 percent allocation to real assets. "The Stanford allocation of 25 percent was an outlier in 2000. When we were loading up on real estate people thought we didn't 'get it.' It would have been nice to have Hewlett at that level too. (Again) It's a bottom-up process finding the right managers, taking your time. Right now is not the time to rush headlong into real estate."

He admits, "I probably do have a bias toward real assets as a good cash generator, good return generator, good diversifier, and a substantial opportunity for value added if you pick the right managers."

Structured to Capture Alpha and Beta   At Hewlett he has implemented a portfolio that differs markedly from his approach at Stanford and from his peers. The Hewlett portfolio has a significant amount of overlay of absolute return of about 20 percentage points.

"Two ways to look at it—one is to look at it as a sandwich. Cash is in absolute return, and we overlay the stock market or the bond market return. So we are looking to get the stock and bond market return plus the alpha of the hedge funds. Another way to look at is that we are leveraged at the portfolio level. We are 120 percent invested and have 100 percent of the beta exposure and 20 percent in absolute return. If you make the simplifying assumption of no beta in the absolute return portfolio, then we have 100 percent beta, 20 percent alpha, 120 percent exposure.

"In reality, absolute return does get some beta so we watch it closely. Either way we can roll the portfolio up and ask, 'What are its risk and return characteristics?'

"There's a lot of discussion of leverage. Leverage is everywhere. The typical U.S. stock has leverage in the company. So there's leverage all over the place and it's hard to assess and hard to evaluate.

"What you can do and what you want to do is look at the risk of the total portfolio including the impact of the leverage. That's different."

Hoagland says he got the inspiration for this approach by combining the "greatest hits" of two leading endowment managers.

"Few people ever have original ideas. Most of my best ideas, I have stolen. Stanford started investing in absolute return in 1989, the early days. As we came into the 1990s, David Swensen at Yale invested a lot in it. He even named the asset class 'absolute return.' I didn't like that I lost the beta if I put the money into absolute returns funds. I then looked at what Jack Meyer was doing at Harvard. He was running a lot of absolute return arbitrage strategies in-house, working the money extra hard, and keeping the beta. So at Stanford and now at Hewlett, we started doing what Harvard was doing except with outside managers—creating a situation where we capture the full beta plus the value we hope to have from absolute return strategies. I give my colleagues full credit."

Investment Manager Selection Based on his stock-picking style from his days in St. Louis, Hoagland considers himself a relative-value investor.

"It could be a growth stock, but cheap relative to other growth stocks. In the endowment area, I just love any investment where you can apply the adjective *distressed*. I like to buy things cheap to begin with, because and that gives you some downside protection. If things go well you can do better. That's pretty simple."

Regarding his criteria for selecting managers, Hoagland thinks David Swensen has the right approach and, like Swensen, tends not to invest with big institutions. He does admit to having brand biases and continues to invest with firms that he has gotten to know over long time periods. He commented on other aspects of the industry.

On Hedge Funds

I was around when the A.W. Jones hedge funds started in the 1960s. The value proposition was: Here's a brilliant manager that will manage one-tenth as many assets as before. The trade-off for paying higher fees of 1/20 instead of 75 basis points is you'll get the best and brightest managers, focused on a small portfolio that will have a good chance of generating good returns.

Hedge funds are not small anymore and unlike Lake Woebegone, they're not all necessarily top decile managers. That puts a lot more pressure on the investor to separate the wheat from the chaff.

On Hybrid Firms with Multiple Products

The managers worry less about returns. As the balance of power has shifted from the limiteds (investors) to the generals (managers), the generals can worry less about generating good return for the limiteds and worry more about running a successful business or maximizing the business.

Currently, more and more companies, instead of focusing on one strategy and doing it really well, tend to be adding multiple strategies and multiple directions. This may create a larger, steadier revenue stream for them, but raises questions for the limiteds.

Managing and Mentoring Hoagland has hired or mentored a number of talented investors that have progressed into leadership roles at other organizations including David Russ at Dartmouth, Dan Kingston at Vulcan Investments (profiled in Chapter 14), and Anne Casscells of Aetos Capital, a hedge fund-of-funds.

To manage and motivate people, he believes that you hire really talented people and give them room to run. He compares his approach to the sport of curling.

"In curling a team member pushes a disc along the ice and other teammates skate ahead and sweep the ice to ease the way. I see myself as sweeping the ice for my team. I like to delegate as much as I can. At Stanford, I was also responsible for the commercial real estate portfolio. I hired the right person and could spend 95 percent of my time on investments."

Peer Comparison and Competition   Hoagland believes there is a huge focus on annual performance or what he calls "the big performance derby" and says it was a significant issue at Stanford in the 1990s that has only gotten worse. He differentiates between universities and foundations, pointing out that university endowment CIOs face the most pressure.

"It's accurate to say that the relative endowment results are significant in the competition among universities for faculty and students. On the other hand, we have to ask, 'What are the implications of every board wanting to be in the first quartile?' What kind of pressure is this putting on? Is there more escalation of risk? It's an issue."

He says that part of the problem in comparing the performance of a CIO at one institution against the CIO at another institution is that focus is usually on looking at 1 year of performance, not 3, 5, or even 10 years.

"In a foundation environment, we have the luxury of less of that kind of pressure. We are spending a lot of time integrating our investment policy with our programs, looking at the amount of risk we are willing to take versus what programs we are willing to cut back."

LESSONS, OBSERVATIONS, AND ADVICE

Despite his stature in the foundation and endowment investment community, that experience represents only one third of a 45-year career. The perspective he brings from his earlier investment experiences not only explains his success managing endowed assets, but also qualifies him more than any other CIO to explain the challenges foundations and endowments have faced and to predict what lies ahead.

11,000 Investment Nights

Hoagland frequently speaks at industry conferences and over time has developed an analogy that sounds like one of the tales of the Arabian Nights to describe past investment conditions and forecast future conditions.

"The really good news for endowed institutions is that the results for the last 15 years, a well-measured period now, are superior. If you took all the returns of all institutional investors in the United States, you would find that the endowed institutions are a step ahead. It has been great that they have generated outstanding results for achieving their purposes. After about 10 years of these results, people began to notice; over the last 5 years people have really begun paying attention.

"Now, let's look at what happened during the 15 years and what's likely to happen over the next 15 years. A lot of what drove this actually goes back 30 years. Imagine a low valley with two fields, one called U.S. stocks the other called U.S. bonds. All institutions, including the endowments, were plowing these fields trying to get good returns.

"The endowed then looked up the valley and saw an orchard with a lot of low-hanging fruit called venture capital and another field called international investments. Some of the first new asset classes they pioneered in the late 1970s and early 1980s. After a few years, they looked further up the valley and found leveraged buyouts, real estate, and absolute return funds, and started plowing those fields.

"During the last 15 years, this valley was fertile and productive. The first half of the 1990s, asset allocation policies were in a state of foment as a number of new asset classes were judged suitable for institutions. The last half of the 1990s, we saw the implementation period as institutions executed their plans by finding and hiring outside investment managers. Between 2000 and 2005, we harvested.

"In the last 5 years, the endowed institutions have looked down the valley and seen the hordes storming up. Other institutions have caught on, and everybody wants to reverse-engineer the Yale portfolio. They're pouring up the valleys, stripping the trees, overplanting the fields. Productivity hasn't slipped yet, but it will be slipping before long.

"Endowments have looked up the valley for the next place to go and haven't found new fields of assets that can take the huge amounts of money we have to invest. It's kind of a box canyon."

Like Scheherazade, Hoagland leaves the conclusion open-ended.

"That's the dilemma we face. Over the next 15 years, instead of having these beautiful fields and orchards to ourselves, there's going to be a lot more money and a lot more competition. One has to predict that it's going to be much tougher for endowed institutions to preserve their performance advantage. That's a little painful, but that's my analogy."

Foundation and Endowment Issues

Hoagland's story brings to the forefront practical and very real near-term investment and organization challenges.

Trickles of Alpha   In response to an observation that many investors seem to be actively pursuing smaller, increasingly more obscure sources of return, he compares the situation to the Glen Canyon dam on the Colorado River.

"All this liquidity is filling it up. We try to get to things before other people do. We think we have a one- or two-year advantage, and it turns out to be a month or two. Everybody now is scouting smaller and smaller tributaries."

Staffing Challenge I   New investors attempting to replicate endowment portfolios and performance are trying to hire experienced people to do it for them. So in addition to the challenge of generating alpha, "a huge challenge is to keep the talent. How do we encourage their passion for our mission? How much should the compensation be? How much of a discount from for-profit compensation can we expect people to accept?"

Global Flooding or Irrigation   When pressed to predict the investment landscape 15 years hence, he says that he does not have one particular view because he questions whether the high level of liquidity and available investment funds is purely a cyclical phenomenon as it has been historically.

"When there is more credit creation than is needed to fuel the economy, the excess flows into the financial markets and runs them up, and then when it's needed, it gets pulled out of the financial markets. We have seen that cycle over and over again. So the question is: 'Is the same thing going to happen again?' In which case, this has been a massive liquidity expansion and I shudder to think about what happens when it gets pulled out. Or, 'Is something secular going on here?'

"Some of the countries that are growing really fast have very high public savings rates, high reserves, and very high private savings rates. The people coming into the middle class in those countries have 25 percent savings rates. So are there structural changes that mean there will be lots more investment funds available? That would mean future returns will be modest. If we have a withdrawal of liquidity or suffer through a collapse, then in the aftermath we will see more historical-type returns."

Staffing Challenge II   No matter what investment scenario transpires, he points out that investing globally with limited resources will be a big challenge. Along with complications like time zone differences, travel requirements, and available energy, he worries how CIOs can run high-quality global portfolios with small staffs.

Staffing Challenge III   Related to the size of the staff is another challenge. "How do we keep up with the demand for talent? Most of my focus is trying to assess what this huge amount of liquidity means for portfolio returns. What does it mean for the demand for investment talent? There's a limited amount of proven investment talent around and a huge amount of money to be managed. Someone coming from an endowed institution is viewed as having the secret sauce."

Given the staffing challenges he sees ahead, he thinks the outsourced CIO model provides a serious and viable alternative for managing endowment assets for many institutions.

Career as a CIO

When discussing the long-term nature of endowment and foundation investment portfolios, Hoagland made this statement on pursuing a CIO career.

"Obviously, I'm trying to discourage people that see this as a good resume builder, come into a senior position for just a few years, and then move on. For young people, it's different. They can come for a few years and they can contribute a lot of intelligence and energy."

Important Influences

When asked to name people who have been important influences in his life and career, Hoagland paused and reflected.

"That's a good question. I learned a lot during the 11 years in the 1980s in the money management business from Dave Anderson, my partner, and from the two of us interacting together. He is a great guy.

"Another person from whom I have learned a great deal is Garnett Keith; we were close colleagues at the family office in the late 1960s and early 1970s, and then he went on and managed the Prudential's investment assets. We continue to compare notes frequently."

He had a lot of good bosses. Then Hoagland happens to remember a 1969 meeting. While in his hometown of Omaha, Nebraska, he visited the home and sought the advice of a local millionaire business leader named Warren Buffett.

"I asked him what advice he would give if I ever wanted to start an investment business. He said, 'Note that it tends to be binary situation. Either it never takes off or it does well.' That advice from Warren was right. Eleven years later, we started our business. We had our Harvard Business School plan and never revised it, because the business went like this [moves his arm in an upward trajectory]. So we had to decide how to manage the business and its growth and decided to run it ourselves."

MIDWESTERN VALUES AND WISDOM

Although Hoagland's brother was a congressman from Omaha and used Warren Buffett as a sounding board, Hoagland and Buffett have not remained in touch.

Nonetheless, the two share several characteristics. They each have the stature and credibility to lead their industry and the experience to know its history and forecast its future. Both Hoagland and Buffett have been known for picking good people, imbuing them with midwestern values, letting them do their jobs, and fostering their success.

Most important, both men have committed their investment accomplishments to supporting the work of nonprofit institutions in perpetuity.

In the endowment and foundation community, Laurie Hoagland is the sage of Omaha.

CHAPTER 5

Doctor, Lawyer, Investment Chief

Dr. Allan S. Bufferd, Treasurer Emeritus, Massachusetts Institute of Technology

Allan Bufferd retired as treasurer of the Massachusetts Institute of Technology in May 2006, capping the last of his 34 years at MIT by earning a 23 percent investment return, top among the 25 endowments surveyed by Bloomberg in an article dated December 4, 2006. For Bufferd, a direct, pull-no-punches, former engineer and lawyer, the achievement may actually have been bittersweet.

On the sweet side, the performance came from long-term investments in alternatives, the asset class into which Bufferd led the organization earlier in his career. On the bitter side, Bufferd abhors the competitive state of endowments and relative ranking systems.

Beginning his career as a doctor of engineering, he then became a lawyer. Bufferd built on those experiences to join the MIT endowment staff, successfully lead it through a period of great change, and achieve the stature of an elder statesman in the industry. Interviewed for the Bloomberg article about MIT's 2006 performance, Bufferd answered a question with a phrase that could easily apply to his entire career and time at MIT, "You learn from your experience."

Before retiring, Bufferd's primary responsibilities included the overall balance sheet, supervision of investment management of assets, formulation and implementation of investment policy for endowment, retirement fund, and other assets, which totaled more than $12 billion; and debt issuance and debt management policies. He was *ex-officio* member of the Corporation of the Massachusetts Institute of Technology and of its executive, investment, and development committees; and also served as a trustee and treasurer of the trustees, of the MIT Basic Retirement Plan. He served as the first president of the MIT Investment Management Company (MITIMCo), since its formation on July 1, 2004.

Dr. Bufferd joined MIT in 1972. Prior to MIT, he was engaged in engineering and corporate management. He currently serves as a member of advisory boards of diverse investment funds including as an investment adviser to the Alaska Permanent Fund Corporation, Computer History Museum, Grayce B. Kerr Foundation, and the National University of Singapore.

He is chairman of the board of directors of the Controlled Risk Insurance Company and the Risk Management Foundation, Inc., a medical malpractice insurance provider to MIT, Harvard University, and its associated hospitals and service organizations; and chairman of the board of directors of The Coop, a retail cooperative serving the Harvard and MIT communities.

Dr. Bufferd serves as the lead director of MassBank (Nasdaq), where he chairs the asset/liability committee and is a member of the executive committee, is a director of RamRe (Nasdaq), and is an independent director of the Morgan Stanley Prime Properties Fund.

He participates actively with tax-exempt organizations, serving as a director and treasurer of the Beth Israel Deaconess Medical Center (including membership on the audit, compensation, and finance committees), of Explorations, Inc.; and as a trustee of the Robert Wood Johnson Foundation and the Whiting Foundation. He is the immediate past chair of the board of trustees of Wheelock College. Dr. Bufferd holds a ScD from MIT and a JD from Suffolk University.

BACKGROUND

Tongue firmly in cheek, Allan Bufferd describes his background as "too much of a shaggy dog story."

How does a doctoral degree in materials engineering from MIT lead to investments? "It doesn't." He was in his 30s in the early 1970s as the world was going through great turmoil and change. One morning, he woke up and decided he wanted a change but was uncertain about what to do. "I wanted to do something different, so I went to law school, and came back to MIT as a way station, initially doing fund raising. A couple of quick short steps later, I moved to the estates and trusts area and subsequently became an assistant to the treasurer."

What started as an interim situation in 1974 turned into a great opportunity. Working with his predecessor, someone he had known at MIT, "in a classic apprenticeship structure," Bufferd got to learn the basics and to work on the new types of investments and asset classes being introduced to the endowment market.

Initially brought in to work on the restructuring of the MIT pension plan following the passage of the Employee Retirement Income Security Act of 1974 (ERISA) because "somebody had to sit with the attorneys," he jokes. "Everything after that just went down hill. One day I said, 'This is not so bad. I don't think I want to leave.' "

Bufferd credits his predecessor, Glenn Strehle, with giving him the opportunity. "I was provided the freedom to explore new areas." Strehle came from the investment management business, a stock and bond person, who delegated private equity and other new investments to him. "In this situation the assistant could not ask the supervisor what to do, for we both were new to the new types of investments."

A good fundamental education, with training in both analysis and synthesis and problem solving, helped Bufferd grow as an investor. "It was a wonderful opportunity." He gained exposure to broad, new areas of investing. "It was full of change, something that always excited me. I was chartered to ask very difficult, and in some respects, simple questions."

BEING CHIEF INVESTMENT OFFICER

Bufferd defers on investment philosophy. "I don't really understand what is meant by an investment philosophy. Nobody wants to buy expensive product. Everybody wants value, a good price, and to know when to sell. Everyone doesn't want to put all their eggs in one basket."

Asset Allocation

Asset allocation at MIT evolved over time and not necessarily from the policy perspective.

"In the investment world in the 1970s, asset allocation was framed very much in terms of mathematical calculations. It seemed to hover around the classic 60/40 stock-to-bond ratio; maybe more daring organizations set it at 70/30." As assets grew and "we all thought we had a better understanding of some of the newer investments, we tended to sprinkle 'salt and pepper' into the mix." An endowment would add some alternatives, including nontraditional alternatives and even real estate.

"What was interesting about the process was that, as we went along over time, we always built in these artificial constraints, limits, or boundaries." For instance, Bufferd would say, "Real estate might be good but we shouldn't have more than 5 percent. Or yes, private equity would be good, but no more than 3 percent." Those judgments tended to be based more on politics or implementation issues. Even if he wanted to allocate more, it often came down to, "I couldn't see how I could get there."

Bufferd elaborates, "It was clear early on that whatever the rigors of asset allocation, there were deep subjective inputs, the perspectives of individuals and of board politics. Some of the rigors of asset allocation went out the window, because of the political, 'small p in a nice way,' and dealing with the realities of interacting with boards."

He observed an interesting phenomenon as they entered the 1990s. "Assuming the data was correct, you ran the optimizers on a totally unconstrained basis. You would get a picture of what would be a great portfolio from an asset allocation standpoint. However, nobody would follow that dictate. You'd look at it and say, 'I'll never get it through the board.' "

Similarly, as the 1990s progressed, "We'd make small allocations to new and emerging areas, then they would be gradually increased over time."

With the staff and the board more comfortable about the increased allocation to alternatives, the overall allocation process became more formal.

Null Hypothesis Approach   In the early 1990s, Bufferd and the staff approached asset allocation using a null hypothesis approach. Starting from the premise that they had only five major asset classes, he presented as the null hypothesis a portfolio divided into five equal allocations of 20 percent. He then asked, "Why should we deviate from the null hypothesis? What do we know that should inform us of how we move off of this allocation?"

Two aspects of this analysis impacted their asset allocation policy proposals. The first is history. "Most allocation studies are done retrospectively. It's about history, not about the ability to predict the future." The result is a heavy historical bias in asset allocation.

"The way you moved off the allocation was by looking into the future." "How did anyone move to consideration of emerging markets when it was well nigh impossible to make any forward forecast about expected returns or volatility since there was no historical data of any statistical significance?"

Bufferd identifies a second important element related to nontraditional investment that would allow an institution to move away from the null hypothesis allocation. "It is an assessment of your inherent ability to execute in that new area. Since the spread of returns is so great in the nontraditional areas, you must have an ability to locate and evaluate, a priori, those managers who will be the high-quality performers."

If an organization "really had to play with the best people" in order for the alternative investment to contribute to the overall portfolio, "you could only move off the null hypothesis if you really understood your ability to execute in that alternative area." When an organization has the ability to execute, by having talented staff members that understand the asset class and have the relationships with managers, then it can structure the portfolio accordingly.

"If you had weakness in the portfolio, you had to look for people to fill those roles." Staff expertise "reflected your ability to move off the null hypothesis." Organizations must determine the importance of a particular asset class if it has limited resources. Because he did not think MIT had sufficient expertise in the area, "pure hedge funds, market-neutral hedge funds, were never a big issue for us—I don't know if I was right or wrong."

Looking at asset allocation across major university endowments and over an extended period of time, Bufferd says, "At a macro level, with the exception of Harvard, I don't think our asset allocations were really that different. However, on a finer level, there was a great difference in how specific programs were executed."

Private equity returns show a wide disparity between the first quartile and fourth quartile of performance. "You don't want to be average; it's not worth it, does nothing. In fact, it's less than the market. The question is, 'How do you get to be first quartile?' If you can't, it doesn't matter what the optimizer says about asset allocation."

While many investors believe that the ability to build relationships and networks makes a tremendous difference in private equity investing, Bufferd believes relationship building is a defining characteristic of an investor's success in every asset class.

Idea Generation

Bufferd defines good ideas by asking a question of his own. "How did I get ideas that differentiated, that contributed, and that fit who we were, where we were, and what we were trying to do?"

He responds, "It's about being an observer. Idea generation comes about from much reading and many conversations. How do you get these inputs? From my perspective, however members of the staff gathered inputs to frame their thinking didn't matter to me. If they wanted to chat with people, read at their desk, run around going to conferences, or run around seeing managers, it was okay. Whatever they do is fine as long as it leads to ideas.

"Idea generation is the sine qua non of the business. The good ideas are not going to come to you on a silver platter."

Bufferd describes an encounter with an investment committee chair that influenced him to pursue new ideas.

"Probably in the late 1980s we had a particular investment we were looking at. I don't even remember what it was. Something in your stomach or head was telling you it had a problem, at the same time we still felt like we should do it. Being somewhat political, I went to the investment committee chair for his opinion, preselling, to talk about it. It was less about being positive; I was talking about it in terms of risk. The chair, a wise gentleman, said, 'You know, Allan, the turtle does not move forward if it doesn't stick its head out of the shell.' I said, 'Thank you very much' and I left."

The chair's pronouncement became a metaphor for his approach to generating ideas and growing the endowment.

"The MIT experience as I describe it was a series of events of a turtle sticking its head out of its shell. Sometimes it got hit! It was all about small incremental changes, less a grand vision, more about finding areas of opportunity and growing programs off those areas."

One example of this turtle approach was their first private equity transaction in 1977, a leveraged buyout (LBO) done as a direct investment. At that point, they had no private equity in the portfolio and participated in the investment even though they had no prior relationship with the manager. It was a successful investment and led to more investments with that private equity manager. He had a similar experience with their first foray into venture capital investing in 1978.

MIT made its first international investment in 1980–1981, investing 100 percent of its allocation in Japan after Bufferd traveled to the country with the money manager who had approached them with the idea. "It was a time of great opportunity in Japan. The 1980s were going to be the decade of Japan. We saw the opportunity for growth of the Japanese economy. We traveled there and walked around like research analysts, visiting department stores and looking at the cost of various merchandise, asking about secretarial salaries, and relating both to our knowledge of the United States. I soaked it up." After executing and performing well, the manager impressed Bufferd further by honestly suggesting when to close down the Japanese investment program. Based on the advice, MIT earned additional profit by establishing a significant privately negotiated put position.

The MIT approach to investing in real estate sounds more tortoise than turtle because of the creativity and complexity involved. They focused on developing real estate projects in the vicinity of MIT. "Based on the thesis of MIT's being an attractor, a magnet, we foresaw how economic development would take place at the periphery of a major research university." They structured transactions to give MIT control of the land into the future and achieved major financial gains with developments above the ground. "We took the development risk and realized value by selling developments and retaining rights to the land, thereby serving an important strategic interest for MIT's future land needs."

When they had interesting ideas, they acted early and started small. "In almost all cases, ideas came from different sources. They came from staff, friends, board members, the investment committee, and manager pitches. Idea generation is a function of being open, listening, and being willing and having a board that's willing to let the turtle stick its head out of its shell."

Manager Selection

When researching and selecting managers, Bufferd preferred that he or his staff conduct the research themselves privately. MIT rarely relied on investment consultants unless they had time constraints or lacked resources in a certain area. "Pasteurized information never struck us as being terribly valuable."

Bufferd trusted his visceral reactions to people and organizations "much more so than the numbers tend to show." He looked for managers with intelligence, a sense of humor, and honesty, and he wants to feel comfortable that the manager is committed to success. Sensing drive, hunger, and commitment to quality, even in large organizations, impressed him greatly. When Bufferd selected managers, he took the viewpoint of "whatever the asset class, there will be people who will be successes." It was not about finding the right asset class; it was about finding the right managers.

"The question is, 'How do you find them?' At least for me, personally, it was very visceral." Bufferd later regretted "doing less belly-to-belly contact in his later years at MIT. I missed it; it was really the part I enjoyed." Today, he says that it's much more complicated. When he started making investments in alternative assets, "there were hardly any consultants, no data, a small group of people, and you could do a lot of work belly to belly." The number of managers today is "staggering. You just can't see everybody. While I miss it, it's really hard."

Even though his visceral reaction helps guide his manager selection process, he cautions against overreliance on it. "You always have to be careful of being full of yourself. I thought I was pretty good at it, but I can react too quickly to manager presentations, like 'Oh my god, this is going to be a terrible half hour.' I highly enjoyed it."

Managing Staff

Bufferd looked to hire bright, energetic people, with complementary styles and skills. "I did not want clones—I wanted contrasts and quants." His approach resulted in a diversified staff portfolio of investment styles. Bufferd gave the individuals freedom to determine the best way to invest in their asset class. "They had to understand and communicate it and then come back and share with everybody else. It was not appropriate for me to direct them to go do X, because I had no idea of what X was. I think overall it worked out.

We were able to build cohesiveness and attract and retain people, because they had the elbow room and could stick their heads out of the shell."

Governance and Decision Making

Bufferd leads off his comments on governance practices, by "painting the backdrop first and showing how MIT benefited by the changes."

"Take a university, a complex organization, all bright people. Faculty members teach, the administration deals with budgets, questions on student life, athletics. All these people make all these decisions about everything going on at a university. But the endowment has to have a board, not overseeing its policies, but actually approving the commitments and the managers hired. What is it that's different? In many places, especially the university world, there's so much fine-tuning and the hand on the wheel."

The types of decisions made in the endowment vary little from the types of decisions made throughout other parts of a university, but with a much higher degree of supervision.

"Some will harrumph and say it's their fiduciary responsibility, but one of the great transitions of the second half of the twentieth century was moving toward framing governance to policy." The shift has resulted in endowments adding staff and fiduciaries and administrations focusing more on compensation and operating budget and less on micro-managing the investment process. He says the shift began in the 1970s, and believes the shift was driven partly by Harvard Management and the formation of other university investment management companies or CIOs with long tenures and the trust of their board.

"If you are going to have professionals, creative people, generating ideas, you must have a change in governance. Creative, capable, and responsible, smart, talented people will not stay in an organization where they have to get approval for each investment, small or large."

Bufferd recommends as a cross-reference *Trustee Investment Strategy for Endowments and Foundations* (John Wiley & Sons, 2006) by Chris Russell. Mr. Russell is a British investment manager and foundation executive whose book advises foundation and endowment trustees. "I had the opportunity to meet him and discuss our experiences and his thesis. He did a good job and I recommend the text for trustees and board members."

Bufferd believes more organizations have loosened their controls. "As I was thinking it was time to step down, I had enjoyed great freedom, primarily because I had been there for 30 years. I didn't need the management company, but I was concerned MIT needed it." He figured that if there was a case for MIT to establish a management company, then it was better for the "person going out rather than the person coming in" to present it to the trustees, get the company approved, and then implement and manage it for awhile.

"I could talk much too long on governance. Governance is one of the major impediments to effective execution in this area and separates large endowments from small."

LESSONS, OBSERVATIONS, AND ADVICE

Given his years of experience in industry and investing, Bufferd has pointed opinions about the state of the world today and his expectations for the future.

Investment Concerns

When it comes to his biggest concerns, Bufferd jokes, "I don't have them anymore, now that I'm not in the saddle." He then expresses two serious concerns about the world and investing today.

"I have concerns as a human being. I listened carefully to my elders when I was younger, now that I'm an elder I don't listen as much. Before I went into investments, somebody told me, 'You probably won't remember this, Allan, but it will be harder to find heroes as you get older.' He was wrong because I did remember, but he was right about the difficulty of finding heroes.

"My concern is that it's the wide-eyed youth that saw heroes, and now there are no heroes. I am very concerned about the world. Everything is an argument; everything is a fight. Reasonableness seems to have disappeared. There are segmented interest groups. I am not impressed with many of the people who have been charged with making major policy decisions for the public sector.

"In a simple word, I am very concerned about the world around us.

"When Boston engages in the largest public works project ever and pieces of ceiling fall down and kill people, or built a convention center and when it opens there are barrels on the floor because the roof is leaking, it's troublesome. There are many people with authority to make decisions and if the people that make simple ones can't get them right, I'm concerned about complicated decisions. I feel like there's much political risk."

At MIT, We Sell No Wine Before Its Time An experience presenting at an industry conference illustrates Bufferd's views on contrarian investment ideas and concerns about investor behavior.

"I gave a paper at an NMS Management conference in 2003 because it allowed me to think about a problem. I turned it into a thought experiment with the attendees. With the assistance of an associate, we labeled four 'investment' categories or asset classes, 'X, Y, Z, W,' so there would be no subjective bias from knowing what each letter represented. We constructed portfolios using these four asset classes with the use of portfolio optimizers, using some historical information on returns that, while not perfect, were reasonably good. Each of the four assets, individually or in the aggregate, increased the risk-adjusted returns of the starting portfolio. Perhaps a bit surprising but it merely speaks to the issue of broadly diversified portfolios."

Bufferd used the example to raise a question similar to his null hypothesis.

"What would it take for us to do an investment in X, Y, Z or W?"

Referencing the factors that made MIT move forward with their Japanese and real estate investments, he asked the audience more specifically, "What would have to be the factors to allow you to move forward in X, Y, Z or W?"

He reached similar conclusions to those he had reached with the MIT null hypothesis portfolio. "We found that where we had confidence and faith in people's ability to execute in their particular area, if they could do that and get past other variables, it could help overall portfolio return, be viable and grow from there."

Two interesting thoughts came out of the presentation.

Laurie Hoagland of the Hewlett Foundation (profiled in Chapter 4), who chaired the session, would not let Bufferd leave without identifying the categories X, Y, Z, and W. "They were fine wines, fine art, antique automobiles, and high-end jewelry. You might laugh about whether these are institutional investments, but there is now a fine arts fund based in London and at least one university has invested in it."

The most important aspect of the presentation that struck him about being contrarian or deciding to make a different type of investment happened when it ended. "The thrust of the presentation was about 'X,' the wine. Afterward, some attendees came over for further discussion. One person asked, 'How long has MIT been investing in wine?' I looked at him and said, 'I'm not at liberty to tell you.' "

Bufferd makes his point. "What this goes to is there are a lot of lemmings. There is a fear of missing something, an inability to stick your head out and be a turtle. With contrarian ideas, you sit, listen, and think. The ability to move forward on those ideas is about the dynamic between you, the staff, and committee and is not about, in my judgment, what other institutional investors are doing."

He adds, "Institutional investors have to find their right place. It's not about what someone else is doing. It is about what their institution needs. What do you need to execute?"

Why Investors Succeed or Fail

Copying or following other institutions also factors into the reasons investors succeed or fail.

National Association of College and University Business Officers (NACUBO) studies show that large endowments outperform medium, and medium outperform small. Larger endowments can spend more absolute dollars on their investments but have it represent a smaller percentage or fewer basis points of cost than in a smaller endowment.

"MIT spends a lot of money on investing. Clearly, large institutions have to spend the money. Travel budgets, we send staff to Asia four to five times a year. In a $500 million fund, the CIO alone goes to Asia, because he or she may be the only one running the money." Bufferd worries that CIOs in those situations get stretched too thin or take their eyes off the portfolio too frequently.

"There is a real problem about understanding the institution and the institutional needs. My predecessor went on to do work sponsored by the Commonfund that relates to this topic. Gifts to the endowment are really very important factors in building the endowment over time. Part of my judgment about the endowment in mid-size institutions is to wonder whether the marginal dollar of the budget should be spent on development rather than on the investment budget. People and organizations have to tune themselves to where they are."

Bufferd says that sometimes success or failure has more to do with luck and timing. "Walking down the wrong path, I have had failures. It's not an easy process or everyone would be making money all the time. You need a little luck."

Foundation and Endowment Challenges

Based on his observations advising other endowments and serving on boards of investment management firms, Bufferd identifies competition from global investors as a challenge U.S.-based foundations and endowments will face.

"The National University of Singapore has assets of about two billion U.S. dollars, a portfolio of hedge funds, private equity, and real estate. They understand alternatives and travel around the world looking for opportunities." Their endowment looks similar to a U.S. endowment, and that creates the challenge. "What I see, one of the problems for us in the United States in general, is that we are quite provincial in our outlook about our strengths and capabilities and how we do things. People in endowments throughout the world are looking at how we do things in the United States and rolling up their sleeves and getting to work."

Besides the National University of Singapore, he has consulted with Australian investors interested in investing their funds more effectively. He has visited universities in mainland China and comments that he received questions about building alumni networks for development purposes and about endowment funds management. Bufferd serves on the board of Makena, an investment management company organized by former leaders of Stanford Management. "Makena manages over $9 billion, with funding that has come from all over the world."

His observations lead to an important conclusion. "Enormous aggregates of capital in the world are sitting outside the United States. These organizations have seen our press, read our books, and want to replicate what foundations and endowments have done over the past 20 to 30 years. The advantage they have is they know our map, because we have laid it out. Not only do they read our map, they read their own map. We have less cognizance of their map. That will be one of the growing challenges for the U.S. foundation and endowment world."

Although he believes opportunities will remain in the United States, Bufferd explains why U.S. organizations should be aware of global investment competitors. "Many investment opportunities will be found in other locations. In general, the U.S. foundation and endowment community is not getting out and seeing much of this." He recently organized a panel discussion to show that "there are people elsewhere who are thinking exactly the same way our domestic organizations are thinking and trying to do the same thing. But they will see other opportunities first, and most of our domestic organizations do not have sufficient awareness of these other opportunities." Bufferd finds these challenges, especially the global movement to replicate endowment investment practices, fascinating. The phenomenon inspires more questions and challenges for endowment and foundation CIOs.

"Why shouldn't we have an office in China? What is the advantage of pooling resources? What is the cost? What is the benefit? Maybe someone should do more of that. There are risks. You have to hold on to people, invest in getting them up to speed. How do you monitor? Running a satellite location is not easy."

Bufferd admits he does not have the answers. "The question was the challenges, not the solutions."

Institutional Goals and the CIO Solution

Asked to comment on the burgeoning outsourced CIO business model, Bufferd brings the discussion back to the goals of the institution. "Whether it is a good idea or a bad idea for an institution depends on what it is that they're trying to do. If they just want the returns of a larger institution, they have misidentified their objectives. They're doing the wrong thing and need to know their own goals."

An endowment approached Makena about possibly taking over its entire portfolio. Makena runs one fund, a single pool invested in different asset classes, and the firm's leaders told the endowment it would be a mistake. Bufferd knows firms with similar models to Makena have already entered the market and expects to see more. "There will be clones of Makena." In the 1970s, MIT had a single relationship or "partnership," giving Wellington Management control of the entire portfolio for many years. Bufferd muses, "If Wellington had grown an alternatives portfolio, I'm not sure what would have happened at MIT."

The decision to outsource the investment office or turn the assets over to a single fund depends on the objectives of the institution. The trustees and committees need to ask questions. "What do they need for success? What does success mean? The objective shouldn't be to do just what the large institutions are doing. How much wealth do we need? Is it free tuition for everyone? Boards need to think about the *raison d'etre* of their institution and where it is trying to go—these are nontrivial questions. We have had such an expansion of asset classes. What are they trying to do?"

Foundations and endowments need to ask those questions and more and analyze the answers before they decide who or what will manage the assets.

Peer Competition

Although he has reportedly spoken publicly about peer competition in the past, Bufferd initially resists commenting on the subject, but given his strong feelings offers his opinion.

"We have created a number of systems and participated in a number of actions which in human terms have driven us to a much more competitive environment. Information about performance and relative position information is all over. Who won the horse race this year versus last year? Who got paid what? Incentive plans make relative performance to peers a component. It's all part of the society. In a situation like that, why are you going to help your competitors?"

Bufferd cites limited capital capacity in alternative investments as a second factor making the environment more competitive. "If you could not get as much capacity, why would you be surprised by elbows being thrown around? You want to reach the bread yourself and get it. It's a big dining table, with only so many seats, and you want to get positioned."

Survivor: Alternative Isle Bufferd and Marty Leibowitz, now at Morgan Stanley, gave a presentation of their dialogue that sounds like an episode of the television competition series *Survivor* to illustrate the shrinking opportunities in alternative investments.

"We described a tropical isle called Alternatives. Early on, you arrived on an outrigger and were greeted by beautiful natives. You found delicious, low-hanging tropical fruit. Now you fly to Alternatives Isle on a 747, land on a paved runway, and stay at a giant Westin Hotel built on the beach. The whole world has found these spaces, they're crowded, and people are now paid on being able to compete on Alternatives Isle."

Back in the real world, Bufferd concludes, "Some institutions believe they have some weight and put heavy demands on managers. There's a really low degree of cooperation and a low sense of community across organizations. I am not happy about it and think we have lost something."

Career Advice

Bufferd knows his advice works because as a young man he followed it himself and built a compelling and rewarding career.

"If you're not happy with what you're doing, then you are doing the wrong thing and should do something else. Like me, I woke up in my 30s and said, 'I don't want to do what I'm doing.' I was able to change with the support of two young children and my wonderful wife. I'm a very strong believer that if you're not happy with what you're doing, you should be doing something else.

"I tripped into it—it was not my plan. I found something and just got more excited about it than I did materials engineering or the law. You have to find an organization and see that it's humming and that you have an opportunity to make mistakes, because you will make mistakes. Find an organization where you'll be treated well and respected."

Bufferd advises future CIOs to become educated in fundamentals of the industry. Even though he lacked investment knowledge initially, 12 years of industry experience and two prior jobs helped him develop applicable skills. "It's good to have not just investment experience, but experience interacting with people."

When he started in the endowment world, many of his contemporaries did not necessarily have investment experience. Future CIOs will more likely have MBA degrees and previous investment experience, a career growth pattern similar to other segments of the investment industry. "There's a raising of the bar of credentials."

Regarding time management, Bufferd says, "I am the worst person to ask. I'm a workaholic. I pull all-nighters and get too little sleep. I love to read, love to talk, and love to find great ideas. I am not great at managing time; I really flunked that course."

Important Influences

Bufferd hesitates to name important influences since he has a long list and does not want to make a retirement speech. "I have had wonderful committees and wonderful chairs and great dialogues. I can't draw comparisons among them because we all have our weaknesses. Everybody understood what they were doing and had tolerance for 'not big' mistakes."

The MIT portfolio consists of 160 managers, some dating as far back as the Wellington partnership with several private equity managers running almost that long. Bufferd values the interaction he had with these good-quality organizations and enduring relationships with their leaders, even as those leaders changed over time.

REAL REWARDS

"There were many things that I valued. We did not always ride the crest of the wave. Where we had deep relationships, we worked the rough ride. We valued relationships, would work through difficult times, and if we were right we would be well compensated for it. We were right more than we were wrong. People had pearls of wisdom along the way that helped shape me."

Allan Bufferd woke up one morning in the early 1970s and knew he needed to make a change in his life. What would have happened if he had rolled over and gone back to sleep? Instead, he stuck his head out, made a move forward in his life, and applied his skills and interest in new ideas to make a significant contribution to MIT and the investment industry.

Some may remember the childhood game with the "Doctor, Lawyer, ..." chant. Luckily for MIT and for investors he has influenced, Allan Bufferd landed permanently on "Investment Chief."

CHAPTER 6

Leading the Evolution

Alice Handy, CIO, Investure, LLC

Alice Handy entered the investment business in 1970, joined the University of Virginia in 1974 as their first investment officer and remained in that role as it grew over the next 20 years, and today runs her own business, doing what she loves—investing for nonprofits. Throughout her career, she has embraced challenge and opportunity. She wanted to work with people and has accomplished that goal, succeeding as a leader, mentor, and money maker. Her career reflects the changes and growth in the foundation and endowment investing community and serves as an excellent model for the next generation of chief investment officers (CIOs).

Alice Handy is the founder, president, and CIO of Investure, LLC, a Charlottesville, Virginia–based investment adviser that serves as an "outsourced" investment office for nonprofit institutions. Investure currently manages approximately $5 billion for a group of endowments and foundations.

Prior to founding Investure, Alice spent 29 years managing the endowment of the University of Virginia. She started as the first investment officer, and later became treasurer and finally president of the University of Virginia Investment Management Company. Alice began her career as a bond portfolio manager and assistant vice president at the Travelers Insurance Company. She also served as state treasurer for the Commonwealth of Virginia from October 1988 to January 1990. She currently serves on several investment committees, including the Virginia Retirement System and the Rockefeller Foundation, and the boards of the Thomas Jefferson Foundation, Shenandoah Life Insurance Company, and Bessemer Securities Corporation. She earned her BA, *cum laude*, from Connecticut College and took graduate courses in economics at the University of Virginia.

BACKGROUND

When Alice Handy received her BA in economics from Connecticut College in 1970, her husband-to-be lived and worked in Hartford, Connecticut, so she interviewed with all the insurance companies and accepted a job at Travelers Insurance.

"They asked me what I wanted to do, and it was 1970, of course, so I said I wanted to work with people, which is what everybody said at that time. They said, 'You're a female with an economics degree and we don't have any women in the investment office.' So they put me in the investment office. The investment business couldn't have been a better fit."

Handy was asked to choose between working as an equity analyst or a fixed income portfolio manager. Having no preference, she let them decide.

"Fortunately, they put me in the bond area. The best thing was there were just two of us in public bonds. Travelers controlled several billion dollars' worth of public bonds, and we went back and forth from corporate bonds to tax-exempt bonds, depending on the profitability of the company. I really learned a lot of fundamentals. More importantly, we had a small trading portfolio, which was really unusual for an insurance company. I learned trading, how the street works, and got very close to a number of brokers. I wouldn't have had that opportunity if I had been focused on a narrow segment of the stock market."

At the time, insurance companies were one of the most prominent institutional investors. Handy valued the experience because she got broad investment exposure, including private equity, hedge funds, and public equity, and worked with talented investors, including Gary Brinson.

In 1974, Handy left Travelers Insurance and moved to Charlottesville, Virginia, so her husband could attend graduate school at the University of Virginia (UVA). She took a job managing the UVA endowment as part of the treasurer's office just when the stock market bottomed and changes in endowment laws began to have an impact.

"It was September of 1974, right at the bottom of the market. UVA had decided to diversify the portfolio from one manager into three managers, hire a new custodian, and do a securities lending program. The program was all set up and ready to go when I arrived. I started out in the corner of the conference room."

Handy handled a number of unrelated tasks initially. "Never having had an investment office, UVA didn't think it was a full-time job." Travel and payroll advances, vehicle registrations, insurance, and investments were her responsibility. "The one thing they wouldn't let me do was trade bonds, and that was the only thing I knew how to do."

When she started, the endowment was valued at $50 million, with $30 million actually available to invest. Handy got on-the-job training, gaining experience in new markets and asset classes.

"Fortunately, they made the decision, which most endowments didn't make at the time, to stay invested in equities. A lot of the big endowments reduced their equity portfolios significantly after the bear market of the 1970s as spending on a reduced base became a huge issue for endowments such as Yale."

UVA had split the $30 million equally among three equity managers specializing in different styles. In lieu of a traditional bond allocation, a portfolio of mortgage loans to faculty represented the fixed-income exposure.

Handy had reported to four treasurers when, in the early 1980s, the university decided the investment office had grown enough to stand on its own. Handy had already been attending board meetings, presenting the investment reports, and becoming more influential in the portfolio by identifying investment ideas. Although she now led an independent investment office, she did not have authority to make investment decisions. She would research managers and present three for the committee, comprised primarily of lawyers and bankers, to choose one. Consulting firm Cambridge Associates advised the investment committee, helping source and review ideas.

Handy began to build a team. "Every time I had a baby I got new help. In 1979, when my son was born, I added an accounting person. In 1981, when my daughter was born, Rob Freer, who is still there now, came to work for me as the first investment person. Then we slowly added more people over time."

University of Virginia: A CIO Evolves

In the early 1970s, Handy joined a very small cadre of endowment investment officers including Walter Cabot at Harvard and David Storrs at Yale. University treasurers generally had responsibility for investments as part of all their duties. Similarly, she reported to the vice president of business and finance and handled numerous responsibilities in addition to the endowment. The arrangement "fit my personality, loving to start things and hating to maintain them."

The side projects included running the university's debt programs. In 1985 she accomplished a "the largest state financing for a Virginia university at that time" for a replacement hospital. In the late 1980s, she managed real estate and other university-owned properties and businesses. Handy ran a golf course, the Boar's Head Inn, and the Colonnades, a retirement home, and renovated fraternity houses under tax-advantaged structures.

As Alice Handy describes her experiences managing the UVA portfolio from 1974 to 2003, it becomes clear that milestones in her career mirrored the changes taking place in the broader foundation and endowment investment community. Her responsibilities, investment philosophy, and achievements evolved following a similar timeline.

1974–1981: Diversify Managers between Growth and Value   Up until this time, endowments often had only one investment manager running all their assets. This is when they began to think seriously about their manager selection and hire multiple managers, mostly in the equity portfolio.

Early 1980s: Diversifying, Growing, and Adding Asset Classes   At the beginning of the 1980s, the UVA endowment had a relatively progressive endowment. Its 75 percent allocation to equity was unusually high. UVA had been a Commonfund client since the mid-1970s and a Cambridge Associates client since 1978. The investment climate began to change.

"In 1981, the markets started changing, and the oils and hard-asset stocks which had performed so well in the late 1970s fell out of favor and our managers started having problems."

Handy began considering alternatives to equity investments. International equities, real estate, and venture capital were coming into vogue. The investment committee decided against adding real estate since UVA owned so much real estate. They made a small allocation to a venture capital fund affiliated with an alumnus that subsequently underperformed but nevertheless was an entrée into the asset class.

"We did some international equity—which was really interesting then—by investing in the Commonfund international equity fund. I had been on the selection panel for hiring the subadvisers. Rather than choosing only the traditional big British banks, in addition we chose GMO, which was just starting its international portfolio along the lines of their successful domestic program." GMO, originally Grantham, Mayo, Van Otterloo & Co. is today a prestigious manager running over $140 billion in assets.

UVA finally hired an outside fixed-income manager in the mid-1980s, because the diminishing mortgage portfolio could no longer function as the fixed-income exposure. UVA staff ran a portion of the fixed-income allocation in-house and performed well enough to bring the entire portfolio in-house.

"Between 1980 and 1986 except for 1981 and 1983, the equity markets had fabulous returns. Some years we were up 40 to 50 percent in traditional equities and would say that this is just too good, it can't keep going. By the mid-1980s, we sold our international equities and put the money into intermediate bonds and global bonds. We didn't purchase portfolio insurance, which was popular at the time. We just took money off the table. Then the market crash came in October 1987."

Governance: Becoming an Issue After the crash, Handy became more conscious of the value of having committee members that understood the markets and the need to respond quickly to opportunities.

"The day after the crash the chairman of the board, Josh Darden, said, 'Let's get back into the market.' The vice president said, 'No, we can't do that, we have a plan,' and Darden replied, 'But we took 5 percent off!' We didn't go right back in—we waited for nearly a year before reinvesting in equities. The market had already run up considerably, so we didn't get the full benefit, but it did dampen the downside. The crash was very interesting in terms of governance."

Board, committee, and investment office governance practices were still committee-centric. "It was a time when you could get decent returns from traditional equity managers, and we had some good ones in the portfolio. We often picked them for the wrong reasons, like someone knew them or had heard about them. We didn't have a full staff to investigate them, weren't equipped to be out there scouring for them. We relied on Cambridge Associates data and information from others. At that time, you tried to learn what Yale, Harvard, Princeton, and Stanford were doing. There wasn't the proliferation of conferences that we have now. Cambridge had an annual meeting of large endowments; NACUBO had meetings. So you generally talked to a few people, but not as many as you do now, without staff you had to piggyback on others' ideas."

Because investment offices had such limited resources, and committees often had limited knowledge, endowments tended to remain invested in funds managed by alumni. It may have been a conflict of interest, but that was how it worked.

Late 1980s: Diversifying Accelerates As the 1980s progressed, different types of asset classes and methods for structuring investment strategies started becoming available. UVA began to delegate more decisions to managers and to diversify the portfolio more broadly.

At one point during the late 1980s, the thought of having investment committees do asset allocation was considered not optimal and that investment managers were better equipped to make those decisions since they were looking at the markets all the time. "The GTE pension plan had hired three global asset allocating managers. We went to Dick Mayo at GMO and told him, 'We want you to tell us when to switch between growth and value and stocks and bonds.' They identified a few big good ideas, putting us into growth in the late 1980s."

UVA began investing in private assets, but avoided typical LBO private equity investments, knowing the committee was cautious about new, illiquid asset classes. Instead, they allocated 4 percent of the portfolio to a new venture capital program, because they had the potential to get a great return from a small investment.

Hedge funds also entered the portfolio at the same time, initially with investments in classic hedge fund strategies like global macro and event arbitrage, adding distressed debt funds later.

The endowment invested in real estate away from the university's holdings. "We went into real estate in a big way in 1991 when the RTC (Resolution Trust Corporation) was selling off properties. We made a lot of money, investing in three managers. We made an investment in TA Associates, as well as two funds to which Yale had provided the initial capital, Brookdale and Shorenstein. The sad part is that we had a great return in the early years, but through the course of the 1990s returns slowed down. In 2000, our chairman said, 'We're not putting another penny into real estate.' We did not put it back into the portfolio while I was there and missed the whole period of great performance in the mid-2000s."

Late 1990s: More Aggressive Investments and Creative Hedging   As the 1990s progressed, UVA increased its exposure to hedge funds, investing in long/short equity, a strategy that was just developing when they first began investing in hedge funds. Because UVA invested early, they were able to invest with such prestigious managers as Lone Pine Capital and leveraged alumni connections to invest in others including Maverick, Blue Ridge, and Tudor.

Venture capital was getting "extraordinarily hot" and Handy believed valuations were not explainable. UVA also began building up a portfolio of private equity funds, but she believes "it was probably five years late." She increased the allocation to emerging markets investments and hired more staff, structuring the team with specialists in each asset class.

1999 to 2000: A Career-Encapsulating Investment Experience   In 1999, as investors continued to push technology stock prices skyward, Handy experienced the highs and lows of that unusual period in investment history. She structured a creative investment strategy that locked in substantial venture capital gains but saw those gains offset by pressures to reverse course in the equity policy allocation. The anecdote shows how the knowledge and relationships she developed over the course of her career culminated in her ability to create and implement an innovative investment strategy.

"Where the experience really got interesting was 1999. When we first invested in venture capital in 1988, Cambridge helped us identify and hire a handful of really good venture capital firms. Returns on those portfolios went through the roof in 1998–1999. When the fiscal year–end statements were received from the venture capital managers in September 1999, the total portfolio of under $1 billion had a $50 million adjustment. I asked the chairman whether I should recalculate the share value and our annual audited statement since it was such a significant difference. He said, 'Absolutely, go do that, and while you're at it, please take a look at these companies because there's no way anything can grow that fast.'

"We conducted analysis and found the stocks were trading at 300, 400 times earnings, if they even had earnings—most of them didn't have any. Ten stocks accounted for over $200 million of the portfolio—just a huge number. The chairman said, 'Alice, find a way to protect ourselves.'

"Having done all the debt for the university, I had relationships with all the major underwriters. Goldman Sachs investment bankers introduced us to their derivatives desk and, working with them, we found a way to sell our securities using our bond portfolio as collateral and lock in our gains on the portfolio. Our intention was only to harvest the gains. We thought, 'We've gotten enough out of these stocks—we aren't going to get piggy about them.' It was a portfolio hedge, not a short to make money.

"UVA executed the transaction early January 2000. The market continued rising, forcing them to keep covering the positions. Some investors heard the idea and implemented it, but many of the shorts were hard to find.

"Putting them on early was good for us. By late March and over the next six months, the market absolutely crashed. Stocks that were trading at $100 in January were now trading at $10. We were able to wait until we received our stock distributions, selling them to cover the shorts. A year later, we were completely out and had realized the gain, but it meant we had a lot of cash."

Handy and her team needed to reinvest, but markets looked "atrociously overvalued." They disliked stocks and found the bond market unexciting.

"We knew we couldn't meet our goals in the bond market. We had this wonderful entrée to hedge funds from our alumni and we had been building up the portfolio since 1998. We went all the way up to a 60 percent position in hedge funds, mostly driven by all the cash we were getting in the portfolio from covering these shorts. It was an extraordinarily interesting time."

Governance practices were not all positive during this period. In early 1999, a board member, dismayed by the value bias in the equity allocation and lack of returns during the boom years of the high-growth stocks of the late 1990s, caused staff to rethink their position: "We subsequently hired some growth managers, all at the wrong time, by selling value. Once the venture portfolio kicked in, the committee and board could see the merit of the original strategy, but that was a year later, so it wasn't all a pretty story."

Having perspective on the experience, Handy says, "But at that time that (market) had never happened before. You weren't really sure it would happen the way it did. It was clearly a bubble. Do I expect it to happen again? No, but it's why you need to be there to take advantage of it and have a little piece of something that can do very well."

2003: Entering the Outsourced Phase   After 29 years, Handy left the University of Virginia at the end of 2003 and formed Investure to offer an outsourced CIO service. Yet again, her next career step mirrors changes taking place throughout the endowment management community.

BEING CHIEF INVESTMENT OFFICER

As the president of Investure, Handy leads a private company, continuing to serve as CIO for a small group of institutions. While still having the same basic responsibilities, she must consider each client's specific investment objectives in a more complex investment environment. Her asset allocation philosophy has been forced to evolve.

Asset Allocation

"I don't believe in asset allocation at all anymore." Handy laughs, and then responds seriously.

"I think it's very, very difficult. I am fully in concert, since joining the University of Virginia in 1974, where it was already reflected in their portfolio, with the belief that you have to invest in equities in order to perform. You have to have equity (company ownership) exposure rather than fixed-income exposure if you are going to make your long-term return goals of roughly 10 percent.

"That's the number that colleges and universities need. They need their 5 percent spending, plus inflation, plus fees, plus a little bit of growth. So they need 10 percent. If we look at all the models, 10 percent is a darn hard number to get in just traditional investments, so you have to look across a broad spectrum. In the last 5 to 10 years, there have been so many different investment tools, call them asset classes if you want, that just weren't available to us back in 1974."

Handy identifies vehicles like derivatives and commodities and portfolio construction and hedging techniques like shorting as viable choices. "They are now considered prudent by the prudent man rule. You just didn't have a prayer of thinking about them before. It also means that it's a very complex world."

As Investure employs an asset allocation model weighted heavily toward alternatives, they have begun to migrate toward a process that analyzes the portfolio by identifying metrics and characteristics driving portfolio risk and return.

Investure reviews the total portfolio, analyzing risk factors like countries, asset classes, liquidity, lockups, and exposures. Veering away from strict asset class definitions can help investors find interesting investment ideas.

"Yale puts a manager in one block, UVA puts it in another, and it's the same manager. One classifies it as a hedge fund and another as a traditional long-only equity manager. Virginia Retirement System puts all hedge fund strategies into its global equity allocation as opposed to a hedge fund box. Asset classes make no sense anymore as they don't really describe enough about the portfolio. The old categories don't address liquidity or leverage. The problem is that the nomenclature academically hasn't caught up with what is happening with investment people."

As an example, Investure decided to increase exposure to Japan because portfolio analysis showed that managers were not invested there. Seeing opportunities in many areas, they allocated to private equity, hedge funds, and long-only asset managers.

"If you start talking about buckets, then you can't do some of the interesting things like activist managers or hybrids that are half hedge fund, half private equity. Not having buckets, being flexible, is okay with our clients. They have bought into the idea that it's the overall risk-and-return profile of the portfolio, not rebalancing individual buckets, that's really important.

"Most important is to help the committee understand that this is a better tool for participating in the management of the fund. They can get a much better idea of where the portfolio is invested. They can do their part of the job, thinking about guidelines and overall risk. It's really important that they have the tools to do their job well."

Strategic Asset Allocation versus Tactical Asset Allocation Handy believes a long-term asset allocation only improves by adding strategically to undervalued areas.

"If you just stick with a long-term allocation, theoretically a good portion in equities and a good portion in bonds, and you pick decent managers, over a long period of time you will do okay, but you will miss the opportunities in the market to do better."

Stepping out of bounds or diverging from the pack can be a risky decision. "To fail conventionally is better than succeeding unconventionally. The market offers a lot of slam dunks in hindsight, but if you're really valuation oriented and you think about it, there's always something to be done."

Handy offers an idea considered for the year 2007. "Investors should go short credit. Everybody is scared to death to do it, because it might take five years before it cracks, but it would still be a good trade if you can stay with it long enough." Endowment investors have a problem holding positions like it, "because we're too geared toward how their colleagues are performing." Endowments with more assets or a mature portfolio like Yale or UVA have the advantage of being able to stick with their convictions.

"Younger portfolios have to find opportunities. Getting into venture capital was great in the 1980s. Should you just keep pumping money into it in the hopes that we'll get another 1999–2000? No!"

In her mind, the next big opportunity or the next big crash will happen in a completely different way than the last event. Investors tend to look for a replay. "We continually play the old game, because we're afraid. That's why I love having had the trader background—what makes this world exciting is trying to find the little niches."

Managing Assets Internally   Managing money in-house provides valuable benefits aside from returns. Having personal contacts in the market can provide information about trades or market trends those investors would otherwise miss. For a number of practical reasons, including high compensation and problems stemming from a failed effort, Handy recommends against managing equity portfolios in-house. She thinks that more foundations and endowments will begin to manage some assets in-house, like the overlay strategies she may institute for her clients.

"I always make sure that the senior people have managed money at some point. They have had to pull the trigger. That doesn't mean they have to be good asset allocators. CIOs must have two skills. They must be able to have their finger on the pulse and network really well. They also need to be able to put the whole thing together, and that's one of the hardest things to deal with aside from governance issues."

Governance   Handy advocates the "smallest possible committee" and repeats advice she heard from a respected committee chair. "I believe the late Dick Fisher from Morgan Stanley, who ran the Princeton investment committee for many years, once said, 'If your committee agrees on everything it's bad. You shouldn't try to get a majority; you're not trying to get consensus. You're just trying to throw great ideas out there.' I think that's true."

The board or the committee should serve as advisers and strategic thinkers. "It's very inefficient to make investment decisions at the board level. The committee should offer advice, but it really should be up to the CIO and the staff to invest the fund. The committee can give you all the parameters and guidelines, those things are important. They can nix directions, but *not* at the manager level. The committee should be thinking at a bigger, broader level, because it's very, very difficult in this environment not to be able to act quickly and appropriately."

Manager Selection   Handy believes a CIO needs extraordinarily smart people on staff in order to succeed at selecting managers. "I have some very strong-willed, very opinionated, smart people that are all really good investors. Maybe we think too much alike, although I think we're all slightly different and all contribute ideas.

"You have to have multiple ways of winning. I'm not saying you can't do growth, but you have to do it when it's down. You don't need to have to have a lot of managers that are really diversified. You can get a lot of diversification pretty quickly in fairly concentrated managers who know what they know very well. That's the advantage of being smaller and why, when we created Investure we didn't want to get larger than $5 billion."

Handy feels investors really need to have fun investing. "Putting people into business or finding the next great investment manager is really exciting and fun. You have to be mentally engaged all the time and really passionate and excited about what you're doing and what you're finding."

They want ethical managers that are tied closely to other people they know well. "We look for people that knew the managers when they were babies, particularly in asset classes without transparency. That's extraordinarily important."

Having a smart team makes an important difference not just in manager selection but in having managers select you. Handy refers to it as "becoming an investor of choice." Good managers want to work with intelligent, nice, ethical investors that don't treat them like a commodity. "If you treat them like a commodity then they will become a commodity. We treat our clients like partners and treat our managers like partners."

Handy prefers not to fire managers when their strategy falls out of favor but instead to hedge the market exposure using derivatives or similar vehicles. "The most important thing is you've got the partner on your side that will come to you and say, 'It's not a great market.' If you have too many managers, you can't do that, you can't know them all that well."

LESSONS, OBSERVATIONS, AND ADVICE

Handy shares her thoughts on the industry and offers her unique perspective on a career as an investor and CIO.

Investment Mistakes

In general, investors have excessively short time horizons and get caught up in "the investment of the moment." CIOs often make the subtle mistake of "thinking and acting like the portfolio belongs to them rather than their institution and become frustrated with their board or committee. You start to think it's yours and it's not."

Without question, "one of the biggest asset allocation mistakes of all time was growth versus value in 1999–2000. People were just flocking into growth funds and venture capital at all the wrong times." She attributes these mistakes to "herd mentality and pressure from people that don't understand the cyclicality of markets."

Advice for Smaller Institutions

Handy thinks that in the future smaller institutions will invest or buy shares in single comprehensive funds managed by firms like Makena, Commonfund, The Investment Fund for Foundations (TIFF), and Morgan Creek. She also expects to see one or more organizations pooling their resources to support a combined office.

"I equate it to the foundations at UVA. They had 20-plus different foundations, some with substantial assets, totaling about $1.5 billion. They each tried to run the money on their own, with their own boards. This approach was viable when all you were dealing with was equities and bonds. When the investment options got more complicated, it got more difficult, so they finally all pooled their assets and now own shares in the UVA pool. I think that's a smarter, better model."

Comparison to Peers

When Handy was starting out in 1974, she met two more experienced investors, Bruce Dresner from Dartmouth and Bob Taylor at Wesleyan. They mentored her, shared ideas, and cooperated for the benefit of all endowments. Now she thinks the organizations are highly competitive and board members like to compare themselves favorably to other institutions, particularly Yale or Harvard.

While she dislikes competitive behavior and thinking, in terms of compensation and investment performance, she finds peer benchmarks useful. "They can tell you how you did versus what was possible in the market at that time."

Being among the First Women Investment Officers

"Early on, I could count on one hand the women—myself, Lyn Hutton. When I started in bonds, there were no women in bonds. I couldn't go to any of the parties or have meetings in New York men's clubs, but it was wonderful. I was a darling; I wasn't a threat. They thought I would quit when I had a baby. Frankly, I thought I would, too.

"For us, it was really fun; you could be the first. With my personality, this was a motivator. You always had balance. If on the one side you had the older generation making sexist remarks, you had somebody else on the other that gave you recognition. That was really really nice."

Handy's two daughters have faced a much friendlier world and have more choices.

"Women have a wonderful advantage that we don't use enough. We don't have the burden that men have of thinking that we have to support our family. We may, but it's usually by our choice, unless you're a single mom and get thrown into it. I supported my family financially all my life, but I never had the burden of thinking that I had to and that I didn't have a choice. I've been blessed."

Handy feels more equipped to talk about balance. "I tell my daughters, 'You can be a good businesswoman, you can be a good mother, or you can be a good wife, but it is hard to be all three at once.' Something always gives, and you have to continually reevaluate your priorities."

Career Advice

Handy learned the most important career advice from her partners and colleagues. "You have to have a passion for investing. You have to have a curiosity. It has to excite you, because it's a tough road. You can make a lot of mistakes. It's not easy and you have to work long hours if you're going to be successful. You can spend more time with this than with your family. I tell my kids this about any job. You have to just love it."

When building a team she says it helps to have a combination of people. You need to balance people that have a strong constitution, can maintain their conviction, and have investment intuition with those good at fundamentals. "Otherwise, you won't take enough chances or will take too many."

Handy urges those early in their career to find a good mentor, a person they can relate to who is also a good investor. "I told my son that he could only go where there's a good investor, because otherwise he'd learn bad habits."

Get training in a large firm if you have the opportunity. "Going to Travelers was the best thing that ever happened to me, because I knew how a big shop works. However, I love being in a small place. If you're an entrepreneur, go to a small place, or if you're a corporate person, end up in a big place."

THE TRUE REWARDS

Looking back on her career and thinking of the future, Handy says, "The best advice I got was from a venture capitalist. He said, 'Make a list of what's most important to you. Don't try to prioritize it. Just make the list. When the right job comes along, the priorities will all fall in line.' It was really interesting for me to do. I wanted to be intellectually stimulated; wanted to work with motivated, fun people; wanted to keep access to so many interesting people I had encountered.

"The best part of the industry is you get to meet fascinating people from all walks of life. Even as young, junior analysts you meet the smartest investors in the world. You won't know the value of it until later. It was important for me to work for a nonprofit. When weighing opportunities after UVA, I looked at a number of options, including starting Investure. Finally, Larry Kochard told me, 'Alice, people are starting to count on you.' When you work for an institution, people do count on you. That's a nice feeling."

The institution matters. "You have got to love the cause and doing something to help its existence. I will teach a class or meet with an alumni group; I really like that. I like dealing with boards, I love the idea of getting ideas from a lot of different people, love the intellectual stimulation of it."

A friend said, "How lucky you are to be working for something that has a happy ending." Handy adds, "My favorite, favorite day at UVA was when the scholarship office let me know that because the endowment had grown so much in 2000–2001, they were able to offer scholarships instead of loans to all the first-year students. That was such a wonderful experience, I am hoping for the same happy story from Investure's clients. That's what it's all about it. If you don't love it, you shouldn't work for a college or university."

An endowment investment professional almost from the minute the institutions began to make the changes that turned them into investment powerhouses, Handy has consistently reached the height of her profession by following her passion toward the next milestone. As one of the few women in the industry, her accomplishments as an investor and businessperson stand out even more.

"A danger, and it doesn't have anything to do with being a woman, is that you can become a dinosaur if you don't constantly reinvent." She need not worry about that threat. Having continually evolved as an investor and CIO, Alice Handy continues to lead the evolution in foundation and endowment investing.

CHAPTER 7

Partner, Patriot, and Performer

Scott C. Malpass, CIO, University of Notre Dame

S cott C. Malpass became the chief investment officer (CIO) of the University of Notre Dame endowment in April 1989 at the age of 26 and with only three years' investment experience. What he lacked in experience he balanced with a willingness to listen and learn and a desire to implement best practices, as well as a deep commitment to the university and its mission. The investment committee took a big risk hiring Malpass as CIO, and it has resulted in big returns. When Malpass took over the endowment pool, it held $425 million in assets. Today, it is worth just over $6 billion.

Stewardship holds great meaning within the Notre Dame culture. Under Malpass's stewardship, the endowment has consistently delivered top-tier investment performance over several different time periods, outperformed other institutions, and beaten its policy benchmarks. For the 10-year period that ended March 31, 2007, annualized return was 15 percent, significantly outperforming its benchmark return of 10.2 percent and the median return of similar institutions of 9 percent. As stated in the endowment investment report, "Looked at another way, the University's investment management program added more than $2 billion in market value to the endowment pool in that time."

For the fiscal year ended June 30, 2000, the endowment returned a record 57.9 percent, the highest return for any American university and the subject of extensive media coverage in the *Wall Street Journal*, the *Chronicle of Higher Education, U.S. News & World Report*, the *New York Times*, and on CNBC.

As vice president and CIO at the University of Notre Dame, Malpass is responsible for the investment of the university's endowment, working capital, pension, and life income assets. Totaling close to $6 billion, the endowment is the 16th largest in American higher education and the largest at a Catholic university.

He graduated from Notre Dame in 1984 and received a master of business administration degree from the university in 1986. He returned in 1988 from the Irving Trust Company and became CIO the following year.

Malpass is assistant professor of finance in the Mendoza College of Business at Notre Dame. In 1995, he helped develop the Applied Investment Management course in the college for outstanding students in finance that has received extensive interest from financial services firms throughout the country. Mr. Malpass is a director or advisory council member for several investment and charitable organizations. He serves on the investment advisory committee for Major League Baseball and for the National Association of Securities Dealers (NASD).

BACKGROUND

Scott Malpass thought he had a different background than other investors, "then I learned that in this business everybody has a different background." He entered Notre Dame intending to go to medical school, rejected that option, but continued studying science and graduated with a BS in science in 1984. Although he knew that he did not want to do research in a lab, he did not know what he wanted to do.

"After I graduated, I took the GMATs, and did better than I expected, so I applied to Notre Dame's MBA program for that fall." Malpass completed the two-year program for his MBA in 1986. "I loved the program, found my passion, knew the campus, and loved the curriculum. A small program fit me, and there were lots of other nonbusiness people. I even worked as an assistant rector in the dorm. It was a great two years."

The stint as assistant rector formed the foundation of his endowment career. The rector, a Holy Cross priest, also served as CIO of the endowment. Irving Trust, the bank custodian of the assets, hired Malpass as a summer intern. He worked in an investment consulting unit that advised pension clients. "It was great. I got to work with Exxon, Warner Lambert, Bristol-Myers; learned how pensions are managed; and got some knowledge of different asset classes and managers."

After graduation, Malpass rejoined Irving Trust full time in the same group. "I worked for Ralph Knisley, a fabulous boss; he got young people involved." Knisley's inclusive management style helped Malpass and inspired his management style. "I try to get young people involved myself."

In 1988, the Notre Dame endowment stood at $400 million and barely had a staff, just the priest that served as CIO, an accountant, and a secretary. The board wanted to modernize and asked the priest to hire an assistant, so Malpass returned to Notre Dame, joining the investment office on August 1, 1988. Nine months later, the CIO decided to leave for a different assignment in the Holy Cross order and Malpass became CIO on April 1, 1989. "I honestly thought they would hire a CIO with more experience; I didn't expect to get the job at the time as a 26-year-old assistant."

Notre Dame

When Malpass took over the portfolio, it had 60 percent allocated in U.S. equities, 10 percent in international equities, 25 percent in fixed income, 4 percent in real estate, and 1 percent in venture capital. While at Irving, he had gained very broad exposure to asset classes but knew very little about alternatives. "Most of the clients were pensions and still very much invested in traditional asset classes; some were in real estate, a little in private equity, but they did not have a lot of exposure to alternatives."

Malpass began aggressively benchmarking other institutional endowments by attending Cambridge Associates meetings for the top 25 endowments, meeting peers managing the large Ivy League endowments, asking questions and learning what others were doing in their portfolios. "I was just trying to think of new approaches for managing the endowment."

Bob Wilmouth chaired the investment committee from 1978 until stepping down in 1994. His replacement, Jay Jordan, continues to chair the committee. "The committee was a very active, good committee. They were playing roles that today we would say should be the responsibility of the staff. In religious institutions, they tend to play a larger role given the smaller asset base. Bob Wilmouth knew it couldn't last, that Notre Dame needed an internal team." Malpass gives Wilmouth full credit for seeing the need, believing in him, and giving him the opportunity. "Probably they were thinking, 'Let's give the guy a shot. If it doesn't work, we'll get a guy with 20 years' experience.' I felt his strong support."

Malpass started becoming more aware of the best practices in institutional money management and started developing his own philosophy. "At that age I was still developing, still learning, and spent a lot of time with existing managers, prospective new managers, and respected investment people across the board. I recently found a report I wrote for the board in 1990 on endowment management best practices. It had investments we should be considering, including a history of how money had been managed. It really helped a lot in developing a new mind-set."

BEING CHIEF INVESTMENT OFFICER

Along with his baptism in the best practices of managing foundation and endowment investments, Malpass engaged in the traditional rituals for becoming indoctrinated as a CIO.

"We conducted a formal asset allocation study, ran simulations, and analyzed trade-offs, correlations, etc. We went about it systematically, bringing in hedge fund and private equity managers, well-respected, experienced investors the board knew. There was a lot of education toward getting the board comfortable with the new approach. Over time, we got into new areas."

Implementing the New Portfolio

Malpass took time to implement new investments, particularly alternatives. "At the time the board resonated much more with private equity than with, say, hedge funds. We didn't want to do everything overnight and cause any unnecessary concern." They chose to build on the existing venture portfolio, with private equity the initial focus. They added new real estate and opportunistic energy investments, but less in hedge funds. "We did participate in the distressed cycle in the early 1990s and invested in a lot of distressed investments in 1990–1991, but private equity was the target at the time."

Adding Alternatives in Private Equity

Fortunately, Malpass started investing with prestigious private equity and venture capital firms before the clubhouse doors closed.

"One of the good things for us as an organization and the board, as we got into less efficient alternative areas, we wouldn't force an allocation. We would only do it if we could get access to the right people." The hallmark of any private investment program is investing in the attractive first quartile; Notre Dame was able to do that. "I went and met a lot of people. They knew about the school because of its strong academic and athletic traditions. We tried to develop a reputation for the university as sophisticated investors. The managers loved the long-term nature of endowments, liked the stability of the money and the institution. We began to have access and built up over time." Malpass says that through the years, his and his team's longevity—his most senior colleague has worked with him for 10 years—have enhanced their reputation with managers.

Malpass gives the example of getting introduced to a top venture capital firm. "Notre Dame was a long-time investor with Capital Guardian. I told

Dick Barker about what we were trying to do, and he said that we should talk to Sequoia Capital. . . . I'd heard of the firm, and Dick Barker introduced us to Mike Moritz and Don Valentine in 1991. We have been in every fund since then, have significant allocations with them, and are now one of their largest investors. It has been a wonderful partnership."

The approach sounds opportunistic, but Malpass made these investments mindful of asset allocation policy. "With boards, you have to adopt some kind of targets, general guidelines, with the caveat of wanting to be with the right people, because of the wide dispersion of returns. Notre Dame developed the right relationships and that worked out well."

Malpass acknowledges that building a top-quartile private equity portfolio today would be a challenge. "It would be pretty hard to get those kinds of relationships today." Notre Dame was in the first wave, along with the largest Ivy League schools, of endowments that invested in private equity. Other Ivy League endowments and organizations similar to Notre Dame came after. "We were there in time to invest in the right funds and make the right relationships. I would hate to have to start this today. We are now reaping the rewards of investments we made 5 to 10 years ago."

Adding Alternatives in Hedge Funds

After their initial foray into hedge funds capitalizing on distressed opportunities in 1991–1992, Notre Dame gradually increased exposure to hedge funds for a number of years, taking a more opportunistic approach. While he continued meeting with other hedge funds, "We were skeptical of the fee structure. We went a little slower, because we were building the team and having so much success accessing and developing relationships with private equity. Hedge funds did not become a major focus until later." As the endowment, team, and resources increased, Malpass increased the allocation to hedge funds.

"As we crossed $1 billion in assets in 1995, we started aggressively thinking about hedge funds, making allocations to multistrategy and long/short equity. By 2000, 13 percent of the entire allocation was in hedge funds. The allocation really grew between 2000 and today; it's now close to 30 percent of allocation." Having more resources made the increased allocation possible. "It was driven by proper compliance and coverage and being able to get out and meet people. That took some time."

Malpass describes key characteristics of the types of hedge funds he seeks. "We seek more value-oriented managers, definitely those more fundamental in their approach. Historically, there has not been much macro, CTA (commodity trading advisors), or trading-oriented strategies. Half the portfolio is in long/short equity, very fundamental stock pickers, people with experience in shorting." He likes Tiger Cubs or ex-Tiger managers, "that's emblematic of their training." Malpass invests the other half in event-driven, arbitrage strategies and distressed managers. "We are not as highly levered in the hedge fund portfolio as some, very fundamental. We are not trying to make money just from leverage, and we analyze how much return comes from leverage, beta, and alpha."

A key component of the Notre Dame hedge fund investment process is a thorough compliance and operations review. "Five CPAs do on-site meetings with every hedge fund, including offshore administrators. We want to know our partners."

To implement the review process, Malpass put "a fabulous operations group" in place starting in the mid-1990s. The group has conducted on-site reviews for the last 10 years. "We made a goal four years ago to have an on-site with every one of the managers and have now done everyone at least once. At some point before or within the year after funding, the team will go on-site and will always get to someone in the first year. It's not an audit—it's partners sharing ideas and best practices with each other."

Asset Allocation

Malpass considers the opportunities created by changing global market and economic conditions and translates his views into establishing asset allocation policy.

"It's an exciting time in investments. It's never been more challenging, never been more interesting. Globalization is the biggest phenomenon we're dealing with. There's the blurring and convergence of asset classes and the talent drain from traditional firms to alternatives. The institutionalization of alternatives means alternatives are now in the mainstream. Traditional buckets don't make as much sense today. It's hard to understand correlations among buckets; it's harder since managers are doing a wide array of strategies."

In thinking about asset allocation, Malpass says, "It's really important people think about risk and how to allocate risk. Alpha/beta separation, getting cheap beta, paying for alpha has some merit to a point. At the end of the day, finding manager skill is pretty tough, very hard work. For example, I've been in China 6 of the last 18 weeks. That's not an easy trip from South Bend, but that's the best way to build a network and find knowledgeable managers that can execute on the opportunities."

Notre Dame revisits the asset allocation policy annually. Malpass has evaluated the asset buckets and the best way to group them and intends to merge some categories. "U.S. long-only, international long-only, and alternatives were in three buckets. Now public equities are all one bucket, including equity long/short funds. Other hedge funds that are more true absolute return strategies, like arbitrage, are in a different bucket. It will evolve. We have a more gradual approach and like to do things in an evolutionary way."

Evolutionary thinking applies to new investment ideas, experimenting with a smaller allocation, gaining confidence and then expanding. "Easing in allows us to be more flexible to try new approaches and to be more contrarian over time."

Regarding investment tactics that eliminate or reduce the role of the investment manager, Malpass and the team do not trade any assets or portfolios in-house, but from time to time seek board approval for certain overlay strategies. The long-term nature of real estate gives Malpass comfort, so they have coinvested and invested directly in the asset class. They have looked at private equity opportunities, but have not invested directly in any private equity deals. "Honestly I don't see as much of an advantage in investing directly in private equity, because we have access to the best people. I don't think we will have a large program of direct private equity investments, but we continue to review and consider the opportunities."

Idea Generation

Continuing the pattern he established when he first became CIO, Malpass relies on meetings and conversations with respected investors and managers to generate ideas, "constantly dialoging with smart people in the current portfolio, thought leaders in our network, and expanding the network over the years. We talk to a lot of people, get their ideas, and share information."

He and the team study valuations and use planning sessions to discuss global events and trends from a contrarian perspective. "Could we do something differently to generate superior returns?"

Malpass gets many excellent ideas from existing managers. A manager may find a new approach to an existing asset class or shift geographic focus. "They might want to do something new, and given our size, we will take the whole thing. We can give $50 million, almost $100 million. That starts to become more attractive to managers in our network. At our size, we can fund new ideas." At times, they have taken an idea, identified the best manager to execute, and approached the manager to start a strategy with Notre Dame as the lead investor. "We limit how much capital they could take in and they would agree because Notre Dame seeded it."

Ideas ultimately come from "intense engagement with smart people all over the world." Being in touch with smart people does not suffice. "You have got to get out there with energy, passion, and enthusiasm."

Manager Selection

When it comes to selecting managers, Malpass considers the personal characteristics of the people and characteristics of the investment strategy before making an investment.

"At the end of the day, it's the quality of the people you're working with. We look for a combination of strong, fundamentally driven managers with good values."

Managers fitting the profile have an edge in identifying and exploiting anomalies in scaleable strategies with aligned incentives. Other important criteria include:

- Compelling strategies that are not overly esoteric or complex.
- Evidence of repeatability.
- Justifiable fees; reasonable given the effort.
- Strong evidence of noncorrelation with other core assets.

Strategies they avoid are characterized by:

- Excessive leverage.
- Being difficult to reproduce over time.
- Secretive or distant managers that limit or withhold information.
- No demonstrable ability to hedge other portfolio exposures.
- Me-too programs.

Malpass shies away from strategies based on paper portfolios rather than real trading and strategies he cannot articulate.

"If I can't understand it, I won't do it, because if it does poorly, I can't explain it. So some well-known investment managers are brilliant, but not for us."

The approach has evolved over time as their ability to identify quality people has been enhanced by their increasing sophistication in understanding the markets and structuring transactions.

"I think we've gotten really good at picking the right partners. It's evolved. We were always good at judging character. Now we are understanding anomalies and inefficiencies and structuring deals as well as anyone in the country. We have more hedge fund separate accounts and have done more seeding of funds as we have grown. At a bigger size, we can give more capital, get good economics, negotiate favorable terms, and create investment partnerships that meet our specific requirements. "

Governance

Malpass believes that appropriate governance standards have been well established throughout the industry. He summarizes the most important standards. "There needs to be a very clear independent investment committee with authority from the board. They need to feel fiduciary responsibility and understand what it means." He recommends structuring the committee with a strong set of intelligent and knowledgeable people. While some members should have good professional investment experience, he finds that a blend of investment professionals and business leaders works best. Malpass advocates manning the committee with 6 to 10 trustees, defining rules and roles clearly and structuring and documenting the investment process clearly and comprehensively.

Even though these parameters seem well established, he finds many violations in actual practice in other charitable organizations.

"Despite how well documented these things are, most people don't follow them, including a few of the top 20 endowments. They have too many people and all the Wall Street alums. They do not provide enough support or autonomy in the investment area, so they are not keeping good people. There's micro management and conflicts of interest."

He expresses surprise that at this point in history such poor practices would occur in major endowments. "For those of us that have been able to succeed, it has been because we have had the opposite."

Fighting Irish

Fiercely committed to Notre Dame, Malpass seeks a similar level of commitment from people he adds to the team, not because he needs clones but because he recognizes it requires a unique sense of purpose to forge an investment career in South Bend, Indiana.

"We're fortunate at Notre Dame to have a very strong sense of mission. That differs from a lot of places. A Catholic university with a very clear, real mission, a residential campus, and strong sense of community—it is easier to get attention from graduates that can relate to it."

The 13 members of the investment team all have undergraduate degrees from the school. Two have Harvard MBAs and nine have CFAs. "All very talented and committed to the school, they have greatly enhanced our community."

Malpass has taught a class in portfolio management called "Applied Investment Management" since 1995. "It's a 'live portfolio' that I teach with other senior faculty. Over time, it's been a source of tremendous talent." The investment office staffs an analyst program every two years and an associates program. "The training programs have given us good stability and some fabulous young professionals to work with."

With the endowment valued at approximately $6 billion, Malpass oversees an investment team comparable to other large endowments. The number of staff is equivalent to the average-size team of the top 20 endowments. "At one point we had been behind, but got more reasonable in terms of staffing. The size of the team is comparable to the top 20. It's driven by complexity. We have 155 manager relationships, and because of our significant global alternative investment portfolio, we need a first-rate administrative and operations group."

Managing the Team

Malpass highly values continuity and stability in the team and the organization. He leads a regular off-site meeting with the team to focus on planning investments and establishing priorities, structuring it to give all participants an equal voice. He and his team find the event extremely valuable and crucial to their success. "We have a really good, sophisticated template for thinking clearly about trends, how the world is changing, markets are changing, instruments are changing. We are looking at allocations, looking at the future, looking at valuations, and developing a list of goals for the year. If you don't have that, then you're at the whim of the market. So we turn down things that turn out to be successful, but we also turn down things that turn out to be terrible. I tell the team, 'It's like stock picking, getting enough of the right things.' Don't worry about missing the good as long as we miss the bad."

The ability to avoid bad investments or decisions improves with the staff and knowledge continuity the meeting fosters. "We do a lot of self-assessment in the session. What worked? What are the lessons learned? We try to institutionalize the knowledge, so we don't make the same mistakes over and over. Continuity helps us." He wonders how other organizations can institutionalize their knowledge with frequent turnover. "It's just different people making the same mistakes. You will make mistakes. What we try to do is limit them. So there's lots of self-assessment about lessons learned and what we should be doing differently."

Having a strong sense of mission helps motivate the team, but it does not pay the bills, so the investment office has an incentive compensation program. "Comparable to other funds and based on a Stanford annual survey, it's the right mix of schools and people." The program includes a bonus pool and incentives for senior staff, with a deferral feature. Malpass structures it so the base compensation is the median of large endowment funds. Adding incentive pay from good performance should elevate them to the top quartile in compensation. "These are patriots and they also know their worth. I don't want them to feel like secondary citizens in the endowment world. I want them to feel like they're competitive with other big endowments."

Team structure has evolved. "We basically have a public team and private team; several that work together. Honestly, it's a very collaborative group overall and across the specialties, with hedge funds in private equity and vice versa. The senior people work so well together, share information, and get involved in due diligence." The compensation scheme had included an incentive for performance in each asset class, but the blurring of asset classes led them to eliminate that component.

Malpass built a discretionary component into the incentive compensation as well. His staff engages in noninvestment activities to support the institution probably more than their counterparts at other schools. He wants to acknowledge and reward that behavior. "There's a lot of good citizenship. It's why we don't have a management company. It just distances you from the school and it doesn't solve anything."

Given the significant growth of the endowment since Malpass became CIO, it seems likely that investment performance has influenced alumni to increase gifts as well.

"Alumni feel there's tremendous stewardship of the endowment program. The numbers have been at the top. We have a more talented student body that leads to more talented alumni. We have a strong investment group and a strong sense of a fiduciary duty." Notre Dame has an opportunity to encourage more gifts to the endowment through the auspices of the investment office. It is one of only four schools with an IRS ruling letter allowing it to commingle assets from charitable trusts and the endowment pool. "It has been extremely well received. In the past, you could not commingle trusts and endowment pools, because of tax issues. We would manage the trusts separately using mutual funds." Harvard, Stanford, and Princeton all have received similar rulings. Malpass expects it to result in hundreds of millions of dollars in new gifts.

Very few members of the Notre Dame community had faith the endowment would even reach $60 million, let alone $6 billion. Father Ted Hesburgh focused on growing the endowment when he became president in 1952. At the time, it was $7 million. "There's a headline from the *Notre Dame Scholastic* from 1944 that says 'Notre Dame Endowment Described as Pitifully Meager.' The article lists five other Indiana schools that had more assets. Yale had $106 million, Harvard $154 million."

LESSONS, OBSERVATIONS, AND ADVICE

Malpass offers his perspective on the management decisions foundations and endowments face in the years ahead and emphasizes the value of a good culture and strong partnerships.

Advice for Smaller Institutions

Since Malpass shepherded the endowment's growth from $400 million to $6 billion, he believes smaller-sized endowed organizations can do more than hope for a miracle to achieve substantial investment returns.

"You have to be creative and think differently to achieve superior returns. The market is more crowded, more institutional, and alternatives are more in the mainstream. That doesn't mean there are no opportunities on a global basis—investors have to go where the others aren't." Private investment in Asia is one example of the numerous global opportunities. Investors now can participate in new forms of investment vehicles like derivatives to get exposure or buy investments in the secondary market.

"There's a lot of ways to get going. If you're creative, work hard, and leapfrog what others have done, you can build a nice portfolio." Investors should be actively looking ahead to identify new asset classes or instruments early. If investors meet and talk to a lot of people, they will find good investments. Although he thinks there are more opportunities today because of global expansion, he admits, "It's just harder."

Malpass believes smaller institutions can and should manage their own investment program.

"This is a topic getting a lot of attention because of firms targeted at outsourcing endowments. At some size, around $500 million, you are better off developing your own institutional approach and memory and an institutional process. Hire somebody young as CIO—maybe our experience shouldn't necessarily be the exception. I strongly believe over the very long term, if you let them have more resources, build a team, and expand into other areas as funds grow, then they will have institutional memory and the relationships they build for the school will pay off more in the long run."

How individuals choose between their commitment to financial income and their commitment to a mission factors into the discussion.

"The problem has been that the economics of hedge funds have caused people to leave. That's very difficult and that's why our mission and commitment to the place is important. I'm the second-longest-serving CIO after David Swensen among the top 20 endowments. In terms of commitment, my number two, Mike Donovan, is as committed as I am. I'm past all of that questioning and will finish my career here. I have been able to get a younger cadre that has gotten offers to go to a number of other places. They choose to be here. Maybe it's unique, but I think our stability is helpful. Maybe that's not what everyone can count on. I would like to think people are going to try to do that first."

Malpass agrees with the suggestion that the situation resembles college sports programs. Schools that can keep a good coach are more likely to have long-term success. Other schools will try to hire those coaches thinking it will bring them the same success. "College sports are a good analogy to endowments. Have good leadership over time and long tenures, develop a more attractive culture, get better people, and build from there."

Proponents of the outsourced CIO model would argue that today organizations cannot single-handedly take a $500 million endowment and grow it meaningfully.

"I think people, if they have the right leadership, can do it. Some of them with these funds are real mercenaries. There is not going to be a lot of stability in those firms."

Reinforcing his point, Malpass tells of being interviewed for the Notre Dame paper. "The headline said, 'Partners and Patriots.' They hadn't told me about it. I loved it. It describes where we are perfectly. I don't think that should be so unique—it can be done with right leadership. What they're feeding on is the very poor governance most institutions have, the lack of commitment to doing it right, to having a dedicated CIO and giving them the right resources to build a team. A university is a complicated organization, and it takes some strong people on the board and in the administration to make it happen. If they can, over a 20- to 30-year period, they'll be much better off."

Future Challenges Facing All Foundations and Endowments

"Building and retaining great teams" will be the biggest challenge for CIOs. "It's all about the people. Organizational design and stability will be a competitive edge. That's where I feel good about our position. Continuity in staff will be a huge advantage for us. I honestly believe with the quality of team, we'll be well positioned going forward."

He urges CIOs and committees to stay focused on the fundamentals of investing and to search for value. "Focus and strong investment planning are essential, and strong relationships with partners are critical." Endowed organizations and their investment manager partners need to find more ways to innovate and invest together.

Investment Mistakes

Malpass advises investors to remember they have a long time horizon. "It gives you leverage, a huge advantage. Think long term, don't be pressured into short-term opportunities. Don't do due-diligence shortcuts. Make extra calls and really work your network." Rushing investment decisions causes mistakes. "I worry about it in today's environment. There's a frenzy to get closed and get legal work done." He recently passed on a potentially interesting investment because he and his team wanted to do more due diligence. "We have got to finish our work if we're going to make a commitment. Understand that you don't have to be with everyone."

Thou shall not chase returns, and thou shall not covet the investments of a larger endowment. "It shouldn't be a me-too game; just because Yale and Harvard do it doesn't mean you have to do it." Investors should not blindly copy investments made by other institutions, because they run the risk of investing in a vehicle they do not completely understand.

"It's harder with globalization. China is a good example. We have a fabulous network in Europe and the United States. Very few have the same network in China. You just have to develop it over time, have an investment process and set of guidelines and stick to them."

Working with Managers

Notre Dame has relationships with 155 different investment managers, and Malpass expects the number of new managers to grow incrementally, but not double like it has over the last 10 years.

"We are trying to displace people more, make tough choices." The average holding period for a manager has increased, indicating their approach to displacing managers has improved. "A lot of firms, most firms, have a life cycle to them. It's hard for people to sustain excellence over a long, long period of time."

Performance is just one reason to displace a manager. Frequently, other issues lead to the decision like organizational changes or a realignment of incentives. "A lot of things like that can come up. We try to anticipate and move on before things suffer. It's hard. We are very close to the partners, and they enjoy working with Notre Dame. We're passionate, well rounded, and have other interests. We communicate so well most of the time, almost all the time, so they'll know where they are and there are no surprises. If they're surprised by a decision, that's our fault."

Career Advice

At Notre Dame, Malpass mentors various students, employees, and others he meets through formal mentoring programs. "I tell them to follow their passion, be willing to think outside the box and try new things that their peers aren't trying. Some are coming out of their two-year banking program and looking for their next idea. I am encouraging them to take a long-term perspective and do something totally different, like go to China."

Once they climb back into the box, he then recommends they get a Chartered Financial Analyst designation (CFA). "I don't think there's any one formula for success; there are a lot of ways people can be successful."

Influences

Despite his concern that the investor he considers an important influence on his investment philosophy and career "might sound too trite," Malpass says, "I recently had a chance to meet with Warren Buffett in his office. I met him once when he spoke at Notre Dame and have read most of the books written about him or by him." Malpass shares Buffett's commitment to principles like having long time horizons and seeking value, even though Notre Dame implements through investment managers. "I clearly can identify with his philosophy and long-term relationships with his partners." Buffett's career has been an influential factor in Malpass's career. "Meeting him brought it home a bit and made me realize he was more of an influence than I had thought."

Malpass cites Jay Jordan, the current chair of the investment committee, as a valuable source of market knowledge and experience, a helpful sounding board and trusted adviser to him and the staff.

When Malpass became CIO, he consulted with several practitioners in various asset classes, including venture capitalists, buyouts, and hedge funds. Since he met and spent time with some of the most successful people in each area, he gratefully acknowledges all their help and influence. Malpass credits people at Cambridge Associates and trustees and investment committee members with helping him learn and succeed throughout his career. "Probably 10 or 12 people have made a difference."

Father Ted Hesburgh

Malpass adds, "I cannot talk about the Notre Dame endowment without saying something about the inspiration of Father Ted Hesburgh. He was the first in our history to talk extensively about the importance of the endowment to the quality of the school. When he became president in 1952, the endowment had $7 million in assets. It was $400 million when he left in 1987. He was the first priest elected to the board of overseers at Harvard University and served two years as its president. He just had an unusual ability to connect our work to the mission down to the students and faculty. He understood what it would do for the institution—transform it for centuries to come. If there was anyone that did inspire me, it was not an investment person, it was Father Hesburgh."

Partners and Patriots

Malpass became CIO at Notre Dame with such little investment experience that anyone unaware of his work ethic and commitment would attribute his successful performance to divine intervention. Having such little experience may have given him an advantage, however, by forcing him to approach the challenge as an outsider and dispassionately analyze the situation and determine the approach, and then passionately commit to executing successfully.

"That's a good observation about the outside looking in. It's hard to put down all the success factors, almost 20 years of a lot of things. We worked hard to observe best practices, what works and what hasn't, and we're very astute about recognizing and institutionalizing that information. Never feel comfortable that we have achieved anything. Last year is history. That was last year. I move on to the next year, July 1, always thinking about the future." Malpass thinks the members of his team share his philosophy. "The business has changed a lot in the last 20 years. The days of waiting for good funds to come pitch their product are long over. We have got to go find them. The reputation that we built took time; it did not happen overnight. It feels good and it's been rewarding."

Often, when the team receives positive news or results, he will say that it happened because "we treat people right and it's coming back to us. We like to make people feel like they're sharing with us. Their work has an impact on our school. We take the investment committee to different cities to host our partners and thank them for their work."

Malpass wants partners to understand the investment team's deep commitment and the unique nature of the school and to express his willingness to work together to achieve their mission.

"We want to think of it as a family fund, and we try to manage it that way, but with the sophistication of any other investor in the country."

COMMITMENT AND PURPOSE

Scott Malpass has devoted his career to an institution he cares for passionately, pursuing it as if he had been called to it. Like his contemporaries, Malpass is an intelligent and astute investor, but unlike others, he expresses a deep and fervent commitment to the institution.

Since Malpass admires Father Hesburgh, it seems fitting to learn more about Father Hesburgh from stories and quotes to see how his words and deeds may have influenced or informed Malpass's life and career.

In an amusing parallel, Father Hesburgh once declined an offer from Lyndon Johnson to run the space program, saying that a "priest with poverty vows should not be running a $6 billion agency." Fortunately, Scott Malpass did not take any poverty vows, because today he runs a $6 billion endowment.

Father Hesburgh once said of being a priest, "It's my vocation, my calling, and my purpose in life," words that could easily describe how Malpass approaches his role as CIO for Notre Dame.

Asked what it means to be from Notre Dame, Father Hesburgh said, "It's having a vision for a good, Christian life. Seeing the world as not just a big secular metropolis, but as the kingdom of God, and knowing that each one of us, especially those who have been fortified by a great Catholic education, can deepen the impact of that kingdom through our personal life and the work we do."

Hesburgh's words describe what it means for Scott Malpass to be the CIO of Notre Dame. He has deepened the impact of the university through his commitment and execution. Scott Malpass is a partner, a patriot, and a performer.

CHAPTER 8

Built an Endowment through Common Sense

William Spitz, CIO, Vanderbilt University

As the chief investment officer (CIO) of the Vanderbilt endowment for the past 21 years, Bill Spitz has influenced the endowment investing community tremendously. Among the first of his contemporaries to leave a comfortable job and a comfortable paycheck to become a CIO, in 1985 he began his tenure at Vanderbilt. Starting with a $300 million fund, no staff, and limited authority, Bill Spitz will leave a legacy of a $3 billion endowment and an investment office run by an independent CIO, staffed with professionals that earn incentives for achieving results.

Among the first of his colleagues to invest in alternatives such as private equity and hedge funds, he paved the way for other endowments and has served the industry as a speaker, writer, and author. It seems fitting that he subtitled one of his books *Building Your Financial Future through Common Sense*, because it describes him and his achievements so well. Like the investors he most admires, Bill Spitz brings rational, logical thinking to the role of the CIO.

BACKGROUND

William T. Spitz is the vice chancellor for investments and treasurer of Vanderbilt University. In that role, he is responsible for the management of approximately $4 billion in assets and the university's technology transfer and business incubation efforts. Bill is a director of Diversified Trust Company and previously served as chairman of the board of Commonfund.

Before joining Vanderbilt in 1985, he spent 11 years in the investment management business in New York, serving as an analyst, portfolio manager, and CIO. Mr. Spitz was president of NSR Asset Management Corporation, vice president of Wertheim & Company, and began his career at Citibank NA. He is a Chartered Financial Analyst, holds an MBA degree from the University of Chicago and a BA from Vanderbilt University, and is the author of *Get Rich Slowly* published by Macmillan Publishing Company in 1992 and *Save Smart for a Secure Future* also published by Macmillan Publishing Company in 1998.

Mr. Spitz was the recipient of the 1993 Rodney H. Adams Award presented by National Association of College and University Business Officers (NACUBO) and the 2005 Hirtle Callaghan Award for Investment Leadership. He currently serves as a trustee of Kenyon College.

Wall Street Analyst Seeking Change

After graduating from business school, Bill Spitz spent his 11 years on Wall Street progressing from roles in research and quantitative analysis to becoming the CIO of a small firm. He says, "I didn't enjoy it and didn't have a passion for analyzing individual stocks. I couldn't care less if IBM made its numbers in a quarter, and that's the nature of the beast. I was not particularly good at it and felt like I was just shuffling pieces of paper around."

His firm managed assets for pension plans and started losing accounts that had become overfunded due to good investment performance. He became frustrated with being terminated for doing a good job.

"I worked crazy hours, commuted into New York City, didn't see my kids. I was thinking about what else to do, didn't feel qualified to do something else, and didn't know what I was going to do."

Meanwhile, he had participated actively in Vanderbilt alumni affairs and ran the New York chapter. When the chairman of the Vanderbilt board approached him and asked him to move down to Nashville and run the investments, his first reaction was, "Don't be silly. I'm a Wall Street big shot. Why would I want to do that?" But the more he thought about it, the more it appealed to him.

Personally, he liked Nashville and the opportunity to change his lifestyle. On a professional level, he felt he was more of a macro thinker, better at thinking about world events, the economy, and different asset classes than picking stocks. He began to see that the role might make better use of his skills. Although taking the position meant taking a pay cut, he thought associating with the university would bring psychic rewards. He was willing to make that trade-off and started at Vanderbilt in 1985.

After serving 21 years and increasing the endowment tenfold—from approximately $300 million to $3 billion—in 2006, Spitz announced he would retire upon the hiring of his replacement.

Vanderbilt University, the First and Only CIO

When he started, the Vanderbilt endowment had more progressive investments than others at that time. The fund had allocated about 8 to 9 percent to international equities, when "almost nobody had anything in international" and had 3 to 4 percent in venture capital and another 3 to 4 percent in real estate. He says, "We started from that base and did more of the same all the way along."

In the mid-1980s, Spitz invested in hedge funds and distressed securities and dramatically increased exposure to private assets like venture capital, private equity, and real estate. Like many others, the endowment moved from traditional to more nontraditional investments, just a little ahead of most. He has continued to move into global investments and has more exposure to non-U.S. than U.S. assets.

Coming Full Circle

As he surveys the investment landscape, he says, "I have to admit today I'm a little skeptical. Long-only approaches aren't so bad. A lot of return has been arbitraged out of nontraditional assets. There's too much money, egregious fees, and egregious terms. When I give talks saying maybe we should go back to a much simpler model without all this funky stuff, I get hooted out of the room.

"Unfortunately, the problem with age and tenure is you get a little bit of perspective. I don't have hard-and-fast data, but I have an incredible sense of déjà vu—been there, done that with other asset classes. It comes into favor, everyone chases it, and returns are horrible. We made that mistake with real estate in the late 1980s. We invested just at the wrong time and got our rear ends kicked."

Spitz serves on investment committees for five organizations with various purposes and investment objectives. "They all had consultants visit and advocate commodity exposure, all giving the same presentations. Portable alpha and alternatives dominate the talk at every conference.

"There is some indication that returns and alpha are trending down in hedge funds, so there may be early signs. I just have a strong sense of massive lemming-like behavior and trampling into assets in a blind way. Early adopters do well; late adopters get killed."

At the same time, he acknowledges, "The problem is where do you go, if you don't like that stuff? Do you go back into stocks, bonds, and cash? Most people find that hard to swallow based on projected returns, but I don't know, maybe that is the right answer. We all look for the truly new, new thing that hasn't been discovered yet. I don't know about you, but I haven't found any of those."

He postulates that investors may have to temper their investment return expectations. "With stocks at 6 to 7 percent, bonds 5 percent, they think, 'Doesn't do it for me; better go into other assets to get the returns I need.' Maybe we better just accept the 5 to 8 percent returns, and that's the reality of the world."

BEING CHIEF INVESTMENT OFFICER

As Bill Spitz describes how his role and his investment approach have evolved over the last 21 years, it becomes apparent that various components of the investment process do not progress in an orderly fashion—they intertwine and overlap. Asset allocation policy begins and ends with governance.

In the early years of his tenure as CIO, Spitz went to the investment committee for any decision. Although they always said yes, over time that became less satisfying, as did the lack of incentive compensation. In the late 1990s he approached the board to propose changes, saying, "I've been here a long time and done well. It's ridiculous for me to have to come to the committee for permission to do things." He asked for broad guidelines. "Let us do the work. If you don't like it, fire us; if you do, we want to get paid for it." After some "pushing and shoving" in 1998–1999, the board approved new asset allocation guidelines and became one of the first endowments to install an incentive compensation structure for the staff.

He received full discretion to operate within broad asset allocation guidelines and select managers, agreeing to seek board approval for new asset classes or dramatic policy shifts. In the course of the next few years, the team began to see tactical opportunities and wanted the ability to implement them.

"When junk bond spreads blew out by 1,200 basis points, I went to the committee, saying that although we had no permanent allocation, we wanted to act on a tactical opportunity in junk. They had concerns. 'What if interest rates rise? What if the world comes to an end?' We didn't act on that or two or three similar situations that followed. Finally, the committee came to me and said, 'You have had some pretty good insights, and made some pretty good calls, so maybe we should give you some more flexibility.'

"The committee widened the exposure bands for each asset class and created a new allocation labeled 'opportunistic.' Up to a maximum exposure of 5 percent, the team has carte blanche to execute trades based on themes or market anomalies, primarily looking for major misevaluations and two-sigma events, not short-term movements."

Spitz recently accomplished another major shift in the asset allocation policy after telling the board, "We have 10 asset classes, a gazillion subasset classes—let's simplify."

Asset Allocation Today

Every year, the committee reviews the strategic asset allocation or policy portfolio and studies each piece to understand the role it plays in the portfolio—how it should behave and how the components should all work together.

Postsimplification, the policy portfolio consists of six broad asset sets with targets and ranges that allow the investment team to adjust or move the weighting as they see fit. This new approach gives them more flexibility and opportunism with less structure and pigeonholing:

1. *Equity.* A single class that can encompass 40 percent of the portfolio. No geographical, style, or market cap targets, yet still diversified.
2. *Private equity and venture capital.*
3. *Real assets.* Real estate, timber, energy (commodities or Treasury inflation-protected securities would belong here if the university invested in those assets).
4. *Absolute return.* Uncorrelated strategies.
5. *Fixed income.*
6. *Opportunistic.* Five percent allocation for executing tactical ideas. "Another arrow in the quiver" that lets the team add value in addition to the managers.
7. *Exceptions.* Certain types of investment strategies can fall under a different category than their asset class or name implies.
   a. *Equity hedge funds.* Long/short equity funds that tend to be net long or directional fall into the equity portfolio. Some equity funds belong in the absolute return allocation, depending on the construction of the managers' portfolios and exposure to market beta. A market-neutral equity strategy fits absolute return.
   b. *Distressed debt.* Included in absolute return, mainly because traditionally it has not correlated to other items in the portfolio.

Adding Value Using Opportunistic Tactics   Spitz and his team use this technique to implement ideas that would be inefficient to execute by hiring a manager. They anticipate having numerous opportunities to add value, having done so in the past.

"Interestingly, over the last fiscal year, manager selection stunk, but we added 160 to 170 basis points from tilts and tactical shifts. We took a stinky year and made it a mediocre year. We had an average year due to the team's tactical strategies. Tactics included overweighting emerging markets and getting international energy right."

Having an opportunistic allocation adds value in another way besides investment return. Spitz says, "One side benefit has been just terrific. The investment team has gotten much more market savvy. In the past, they looked at their little area, focused on the nitty-gritty, nuts and bolts, not thinking very strategically or tactically. Now they are paying attention to asset classes and relative value."

He eventually wants to simplify the allocation to three asset profiles:

- Return generators
- Inflation hedges
- Deflation hedges

"That's where we want to go conceptually—don't know if we'll ever get there."

Back to Governance

The investment committee has statutory terms with relatively low turnover. Because the board has few members with professional investment experience, they recruited four nontrustee alumni with expertise in particular asset classes, including private equity, venture, and hedge funds, to serve on the committee. Spitz says, "They are really helpful."

He reflects on how governance has changed over the years "for good and not so good." Early on, the board was very involved in the decisions.

"It is very interesting that we have achieved the opposite problem. Our committee is no longer very engaged. We have taken on much responsibility as a team and have done well. I've been there a long time, so I have a lot of stature and credibility. They assume we'll take care of it, so it can be hard to get a quorum. It's an interesting problem. I don't know what's worse, having a committee that's meddling or disinterested."

Portfolio Construction

The approach to portfolio construction and manager selection also demonstrates the overlapping responsibilities and concerns of a CIO.

"The approach evolved over time as I made mistakes and learned. I have become really comfortable with a core-satellite approach that I have used in some form or another for very long period of time. It includes a core of passive or semipassive managers just to make sure a significant part of the portfolio gets market-like returns. Then we add some very concentrated and, we hope, high-alpha-generating satellites, around the core."

When he deviated from the approach, he regretted it. "I brought on new people in the equity area and they didn't like that approach, so we moved away from core into more satellite managers, and the results stank. So two things happened: First, I fired one of the people, and second, we have moved back to more of a core position."

Core: Passive Managers   Managers with low tracking error make up the core. Forty percent of the global equity is invested purely passively in a global index that includes emerging markets.

"I really believe that passive funds are okay. I'm not embarrassed to admit to putting passive managers in the portfolio. Unless you can look in the mirror and really convince yourself that you've got something that's really providing value added, passive is great. If you just do passive managers, then you will outperform most of your peers. We know that, so that should be the starting point."

The equity portfolio also contains some enhanced passive managers like quantitative managers. He blends in fundamental managers. For instance, they invested in a fund called Adage that runs an enhanced index using traditional, fundamental stock-picking methods.

Satellite: Active Managers   Around the core or the satellite part of the portfolio, the team invests in concentrated, sector-focused, "high-octane" managers. Spitz says, "We are not afraid of concentration. Some of the managers hold only 10 to 12 stock holdings." Spitz is attracted to global unrestrained managers, with broad mandates. He prefers to find smart people and tell them, "Here's our money; go do your thing." He likes activist managers because "they can make things happen and impact the results across all asset classes. I don't look at activism from a corporate governance point of view. When I am paying people to earn returns, it's better if they have the ability to influence the outcome."

On Selecting Managers

First, we ask, "What's your edge?" If they haven't thought about it or can't answer, then it's a short conversation.

If they do have an edge, why is it sustainable? Why is it systematic? What is it about your firm that allows you to produce that? We are not doctrinaire about what that might be; we just want them to be able to say they have a proprietary skill, proprietary information flow, or proprietary something that is sustainable, ahead of the pack, and always being fine-tuned. We need to hear that they've got *something*. If they can't articulate that, it's a short conversation.

We care about risk management, systems, and any conflicts. We like them to have a lot of their own money in their strategy.

On Sourcing Ideas

A few conferences are really good. Certain managers are good. Highly focused managers aren't as good for ideas. A firm like

Grantham Mayo is good because they invest in a lot of asset classes. We talk to peers and get some ideas from Cambridge Associates, Commonfund, and general reading.

We are trying to develop a series of internal indicators to help us generate opportunistic investment strategies. We will track the performance of growth versus value, large cap versus small cap, domestic versus international, relative valuations, and volatility.

Hiring and Managing an Investment Team

For the first 15 years of his 21 years at Vanderbilt, Spitz ran the whole fund by himself. He began building a team that now includes five people running $3 billion—an unusually small team compared to other funds of the same size.

"Not a denial of resources, it's a function of one thing. I personally hate managing people, hate managing an organization. I want to be an investor; I don't enjoy dealing with a big staff.

"I am still very actively and always involved in the investments. I have no interest in being someone sitting on high, presiding over the team and the process. I want to be engaged and involved in investment and decisions."

He concedes his approach may be outdated, given the complexity of asset classes and portfolios, compliance issues, and accounting regulations. He thinks it appropriate that his replacement will likely have a bigger staff and more structure.

"I just don't want to do it."

He believes that having a smaller team hasn't hurt them, especially since they have worked together for a long time and have had good performance.

Having a smaller team does not necessarily mean the endowment has a smaller set of managers. He says that his team members want to pursue interesting ideas, so he constantly pushes them to concentrate and have conviction.

The smaller size has forced them to network and rely more on peers for advice and "hopefully give them an idea here or there, too." He also doesn't use consultants because "I don't believe in off-loading responsibility."

On Avoiding Groupthink
There is a fine line between sharing ideas and being seduced into doing what everyone else is doing.

I don't have the right answer. I think you need to do a couple of things. First, be cynical and skeptical, because everyone is very adept at marketing and you hear great pitches, see great stats. People will come in and make very good cases for anything. So you always need to start from a position of being cynical and skeptical. It's a bad way to go through life but . . .

Second, you need to have your antennae out and when you begin to hear the same discussion or the same argument repeatedly, you need to process that. When every single investment committee I'm on had a presentation on commodities, a bell went off in my head. The networking we do tends to be more focused on specifics, like specific managers. We don't call our peers and ask them what they're thinking or what they're doing.

On Structuring the Team and Making Decisions

I experimented with having staffers as specialists and having them as generalists and ended up with a hybrid I think works really well. The way we operate, except for me, each person has responsibility for a specific asset class and then everybody makes the decision.

So the private equity person finds an interesting fund, invites them to meet, the whole team sees the presentation, asks her to do more due diligence, and the whole team decides whether to pull the trigger. We benefit from someone that spends all their time in an area and from others with different views and perspectives.

Incentive compensation is based on portfolio performance not on an individual's asset class. No one can point to you and say "You made a crappy investment," because we made a crappy investment.

Because we did really well for a long time, we got accustomed to very nice incentive bonuses. Last year when we didn't do well there was no incentive bonus, so there has been a lot of tension. The rest of the team is all over those in the areas that underperformed: "You've got to fix that portfolio." And it's healthy and constructive. The pressure and tension is a good thing.

On Balancing Authority with Experience

Unless I have incredibly strong feelings, I think it's hard to build a staff when you overrule them very much. My strong tendency, to my chagrin, has been to agree to things that I wasn't crazy about.

It's hard for me when I really disagree, I think, "I'm the CIO; maybe I should squash it." On the other hand, if I squash it too much, then it takes away their incentive to be creative and successful. Getting that balance right is really hard.

Biggest Investment Success

Spitz finds it interesting that his biggest success and worst mistake are the exact mirror image of each other. He says his biggest success came from being willing to do investments that were "unpopular, contrary, hard to do, and messy." Around 1988 or 1989, he invested in distressed debt for the first time shortly after Michael Milken went to jail, the United Air Lines leveraged buyout failed, and savings and loans had to sell off their high-yield positions. He says, "You can imagine going to the committee to convince them to invest in the debt of bankrupt companies. That was an interesting sell. The investment ended up delivering an internal rate of return of 40 percent over its life. But it was a hard sell and painful to do."

Worst Investment Mistake

Spitz attributes his worst investment mistakes to not realizing when investments were late in the cycle and overly popular, then "getting seduced along with everyone in the world."

He says, "In 1986–1987, we got seduced by real estate. At the time, we had modest exposure. Salesmen came in with wonderful charts showing the diversification benefits and the same historical return as stocks. That turned out to be the top of the cycle, and we earned horrible returns over the life of those funds."

He learned to pay attention to investment cycles and recent patterns of performance, popularity, and valuation. Spitz advises investors, "Try to have the courage to invest when assets are unpopular and in the worst part of the cycle and not to invest at the other end of the cycle. That's easy to say and hard to do.

"No matter how long you've been doing this, you can still get seduced by the great pitch, the great returns. You look at it and say, 'I'm the only dumb ass in the country that hasn't made a lot of money. How did I miss this? I better jump on that bandwagon.'

"I've become a huge believer of regression to the mean, a huge believer in cycles. I am not saying that you should be trying to time things exactly, you should just be aware of where you are.

"And try to make sure you're not the last person in the world figuring out that this is an interesting thing to do."

Comparison to Peers

As CIO, Spitz has felt the impact of competition between universities—for students, professors and gifts—even at the endowment level. The desire to outshine peer institutions has not only increased pressure to replicate the portfolio and performance of other endowments, but also added an element of competition to the endowment staff's compensation plan.

Spitz says that to outperform peers "we have to have better asset allocation or better manager selection."

The asset allocation is in the middle of their peers. "We are not doing anything unusual there, although if we do shift back into more traditional assets that might differentiate us.

"I'm hard pressed to think we have better manager selection than our peers. Of course, every endowment works at it. All have smart people and lots of resources. I have no a priori reason to think we're going to be more successful.

"The board thinks I'm sandbagging when I tell them we should be in the middle of the peer group. If we're doing that, we're doing well. How can we expect to outperform Harvard, Yale, Princeton, Stanford, and Duke? They have all and more of the resources we have. (Like Vanderbilt), they also have smart, great alums and strong networks. Why do we think we should beat them?

"Hard to accept and hard to swallow, but that's the reality of the situation."

Spitz says that the investment environment has gotten more challenging. For one thing, early adopters of nontraditional and alternative investments had an advantage. As early adopters, the Vanderbilt endowment got the opportunity to invest in venture capital funds like Sequoia and Kleiner Perkins, "that you can't get into today if you're not already in the club."

According to Spitz, for a long time few endowments had staffs; now they have built staffs of capable people. With many opportunities widely available and all his peers seemingly invested in all the same types of funds, the environment is tough and will be a lot tougher.

Impact on Compensation   When the board originally implemented the incentive compensation policy for Spitz and his team, the bonus formula only measured performance compared to policy benchmarks. Today, the calculation includes those benchmarks plus performance compared to similar institutions.

"In 2001–2002, we beat the benchmarks pretty handily, but were in the bottom one third of the peer group. The trustees said, 'This is ridiculous; we're paying you incentive comp to be in the bottom of the peer group.' I said, 'Yeah, but we beat the benchmarks and we added value.' After some pushing and shoving, we ended up adding a peer group measure—the Cambridge Associates universe of institutions with $1 billion or more—as a small component of the incentive comp.

"It's a broad universe that outperforms most other types of institutions like pensions. It's a tough group. Is that exactly the right peer group? Who knows? Is the data readily available and easy to use? Yes."

Relationships with Peers   He says that despite similar incentive policies at other organizations, they haven't experienced any competitive behavior when they interact with their counterparts at other institutions. Their peers remain very forthcoming with information and ideas. Besides comparing notes on potential investments, Spitz's team will sometimes join due-diligence efforts.

At the same time, though, "Does David Swensen call me up and give me his best ideas? No. When David Swensen speaks, everyone listens, but I think he tells you what he *was* doing. Everyone thinks they're getting the great idea from the oracle. You're getting a year-old idea."

Spitz thinks there tends to be more pressure at institutions with clearly identifiable, direct competitors, and that leads to more competitive behavior among their staffs.

"All the Ivies are usually competitive. What is the direct competition for Vanderbilt? Maybe it's Georgetown, Washington University in St. Louis, but no clearly identifiable group. So we don't quite have the same problem. I know one CIO that ran a smaller Ivy League endowment, and he got a hard time about what he did in comparison to Harvard or Yale."

LESSONS, OBSERVATIONS, AND ADVICE

Spitz shared his thoughts on a variety of topics impacting investments, governance, and the future for foundation and endowments.

Concerns about Investment Managers

Spitz took an opportunity to admonish investment management organizations for galling terms and fees.

"One thing I will say is that I'm really frosted about terms, about hedge fund terms in particular. You just can't convince me that shorting stocks is very much different from buying long-only. Yet fees go from a total of 50 basis points to 2 and 20." [That is 2 percent management fee and 20 percent performance fee.]

"Lockups are really egregious. In an esoteric strategy, with hard-to-unwind positions, I'm fine with a two-year lockup. For a big-cap long/short manager to ask me for a two-year lockup, he's just asking me to guarantee his revenue flow, and I have no interest in doing that.

"I told my team, 'Don't bring me a manager with a hedge fund format unless they walk on water.' We will not agree to the fee structure, will not agree to the lockup unless there is something so unique and outstanding that I've got to put my last dollar into it.'"

He expresses dismay about experiences exiting investment funds.

"We have had couple of occasions in the last few years in funds that performed poorly and we wanted to get out and couldn't. When we reached the end of our term, they distributed 80 percent of our assets and told us we'd get the other 20 percent in three months when the audit's done. All that stuff, it's ridiculous."

Spitz chuckles at the absurdity of a conversation with one manager, "A private equity partner tells me, 'We don't make money off the 2 percent management fee, just the carry (performance fee),' and I'm sitting there saying, 'Wait a minute, I can do that math—$5 billion times 2 percent is $100 million, and there are 10 of you. . . .'"

Meanwhile, "there's a lot of data that shows if you're not invested in the top handful of firms, you shouldn't be invested in the asset class. The problem that creates is that if you're not in these funds, you can't get into them.

"One tension arises if you have a private equity specialist on your team out looking for new, interesting private-asset managers. Can you convince me that they can really add value? That's very hard to do. Yet, on one hand, you want your staff to be motivated to look for new managers. On the other hand, you must be cynical about how much value they can add."

Endowment and Foundation Management Issues

Regarding the rising trend of outsourcing the management of small and medium-sized endowments, Spitz says, "I have thought about it a lot recently. It raises a lot of really interesting questions. If you have an endowment of $100 million, with no staff and a committee, it's perfectly reasonable for someone to say to you, 'Why in the world don't you outsource? You don't have any resources, don't have any expertise, and there are outside firms with expertise to do it all.' For best practices, the burden of proof may shift to the endowments to show why they are *not* outsourcing."

He believes the largest endowments will face a huge staff retention issue. "People work at endowments not just for money; there's the mission and quality of life, but that only goes so far. I think if they can join an outsourcing firm, get a higher salary and equity stake, and do the same job they have at Harvard, Duke, or Vanderbilt, there's going to be tremendous pressure. In addition to upward pressure on compensation, this raises big issues for small endowments for determining what they should be doing and for the larger ones for retaining their staff."

He grins and says, "Nick Sabin just got $4 million to coach football at Alabama; so I don't feel too guilty about my paycheck."

Spitz believes there will be many new pressures. He cites more student activism related to investments, new auditing standards, and increased Sarbanes-Oxley focus on disclosures and conflicts. He expresses concern that compensation pressures may cause the IRS to scrutinize nonprofit organizations if it believes their employees are earning too much money. Finally, he believes that in a modest return environment a spending rate of 4 to 5 percent is unsustainable and should be lower.

Working with the Investment Committee

Although the investment team picks managers, Spitz has tried reenergizing the committee by having the members meet potential managers or seeking input when the staff is uncertain about a manager. He finds them very engaged individually and responsive to calls for help with ideas, research, or references. Or they will call him with an idea.

He says, "What will be fascinating is what happens when I leave since I have been there for 21 years and have stature and credibility with the committee. Basically, they look to me to run the portfolio and that's been fine. When the new CIO begins, there will be an interesting dynamic. The board will not be able to hire a good candidate if they don't give plenty of latitude and flexibility. On the other hand, will the next CIO get the flexibility and latitude I have had? Probably not; getting that right will be interesting."

Investment Influences

Spitz identifies Charles Ellis as an investor who had a big impact on his thinking, and Jack Bogle as another. He names his friend Hunter Lewis of Cambridge Associates, adding that Cambridge on the whole has done a good job of influencing the endowment world to think carefully about what they are doing and how they approach the business. He also cites Jeremy Grantham as an investor he admires tremendously.

They all have "ability to cut through all the BS and analyze things from an economic, analytical, intelligent framework. There's so much BS, advertising hype, and spin, and not many people that carefully cut through all of it and really think. They're all rational, logical thinkers with some sort of quantitative bent. I guess that tells you what kind of person I am."

COMMON-SENSE REWARDS

Spitz offered some closing comments on his career as an investor and advice for those that would like to pursue this role.

Asked to summarize his investment philosophy, he says, "The thing that drives me the most is that there are very few things you can control in investing and very few things that can impact the outcome, but the one thing you can control is the price you pay going in. So I try to make sure we get in at the right price. I don't always do that so well, but I view it as the one major controllable at your discretion. So I guess that means I'm a classic value investor.

"I don't think I or my colleagues are particularly good at picking equity and bond managers. We haven't found it to be a particularly easy thing to do, so we take a quantitative passive approach. We take the time and put the energy into investments where we have shown that we can add value like private equity and real estate. Focus on things that have the biggest payoff."

Asked to offer advice to those preparing for a career as a CIO, Spitz says, "Don't try to copy anyone. Don't try to be Dave Swensen. Develop your own approach and your own style; try to figure out what you're good at and take maximum advantage of it."

CHAPTER 9

Investment Artist with Her Own Perspective

Ellen Shuman, Vice President and CIO, Carnegie Corporation of New York

When Ellen Shuman graduated from Bowdoin College in Brunswick, Maine, as an art history major in 1976, if you had asked her to paint the picture of the career ahead of her, she probably would not have envisioned succeeding in the investment arts. By learning from the best and applying her own perspective, Ellen Shuman has made a fine art of foundation and endowment investing.

BACKGROUND

In 1986, David Swensen recruited her from the finance office at Yale, just across the hall, to join the Yale investments office. Over the next 13 years, she rose to become a director of investments with responsibility for real estate and capital markets activities and joined Carnegie Corporation of New York as vice president and chief investment officer (CIO) in January 1999. Managing a multiasset portfolio valued in excess of $2.5 billion, she has significantly outperformed her policy benchmark and peer universe and earned the respect of her endowment and foundation colleagues. Shuman received the Foundation of the Year honor from *Institutional Investor* magazine in its 2006 Awards for Excellence in Investment Management and serves on the Bowdoin College Investment Committee, among others.

While undoubtedly influenced by her experience investing along with Swensen at Yale, like most artists, she has her own vision. She says, "A lot of investment styles work. and it's important to find the style that works for you. If you're a growth investor, stick to growth; if you flip-flop, you will do it at the wrong time. Be true to yourself, have the conviction to stick with a consistent investment philosophy, and you will do well."

D. Ellen Shuman reports to Carnegie Corporation President Vartan Gregorian and serves as a member of the senior management team. While at Yale University, in addition to her investment responsibilities, she taught several finance and investments courses at the Yale School of Management and Yale College.

She is a member of the board of trustees at Bowdoin College, serving as vice chair from 2000 to 2004. She also serves as a director of The Investment Fund for Foundations (TIFF) (2001), and is an investment adviser to the Edna McConnell Clark Foundation (1998), the Community Foundation for Greater New Haven (2004), the American Academy of Arts and Letters (2005), and Brandywine Trust (2006).

In 2004, she joined the board of directors of General American Investors (NYSE: GAM), one of the oldest closed-end funds in the United States.

Ms. Shuman received her CFA in 1992 and an MPPM from the Yale School of Management in 1984.

Yale University

A few years after receiving an art history degree from Bowdoin College and evaluating her career options, Ellen Shuman decided she needed to be "repackaged," and entered the Yale School of Management in New Haven, Connecticut, earning a master's in public and private management, the equivalent of an MBA, in 1984. The program was differentiated from other business schools because of its broader focus, emphasizing nonprofit and public-sector management issues more than other graduate management degree programs. She developed an interest in higher-education finance and joined Yale in its Office of Finance upon graduation. After about a year, "I began to think that the investments office across the hall looked more interesting and fun."

Shuman appreciated the importance of endowments because of course-work on education finance, but the field of endowment management was quite undeveloped at the time. Pensions, endowments, and foundations all pretty much utilized a 60/40 equity/bond allocation, and international equity was still considered an alternative asset class.

Swensen recruited her to join the investments office in 1986. He himself was new to the field of endowment management, despite having a PhD in economics and significant Wall Street experience. "We all grew up together under David's leadership." Shuman recalls that Swensen, a Wisconsin native with solid Midwestern values, was "appalled by the principal/agent issues brought to light by his work on Wall Street." At the time, it was uncommon to emphasize the alignment of interests between investment managers and investors, but this soon became a hallmark of Yale's investment approach.

"One of my weaknesses had been that I had never been on Wall Street. Being aware of principal/agent issues was a big part of my Yale experience and remains a significant influence on my outlook. Working with David made up for not having been through a sausage factory on Wall Street."

Real Estate and Oil and Gas: The Ground as Training Ground   Shuman handled real estate and oil and gas investments. She says, "They were pretty immature asset classes, typically managed by talented, self-made deal makers who were not schooled in the fiduciary world of institutional investing. The principal-agent issues then were most egregious in real estate, whereas today I would say that honor rests with many hedge funds and private equity firms, particularly those that seek 'permanent capital' from the public markets.

"Examples of some common practices we observed were that real estate managers utilized separate accounts with fees based on the value of the assets, but they were responsible for valuing the assets. Managers did not receive incentive pay at that time, so they were motivated to hold assets to maintain fee income and thus rarely sold properties. They would run a commingled fund alongside multiple separate accounts—who got which deal?—and if the accounts didn't want a particular investment, they'd put it in the fund. They received acquisition and disposition fees. It was altogether an unhealthy situation."

Yet it also was a great time for Shuman because institutional investment in the asset class was in its infancy. Foundations and endowments had little exposure to real estate, and investing in it was somewhat controversial. The savings-and-loan crisis and resulting real estate fire sales ended up being fortunate for Yale. "We took a contrarian approach that was very unpopular at the time, focusing on real estate in a serious way because of all the distressed sellers in the marketplace. It was the beginning of a long and profitable investment opportunity for the university because of our willingness to question the status quo. Yale took a leadership role that drove permanent changes in the structure of the industry.

"Swensen asked questions to which the answers are obvious today, but at the time represented a new way of thinking. 'Why can't the structure of real estate vehicles be like those in private equity? Why not have a manager who is an operator, not an adviser? Why can't an operator raise a fund that represents their sole investment vehicle, just like a private equity manager, which owns and manages the properties?' Investors don't tell their buyout manager, 'I like this kind of deal but I don't like that deal.' It's so obvious now that the same thinking works in real estate, but at that time they didn't do that. The large pension funds all required that they approve each investment that went into a separate account. By the time it had been approved it wasn't a good deal because, if it were, it wouldn't be sitting around waiting for a pension fund and committee to approve it."

According to Shuman, the Yale endowment was the first institutional investor to support real estate managers raising a fund that represented the firm's sole investment vehicle, and importantly, giving the manager full investment discretion, which was "unheard of" at the time, but it worked because the fund was structured to align financial interests of the general partner and the limited partner. They were the first to invest in organizations such as Shorenstein, Avanti, and Brookdale and were responsible for changing the institutional approach to real estate investing.

This experience formed one of the core tenets of her investment philosophy. "One of my biases comes from the Yale model. I like focused managers. Especially in real estate, you need local sharpshooters, people that aren't trying to be everything to everyone. Brookdale dominates the southeastern United States, while Shorenstein always invests in a dominant office building in a market. Superior managers don't try to be good at everything. Real estate is still a local business so that operators trying to be active in every property type in every market are doomed to be average.

"The truly local investors know that one side of the street is better than the other or that one floor plan is better suited to the local tenant market than another. I learned how critical it is to find 'the local sharpshooter'—someone with very, very detailed knowledge that is differentiating. I try to apply that thinking to other asset classes, particularly country-focused investments."

Shuman stayed at Yale in the investments office for almost 13 years, eventually adding capital markets to her area of responsibilities. Given the investment skills she developed over this time frame, Shuman was well positioned to become a CIO at another organization. On January 2, 1999, she brought her investment artistry to Carnegie Corporation of New York, joining the organization in the newly created role of chief investment officer.

Carnegie Corporation of New York

Carnegie Corporation of New York is a private grant-making foundation funded by Andrew Carnegie in 1911 with a $135 million gift, which was invested in 5 percent coupon fixed-income securities. Eighty percent of the assets were in U.S. Steel bonds, a credit Mr. Carnegie knew extremely well. According to Shuman, the foundation weathered the Great Depression because of its heavy bond allocation, increasing its equity allocation by approximately 10 percent each decade since inception.

Shuman quickly observed that foundations have historically undermanaged their financial assets compared to universities.

"Foundations continue to evolve behind endowments. Foundations have mostly been led by people who focus on the mission and programs. They're typically less financially savvy and have had the luxury historically to emphasize program. Private foundations are required to spend at least 5 percent of average assets every year. If assets go down in value, then the foundation spends less. At Carnegie and other foundations, fixed costs are relatively low, while variable costs (primarily grants) are high. For example, at the corporation, fixed costs for staff, travel, office expenses, and other overhead represent approximately 15 percent of the budget. People often think that foundations should have a more conservative investment portfolio because it is the only source of income. But if valuations decline, you have the ability to reduce variable spending."

Conversely, Shuman says 85 percent or more of costs at colleges and universities are fixed, causing administrations to focus on their endowments and creating pressure on performance, as it is very difficult to reduce expenses. Shuman feels fortunate that President Gregorian is a former university president, and for that reason appreciates the importance of endowment management at a foundation.

"Endowments face fewer constraints than foundations with respect to the management of their portfolios, including excise taxes, and UBTI [unrelated business taxable income] that precludes the use of leverage. Carnegie Corporation is a totally closed system with more liquidity constraints, as we don't receive gifts, unlike universities. We haven't received a dime since 1911."

Before Shuman joined Carnegie, the organization utilized a committee-driven, as opposed to staff-driven, investment process. The investment committee functioned as a subset of finance and administration rather than on its own, with the treasurer spending half her time on investments and the other half on budget and administration. Vartan Gregorian, the former president of Brown University, joined Carnegie as president in June 1997. Coming from an academic environment, he understood the need to manage the underlying investment assets more actively and hired Shuman, the first full-time investment professional at the corporation. Shuman inherited a portfolio worth approximately $1.6 billion. Fortunately, over the years, the foundation had benefited from having many astute investors among its trustees, including Robert Rubin, John Whitehead, Dick Fisher, Vincent Mai and Larry Tisch. The committee members were surprisingly hands-on. "During the tech bubble, we received a high volume of venture capital distributions. One morning, after getting another distribution, the broker called to see if we wanted to sell the stock. Then he said, 'I really need to update the signature card.' I asked him, 'Who signed it?' and he replied, 'Robert Rubin.'" Rubin served as secretary of the Treasury from 1995 until 1999.

An investment committee led by Vincent Mai, chairman and CEO of private equity pioneer AEA Investors,[1] had been formed in the fall of 1998 in conjunction with creating the CIO position. An investment advisory committee that included David Swensen had begun to retool the portfolio from 1996 to 1998, establishing asset allocation policy targets and diversifying into alternative asset classes.

While the portfolio was still light on alternatives and heavier on fixed income and long equities, Shuman found a thoughtful portfolio structure in place and was able to focus on fine-tuning each asset class.

BEING CHIEF INVESTMENT OFFICER

Shuman seems to have embraced the role of CIO. "It's fun to join a new organization or participate on another investment committee and see that there are different ways to do things. I saw that I could do things on my own and make my own decisions. I enjoyed exercising my own views and evaluating opportunities with a new perspective."

Asset Allocation

Initially, Shuman focused on adding alternative investments because she believes they are less efficient and can add incremental value relative to traditional asset classes. Meredith Jenkins joined the staff in July 1999 and "has done an unbelievable job with private equity." As the two senior investment professionals, they worked together to retool the portfolio in the early years. First, they focused on adding hedge funds and engineered a significant strategic shift to absolute return investments on January 1, 2001, just as the tech market boom was ending.

"The move was very fortuitous, in retrospect. It had taken almost a year to educate ourselves and the committee, which was reluctant to reduce exposure to a buoyant market. Moreover, we had a value bias, and our timing was very lucky. It allowed us to weather the tech storm very well."

The foundation has a formal asset allocation policy that the staff and the investment committee evaluate annually. Most changes, if any, are incremental, taking into account execution challenges and avoiding market timing. They adjust the private equity and private real estate policy allocations to be close to the actual. "It's meaningless to have a 15 percent policy allocation to private equity when in reality you only have a 10 percent allocation."

Rebalancing Shuman's experience at Yale instilled a strong rebalancing discipline that was tested almost immediately after she joined Carnegie in early 1999. The combination of the Long-Term Capital Management and Russian ruble crises in late summer of 1998 devastated emerging-market valuations, causing the foundation's 5 percent allocation to drop to 3 percent. She suggested to the committee that they rebalance. While they were reluctant, they supported her recommendation, which paid off handsomely. Afterward, colleagues told her, "That was really risky" or "You are so brave," but she says, "It was just rebalancing. People are often reluctant to invest when prices are down, but it merely represents valuation discipline."

Rebalancing has become an ongoing issue for investors. It is difficult to implement because many investment managers impose long lockups or are closed to new investors. With respect to the latter constraint, "If you take money out, you can't put it back." And with high valuations across all asset classes, the reinvestment decision is very problematic.

Shuman went through a two-year period recently in which she consciously did not rebalance her emerging-markets exposure. "Where do you put the money in an environment where everything is fully valued? Emerging markets are still more attractive than other equities." Fortunately, Shuman has observed that some of the investment managers employed by the corporation rebalance their own portfolios, allowing her to worry less about this issue. Examples include firms selling fully valued securities or private equity firms selling portfolio companies. Carnegie has received substantial private real estate and private equity distributions the last couple of years because managers are "taking money off the table." She says, "Our managers are generally very disciplined buyers and willing sellers. If they can't find anything to buy, so be it."

Portfolio Construction and Management

Because foundations must consider myriad tax issues, portfolio construction becomes much trickier and requires them to exercise more care and avoid certain tactics. For example, leverage creates UBTI for foundations but not for endowments in most cases.

Shuman didn't know it was going to be that much different. She remembers needing cash early in her tenure and blithely saying, "Oh, we could just borrow from current funds." Unfortunately, foundations do not have current funds that are separate from endowment, and even if they did, borrowing would generate tax. On the margins, foundations must be particularly conscious of liquidity, which is potentially "the weakest link in the chain."

Foundations often have higher allocations to bonds in the portfolio than a university, and must manage cash flow and capital commitments very carefully due to the 5 percent spending requirement, a lack of gifts, and in the case of the corporation, substantial unfunded commitments to private equity and real estate. "In the summer of 2002, I was extremely nervous because values kept going down and down and down. In market downturns, assets are cheap so we expected a large wave of capital calls, based on a high level of unfunded commitments. I thought, 'Where will we get the money?' You don't want to sell equities at the bottom."

When determining asset classifications, Shuman does not get overly concerned because of the way she has structured her team and their compensation. Each one of her senior staff specializes in a different asset class but is compensated on the entire portfolio performance. She does not want the staff to worry about where a given manager might fit into the portfolio and estimates 15 existing investments could be classified in more than one asset class. On a practical note, she finds it important for managers to know who their primary contact is: "When everyone's a generalist, who does the manager call?" She notes that the hybridization of certain asset classes has naturally led to much more collaboration among the staff at the corporation.

Governance

From day one, "wonderful governance" has been an important factor in her ability to manage the portfolio successfully. "I have had great, very supportive committee chairs, Vincent Mai, Marty Leibowitz [the vice chairman and chief investment officer of the Teachers Insurance and Annuity Association–College Retirement Equities Fund (TIAA-CREF)] and now Geoff Boisi. In addition, President Gregorian attends every investment committee meeting. They probably trusted me more than they should have, given that I did not have CIO experience. I was my own emerging manager."

Staff   In addition to forging excellent working relationships with the investment committee, Shuman has managed to retain most of the individuals on her staff for periods of six to eight years. In the competitive New York City market, keeping a team intact is an unusual achievement.

Believing in a collegial approach, Shuman empowers her team, making each of them responsible and accountable. Even so, she remains "very involved with portfolio management and construction, as the buck stops with me.

"The approach works really well by allowing the team to build and maintain good, consistent relationships with investment managers." More importantly, the investment committee has been "very supportive, asks constructive questions but does not micro manage." The team has selected "a lot of emerging and niche managers. The investment committee has embraced our efforts to identify less efficient opportunities, which we appreciate very much. It has enhanced our performance."

Investment Committee Relationship   Unusual investments have been some of their best successes. In 2001, only two years into her tenure, Shuman recommended a manager that invests in sub-Saharan Africa and the Middle East, an esoteric and highly inefficient market. "That was unconventional at the time," she says, especially because the manager was recovering from a patch of poor performance. "Because we have grant programs in Africa, I think the committee was more open to the idea of investing in this region." The fund ranks as Carnegie's single best-performing public equity manager.

The investment committee approves all manager hires, a practice some of her colleagues avoid if possible, but she prefers it because she finds that it allows the committee to buy into the portfolio. In addition, the process of writing the recommendation and then presenting it to the committee provides a good discipline for the staff. A key reason to get buy-in: "That way, if things do go wrong, the committee won't come back and say, 'What were you thinking?' "

Manager Selection   When sourcing investment ideas, Shuman takes an opportunistic approach, tapping her network for referrals from high-quality sources. When selecting managers, she is decisive, trusting her experience and using her contacts to ascertain quickly whether a manager fits her parameters. Shuman says, "We don't feel the compulsion to do a comprehensive manager search in a particular area if a manager meets our rigorous criteria."

Conscious of principal-agent issues, she seeks principal-owned firms where the principals, not shareholders or financial sponsors, earn the profits. "We don't want financial sponsors taking a portion of the incentive compensation." Shuman prefers managers with a focused investment strategy regardless of their asset class; concentrated portfolios; and a hungry, stable team that's passionate about investing.

Regarding terminating a manager, Shuman says, "I don't think I've ever fired a manager for performance. It's usually because of organizational instability or style drift. For example, we terminated a small New York–based hedge fund manager; they began buying stocks in Greater China and Brazil, which clearly was not its competitive advantage."

When an investment performs poorly, she reviews the situation to determine if it could be an opportunity. "If a manager's performance is poor but they are being true to their style, you may want to think about giving them more money because it probably means that their style is out of favor. Patience is often rewarded in this situation, but you will have to work with the committee, because they will question why such and such manager is doing badly."

Shuman believes in supporting investment managers in sickness and in health. In the case of a poor performer, "I try to work with the manager in a supportive way. The last thing you need to do is undermine their confidence."

LESSONS, OBSERVATIONS, AND ADVICE

Shuman shared her thoughts and opinions on investments and industry trends and offered constructive criticism and advice for investment management firms, colleagues and budding CIOs.

Investment Themes

Investment themes that drive her portfolio construction continue to include emerging markets and focused private equity strategies. While mega buyout funds have been in favor and the driver of performance in the asset classes, the foundation has exceeded its private equity benchmark, despite being underweighted in these large funds. They are attempting to identify the winning private equity firms in India, China, and other developing markets where she believes it is possible to generate multiples on invested capital.

Venture Capital: Death by a Thousand Cuts

Shuman believes that the smaller fund size of top venture capital firms, and correspondingly dwindling venture capital allocations, have become an ongoing issue for institutional investors. "It is challenging to get a meaningful allocation in a fund sponsored by a premiere firm, especially because the corporation had few legacy relationships." She offered the example of a firm that recently awarded Carnegie an $8 million allocation; despite its modest size, it is meaningful for the corporation's $2.5 billion fund. Proportionately, it is the equivalent of a $32 million allocation to a $10 billion fund. "It will be interesting to see how larger institutions deal with the problem of obtaining meaningful allocations to early stage venture."

Venture capital and private equity performance studies show that top-quartile managers consistently remain the top-performing funds and significantly outperform the rest of the pack. "Investors all want allocations to the same handful of firms. We are all receiving fairly small allocations; meanwhile, the firms have cut fund sizes." On top of that, she says, "You are unlikely to get an allocation if you are not already an investor."

Shuman acknowledges that firms are being fair, and underallocating equally to existing investors. She just wonders if small allocations will have an performance impact on larger portfolios, and whether it is logical for larger institutions to continue to invest in the asset class.

Manager Proliferation

Shuman identified "manager proliferation" as a "problem for all of us." She says, "It's easy to keep adding managers, but potentially unproductive. We are overdiversified, way overdiversified. The top position in the portfolio, which will often be held by multiple managers, might represent a maximum of 70 basis points."

Shuman believes overdiversification happens because CIOs want to keep hiring new managers to freshen their portfolio. "It's fun. And you don't want to fire people." Although concerned about having too many managers, she continues to review new managers as it is critical to stay abreast of the marketplace.

At the same time she questions how foundations and endowments will be able to continue to conduct the necessary research and due diligence given the geographic expansion of markets and relatively small staff resources.

"Carnegie invests in emerging markets because we think it will be a driver of long-term performance. How do you do that with limited staff resources and the global travel that is required for this asset class?" One of her key staff members is moving to Hong Kong, and will continue to work with the corporation so she will have someone on the ground in Asia.

Competition and Comparison to Peers

The competition for allocations and a compensation structure that measures CIOs against peers at other institutions make it difficult to share resources and information. For Shuman, the collegial environment is one of the more attractive aspects of working in the endowment and foundation arena. She feels these issues have been eroding the camaraderie. "I will tell people about an exciting new manager *after* the corporation has an allocation, but not before."

Working with Investment Managers

Carnegie Corporation has served as a lead investor on a handful of transactions but does not have enough staff to do so regularly. "It is a wonderful opportunity to set up a great long-term relationship and establish mutual loyalty, especially for an institution with a relatively small asset base.

"It is increasingly difficult to find new, high-quality managers, particularly in the hedge fund arena, where most choices are either a 26-year-old or an 'uber launch.' There's very little in between. We don't need to hire someone that cannot match the quality of existing high-confidence managers in our portfolio. I'd rather have a lower hedge fund allocation. When you do the math on hedge fund fees and calculate the gross return that is required to generate a net return equal to the equity index, a manager has to outperform by a wide margin. Fees are way too high in aggregate, given the zero-sum nature of the market." Shuman worries that investors are setting themselves up for disappointment, as higher fees shift risk from the general partner to the limited partner. "Fee creep," an offense committed primarily by private equity and hedge funds, is also very concerning. "Not only are they charging higher fees, but also they are charging us for services previously covered by the management fee."

Shuman describes another scenario that could be titled, "Heads I Win, Tails You Lose." There should be a symmetry between the lockup of the investor and the lockup of the manager. "The investor has a three-year lockup, but the manager can take out carry (performance fee or profits) every year. We are setting ourselves up for a fall!" Always conscious of principal-agent issues, Shuman seeks a solution that would align interests. "If we have to lock up for five years, then the manager should lock up for five years. We generally favor lockups, as they screen out short-term investors. But what does concern us is that the corporation must fund its legal spending requirement. We would like managers to allow a 5 percent withdrawal annually when a longer lockup is in place, as we are not getting any new gifts into the portfolio. It's a very reasonable request and critical on the margin to help manage the payout."

Shuman believes such a policy would benefit managers, too. "When investors can take money out only once every five years, we are inclined to redeem a greater amount than if we had more than one bite at the apple. We encourage managers to stagger the lockups of their investors, because there could be a problem upon a five-year anniversary if there are more redemptions than they were expecting. It will be interesting when that happens."

Investment Mistakes

Shuman expresses concern about groupthink. "Hot new managers or asset classes are often problematic." Investors should protect themselves from groupthink by keeping in mind their own goals and biases.

"It's human nature to want to be part of the pack. Especially with compensation being based on peer comparisons, it can seem safer to have a similar portfolio to your peers." Shuman points out that peer comparison may have unintended consequences. "Our asset allocation, manager selection, and performance may converge. We are becoming less, not more, differentiated."

Shuman cannot understand the appeal of "uber launches" when large teams come together, form global firms, and start big funds. She suspects such funds may meet investor needs for capacity rather than return and feels fortunate not to have that issue.

Career Tableau

On the subject of mentors and influences, the discussion skipped immediately to David Swensen, her mentor at Yale.

"I received great training from David. One of his best qualities is that he loves mentoring people. David and I held a reception in New York in December 2006 for Seth Alexander, who left Yale recently to become the president of MIT's management company. It was a mini reunion of our former colleagues from the Yale investments office. I spoke briefly about David and what he has done for the investment community by training so many great people that are now sprinkled throughout the nonprofit community. If we weren't independent-minded and ambitious, we wouldn't leave, so it's a natural evolution. He has performed a great service for the industry, because he trained and sponsored so many of us."

Commenting on being a woman in a male-dominated field, Shuman does not seem to feel disadvantaged, noting that today there are a lot of women CIOs. However, she does say, "But what's really interesting is very few of us have had children. It is a fulfilling and interesting career path. And over recent years the compensation has become more attractive. We are never going to get rich, but we are very well off and have privileged jobs."

Having spent the first half of her investment career in real estate and oil and gas, Shuman literally got "on-the-ground" training in alternative investments. It gave her a great platform for learning to conduct due diligence, structure investments in new ways, and identify managers with focused strategies.

"At Yale, my colleagues and I had to work very hard to create an entirely new real estate structure. We took the lead when there was no capital in the industry because of the savings-and-loan crisis, which created a tremendous contrarian opportunity. This environment gave Yale leverage for defining the terms and structure of the funds. As a result, our real estate deals were among the most favorably structured in the portfolio. While it is more difficult today to create an attractive investment structure, this early lesson was critical to my training and has had a lasting impact on my career."

COMPLETING THE PORTRAIT

Ellen Shuman has taken the raw materials of her experience and training at Yale and applied her own skills and perspective to shine on her own as one of the most successful investment artists in the foundation and endowment community.

CHAPTER 10

Master of All Trades

Bruce Madding, CIO,
Henry J. Kaiser Family Foundation

An active leader in the foundation and endowment investment community, Bruce Madding has served one of the longest tenures in one organization of any CIO and faces some formidable challenges. As senior vice president and chief financial officer (CIO) of the Henry J. Kaiser Family Foundation, Bruce Madding serves as both the CIO and chief financial officer (CFO) of an operating foundation dedicated to informing health issues in the United States and abroad. While his role is described simply as being responsible for the financial administration and investment management of its $600 million portfolio of assets, because the foundation has higher operating expenses, he has higher investment performance targets than many of his colleagues in the investment community. His ability to successfully execute is crucial to sustaining the work of the foundation.

As an operating foundation, Kaiser's required distribution annually supports primarily its own activities, not outside grants. Receiving only modest outside support, every activity and every employee is, for the most part, funded by investment performance. He never put it this way, but Madding basically serves as the organization's sole source of support while also overseeing much of its administration. His 18-year tenure and industry leadership show that he has mastered his roles.

Madding chaired the investment committee for the American Red Cross and was president of the Foundation Financial Officers Group (an affinity group of the nation's largest foundations). He serves on the investment committee of the University of California–Berkeley Foundation and on several advisory boards, and also has been a member of a Financial Accounting Standards Board's not-for-profit task force.

He began his career at Price Waterhouse & Co. after receiving an MBA from the University of Southern California in 1974 and holds a BS degree from the University of California–Berkeley. Bruce Madding is a certified public accountant and a member of the American and California Institutes of Certified Public Accountants.

BACKGROUND

Bruce Madding spent over a decade at Price Waterhouse working on domestic and international assignments. An international-based stint required him to travel extensively.

Developing Valuable Skills in Accounting

"Spending time overseas working with international accounting laws and reporting requirements provided a global education in financial systems and policies. Internationally, accountants are often seen as the financial experts, in contrast to the United States. My last two years with Price Waterhouse were with its internal Technology Research Center in an operating role. The firm was taking the step of looking at emerging information technologies and their impact on financial services.

"Coming to the foundation was a complete change and provided me the opportunity to work with seasoned investment professionals on the Kaiser board in managing one of the foundation community's largest portfolios. I saw an opportunity to step in—expecting to be there three years. Instead, I began to learn what it took to manage an investment portfolio and have now been at the foundation for 18 years."

Although he has not taken the typical path of his investment colleagues who have direct investment experience, Madding believes there are advantages to his background.

"My accounting experience allows me to bring a more forensic approach to evaluating investments. When you train as an accountant, you're taught to observe, question, and generally be skeptical. You learn to drill down on the details. One looks for corroboration and does not rely on a single answer. The effort occasionally leads you in different directions. At the end of an evaluation, you are able to bring into view a full picture of the organization based upon its structural blocks. I need to fully understand an investment before committing the resources. If you can't explain it to someone else, then you don't understand the risks you are taking. Black boxes are not going to pass the screen."

Getting Started at Kaiser

When he joined Kaiser in 1988, the $300 million portfolio had investments in a few core equity managers, and one fixed-income manager. Outside of these managers, tranches of money had been invested in real estate, venture capital, and a small-manager equity fund (SMEF) that invested small amounts in emerging managers or new assets classes. The philosophy behind SMEF is that the foundation could use the emerging managers to add to their portfolio or replace existing ones. Usually known today as an "emerging manager fund," it was an uncommon strategy in 1988.

The foundation invested early in international equities, and began including hedge funds in 1988. When he joined, they already had a small allocation to venture capital, which was then increased. Kaiser had a much heavier weighting in venture capital much earlier than other institutions.

"The venture commitment relates to our location; it's part of one's education being in northern California and the heart of Silicon Valley. Early on, you felt the buzz; saw the changes technology was making and watched the start of new small businesses. The community was energized. It was special and we were in a great position to engage in it."

Madding agrees with the comment that the difference between successful endowments and mega-successful endowments has often been the private equity portfolio. "Venture capital has added significant value to the foundation. Being located on and owning 20 acres of Sand Hill Road, which has been called the home of venture capital, has made a difference. Many of the well-known firms are our tenants. It would have been difficult to engage in venture if you worked in the Midwest or South. Proximity continues to provide an enormous edge. You live, breathe, talk, and socialize with people creating new businesses in innovative fields. It's a wonderful environment that I am fortunate to have benefited from. Location alone would not have allowed us to proceed had the members of my investment committee been unwilling."

"From day one, the board has allowed the inclusion of esoteric strategies in the portfolio. We were early in VC [venture capital], early in hedge funds, early internationally. We were the first U.S. money for an international manager, who today has over $30 billion under management. The committee was generally more willing to engage in other types of opportunities—commodities and emerging markets—sooner than other foundations."

In 1988, Madding believes, foundations generally approached investing more cautiously. "The mind-set focused on minimizing the risk of loss. Boards imposed self-constraints when considering new investment strategies.

Foundations willing to go forward needed the leadership of a skilled investment committee. I was very fortunate to have had, and still have, such a committee. I wouldn't have said that was the norm."

Another change that Madding has seen take place is the hiring of more sophisticated investors into the role of CIO. He views this as positive. These managers approach their jobs with strong financial backgrounds.

"Twenty years ago the majority of professionals overseeing endowment assets were CFOs. There were very few dedicated CIOs. Today, foundations engage professional managers with strong investment backgrounds. The CFO who wears multiple hats will gradually disappear. Small foundations trying to hire someone who is competent to handle the operations and invest the portfolio will find the task difficult.

"The complexity of these organizations, on both the accounting side and the investing side, will lead to the separation. It was easier when foundations just had a 60/40 split of long equity and fixed income. Now we're trying to evaluate hedge funds and commodities in addition to traditional long equities and fixed income. We are looking geographically and trying to keep on top of derivative transactions such as collateralized debt obligations."

BEING CHIEF INVESTMENT OFFICER

Managing the financial resources of the foundation is inextricably linked with managing the human and programming resources of the foundation. As an operating foundation, Kaiser makes few grants. Spending goes to paying staff and expenses in support of its own programs. Kaiser retains a staff of 110 people, many of whom travel frequently across the United States and abroad. The foundation maintains two office facilities, one in Washington, D.C., and the headquarters in California. Its Washington, D.C., space includes broadcasting studios and conference facilities. All this means that the foundation has high operating expenses.

Kaiser's structure also means that "without the steady, strong returns, the staff member that happens to share the offices next to you may not be there."

As an outside observer, it is easy to see that Bruce Madding has a lot of mouths to feed. Because his institution differs significantly from his contemporaries, so do the investment objectives, philosophy, and policies.

Investment Objectives

The Kaiser Foundation has approximately $600 million in assets from which to generate the cash flow to meet its operating expenses. Not wanting to be dependent on outside capital, it receives minimal funding from outside organizations. Unlike most grant-making foundations that spend only the required 5 percent annually, Kaiser spends around 8 percent, and has spent as much as 12 to 13 percent of its endowment in a single year.

"The need for consistent, strong returns frames our investment strategy. You must continually balance liquidity and downside protection with the need for high growth. I can't call on a development officer and say, 'Let's go out and raise more in a capital campaign or annual fund.' The only resources I have to meet our obligations come from the growth in the portfolio. Therefore, you are continually challenged to take risk, pushing the envelope for returns. The minimum goal year in and year out is to cover the 8 percent spending rate, inflation, and investment management expenses. This equates to needing a 10 to 11 percent return in a low inflationary environment. To put this in context, studies have shown that over long periods foundations that distribute more than 5 percent annually have a high probability of spending themselves out of existence. To date, we have successfully weathered this challenge and even grown the portfolio."

The investment objectives and constraints forming the investment philosophy include:

- Large payout
- Capped pool of capital
- Stable returns
- Protection from downside exposure

The need for downside protection is critical when the pool of capital is capped. "In a period like 2002 when the S&P 500 was down 22 percent, if you matched that loss and paid out 10 percent as we did, the quick math is that your portfolio would have been cut by nearly a third. Our diversified portfolio meant we were down only 5 percent, but the overall decline of 15 percent still caused great concern. With a capped pool of capital, you can't have too many down years and still be a viable entity."

Investment Strategy

The overall investment philosophy includes the following considerations:

- Diversification by investment strategy and geography.
- Looking for noncorrelated returns.
- Strong management teams—don't be afraid of being early money if you can become comfortable with the strategy and professionals.
- Taking advantage of the longer-term nature of a foundation's capital.

- Being mindful of liquidity needs and risk mitigation.
- Tax considerations.

"At present, we are not carrying any fixed income. In the current low-interest-rate environment, I cannot afford the drag on returns. Minimum levels of cash are kept for operations. When funds are needed, we will either liquidate securities or take from the steady cash flow we receive in rental income from the 26 percent of the portfolio we hold in directly managed real estate investments. Owning and operating real estate adds a layer of complexity to your investment program. After the initial purchase of real estate to house the foundation, we have continued our expansion by developing nearly $100 million worth of new buildings. Through development we have been able to achieve larger returns."

By investing in real estate, Madding hopes to achieve a combination of equity-like upside returns as well as provide deflationary control and cash flow.

"Owning real estate has not always been a riskless endeavor. We have been subject to large swings in the investment's valuation. Foundations have to mark their assets to market on an annual basis. The size of your asset base then affects your required payout and potentially has tax computations. What holds true for equities holds true for real estate. We are always pleased to see the assets go up, but must reflect the write-down during declines. We own a complex of buildings on Sand Hill Road [home to the Silicon Valley venture capital community]. As a consequence of the dot-com bust of 2000–2001, we took a 25 percent write-down on our real estate valuation. While it caused concern, the write-down did not change anything in our operations. It did result in a higher payout percentage, close to 13 percent.

"We are all subject to taxes and, despite being considered tax exempt, the impact of excise taxes that foundations pay plays a small part in their investment strategy. When managing a portfolio seeking incremental returns, you need to consider them." As an example, Madding explains that if a foundation spends in excess of its rolling five-year average, instead of paying the government a 2 percent excise tax, the foundation can pay 1 percent and use the other 1 percent for grant making."

Madding has to be extremely conscious of liquidity since he extracts cash regularly. He therefore monitors heavily the treasury functions. He continually tweaks the portfolio, looking at monthly cash flows to make sure he knows exactly when to withdraw money because every investment manager has different withdrawal periods.

The need for liquidity impacts one third of the portfolio annually and involves liquidating or redeeming investments to pay bills, making commitments to private equity and real estate construction projects, or redeploying to different investments.

"We probably give up a couple of hundred basis points of return annually when compared to other institutions that don't have these same constraints. We can't take liquidity risk. With the high payout, I am limited in my ability to build up reserves for investment into other areas the way I might want."

Risk and Return Expectation　　While cognizant of its goal to live in perpetuity, the foundation's leadership realizes the importance of its mission and the impact of spending on programs today. This has driven their willingness to spend more than the required 5 percent annually.

"A social dollar spent today may well have a greater impact in society than one invested and grown for future distribution. Kaiser's mission focuses on health care. With 42 million uninsured in America and problems with access to care globally, the need is clearly great. The board views the opportunities they have now. It is comforting that we have achieved not only the goal of meeting our payout requirements, but also have grown the portfolio." Madding has achieved his goals regularly, which will make him a hard act to follow. Madding also recognizes that you cannot have "double the payout of other institutions without taking more risk." He has significant risks embedded in the portfolio and ensures that the board is fully aware of such. Regularly, he reviews the portfolio construction and discusses the implications of the positions taken. His macro discussions focus on structural issues in the economy and how they may stress the portfolio. Downside risk is weighed against the upside potential. "The investment committee is comprised primarily of generalists who are extraordinarily bright. While they are not 'financial experts' in the investment sense, their business knowledge allows them to raise important economic issues."

To help his board members understand the risks in the portfolio, he engages in an ongoing educational dialogue.

Asset Allocation

The investment committee is scheduled to meet quarterly to review the investment portfolio. At one of these meetings each year, Madding holds a detailed review to focus on the recent past, present, and future asset allocation policy.

Assets are broken down into equities and fixed income. Under equities, there are an additional seven categories. "Broad" targets have been set for these categories. The broad targets give him great flexibility and opportunity to adjust the portfolio regularly. So even though the asset allocation has a place for fixed income, he says, "At the moment I have no conviction that I need fixed income in the portfolio as either an income generator or a protective device. Real estate provides me with higher current income and upside potential. One can't forget the need to make the 8 to 10 percent return."

The foundation's strategic approach to asset allocation is exemplified in their real estate strategy. Kaiser, one of the largest real estate owners on Sand Hill Road, includes that 20-acre parcel in the real estate allocation. The performance of those assets has varied. In 1999, Kaiser could charge rent of $200 per square foot, while today they charge $100 per square foot. Yet the area continues to grow and develop, so the assets continue to appreciate. Madding says valuations today would more likely exceed those available in 1999. In the past, the foundation has generated roughly an 8 percent cash return on the property's appraised value. For the annual portfolio valuation, Madding has the real estate appraised conservatively. He could probably sell the assets for substantially more than they are currently valued, but while a higher valuation would boost portfolio performance, he is not sure where he would invest the money. He jokes that there is a price at which all assets would be sold.

In addition to reviewing and evaluating the asset allocation policy with his investment committee, he provides a monthly two-page report that details investment managers, assets, and important highlights.

The current question in his mind is, "Where should we be going? I attempt to look out over three to five years rather than concentrate on today. I weigh what's currently in the portfolio against future obligations. First and foremost I focus on covering the spending objectives." In practice, he reviews the asset allocation regularly as part of managing the portfolio.

Portfolio Management

Higher performance targets have led Madding to invest in more aggressive asset subcategories or strategy styles. Relying on low or noncorrelated strategies tempers his risk.

"We are seeking returns aggressively, which is somewhat contradictory with my value tilt. Equity long/short managers are expected to achieve equity returns on the upside while protecting the portfolio on the downside."

In the absolute return allocation, Madding currently likes the distressed category, which appeals to his value orientation and acts more protectively than other alternatives. In the past, he has tactically pulled assets from distressed debt and then reinvested it when he again saw opportunity. He has also invested in distressed debt funds as a fixed-income substitute. These are nonleveraged transactions invested in senior debt securities. These investments had a higher likelihood of earning income with lower, but still attractive, rates of return than more common distressed debt strategies. Because he expects more companies will start having financial difficulties, he has begun taking a more aggressive approach toward distressed investing, believing he needs to invest ahead of the market.

Generating and Evaluating Ideas Madding balances qualitative and quantitative methods to generate investment ideas. He largely sources ideas from networking in the industry. Participation with other leading investors on private equity and other not-for-profit boards have been particularly useful.

The Foundation Financial Officers Group (FFOG) that he led at one point provides an educational and networking resource to foundations. Madding said, "Foundations are not competing with each other for the best ideas; they seek to collaborate with each other recognizing that better outcomes are good for the entire sector."

His network makes a difference. By talking to his contacts and attending conferences, he discovers new or unusual opportunities. He also will source ideas from public records, reading and receiving calls, and printed information from investment managers.

Investment ideas funnel into a structured research and due-diligence process. He estimates that he and his two-person investment support staff annually process 400 to 500 ideas derived from inquiries and calls, and meet four or five managers a week. They distill information from other databases into their own system and then analyze and model the data, graphing performance over 3, 5, and 10 years in evaluation of the manager's performance on a relative risk/return basis. The system also monitors ongoing manager performance.

"We're willing to listen and respond. There is continual analysis leading to the selection of a few from this enormous effort. From 400 managers we will distill down to, say, 30 that you will have any interest in. After internally evaluating these 30, we will reduce the number to 10 to 15 that you actually will want to spend the time in person with conducting due diligence. From that, you might find 3 to 5 you will eventually invest with. It's a long process." Madding has a preference for smaller managers, but not ones without the requisite strong operations.

On Evaluating Investment Managers' Operations

Looking at small managers versus large ones, coming from a small organization, I want to reward entrepreneurship and individuality. This cannot though come without risk controls and redundancy. Here's where my accounting background comes in. I also prefer small teams rather than solo operations. There needs to be adequate dialogue among the investment manager's professionals. Challenging debate among professionals often brings positive outcomes. Infrastructure clearly has to be in place. I will spend time examining the back office and in understanding how trades are being made, how decisions are being processed. Who is going to control the process? Whether there are a single or multiple points of review, under what circumstances can a group or an individual make a different decision than the senior officer or change a decision that has been made? Hedge funds often have a single point of reference—the sole portfolio manager—and you have to have comfort that enough discussion occurs and that myopia and arrogance do not filter into their decision making.

On Evaluating Investment Managers as Partners

So the question is, "What makes a bad presentation, and how do you evaluate managers during the initial interview?" I find the worst presentations are ones that are too general or demonstrate that the presenter doesn't understand the business. It tends to occur most often with marketing representatives. It is unfortunate, because we may miss out on good managers that way. It is incumbent upon the managers to train their people to represent the firm effectively. Going back to my background, if I don't believe they truly understand their business and can't explain it in a clear and concise manner I would write them off quickly as a potential investment. My technique is to sit in a meeting and listen more than interrogate. I have read the material before and want to hear how they describe their strategy. I will often challenge or question their assertions. Invariably, it's a dialogue. What you're judging in that meeting room is not just performance and background, but also who the person really is. Is this someone you're going to want to work with? How do they respond to your questions? If the meeting is a success, it will lead to further discussions before making an investment.

Managing Responsibilities   It seems like it would be almost impossible to function as CFO and CIO when the CIO role requires such an active commitment. How does he allocate time between the two roles?

Madding laughs, "In a 125 percent day? It's like anything else; I probably spend 75 to 80 percent of the time on investments and then spend the remaining 45 percent of the time on operations."

As CFO, he has responsibility for much of the foundation's administrative functions, including human resources, accounting, and legal. On the administrative side, he is supported by a strong, tenured staff. Two invest-ment support staff come from an intern-like program that Madding created. The analysts join the investment office right out of college for a three-year period to support Madding and learn investments before attending business school or moving on to the next phase of their careers. The program has attracted as many as 400 applicants in one year from major universities and hired graduates of University of Michigan, University of Pennsylvania, Uni-versity of California–Berkeley, Stanford, and Harvard. While Madding gets the support he needs from these "extraordinarily bright and energetic" staff members, they get an opportunity to learn about investing and participate in the process—a rare career experience for a recent college graduate.

Board Governance Since Madding has had such a long and successful tenure, the Kaiser board provides him ample latitude and more authority to make investment decisions than many of his peers. He works closely with the committee chair to review and implement investment strategies. The investment committee is structured to meet formally four times a year, but does not require monthly review meetings or reporting.

"It has worked well and gives you latitude to function at a small institution. The plate is full and it would be difficult to add a monthly meeting or monthly review. Not having that responsibility is a luxury that others do not have."

One difficulty he and his contemporaries in smaller organizations do have is getting broader investment insights. "You have to seek it out from colleagues, conferences, and boards that you're on."

LESSONS, OBSERVATIONS, AND ADVICE

As one of the most experienced CIOs, in particular one that has managed a small to mid-sized foundation for many years, Madding seems well positioned to advise similar-sized institutions about their asset management. But he has no easy answers and questions of his own.

"One question I struggle with often is whether we are too small? What is the minimum amount of assets needed to justify having a CIO on staff? Put another way, what is the minimum commitment that an organization must make and be willing to spend on their investment staff if they're going to tackle the challenges of investing in today's environment? Today's $500 million foundation may be as complex, or more, than one two, three or four times its size. One must consider all investment strategies. The only difference may be the size of the organization's commitment. Some studies recommend sizing staff based upon a percentage of assets. A small percentage of assets spent annually may be fine for a large institution, but it is not adequate for smaller organizations, unless, of course, they're willing to take lower returns and be less competitive. There is a minimum level that needs to be spent on the internal infrastructure regardless of the organization's size."

Though even his own organization has had a relatively long commitment to its investment office, and has had strong returns, he wonders if it is too small to effectively maximize the portfolio's return. "If it wasn't me, I'd recommend outsourcing it."

His experience and tenure cannot be discounted. "There are benefits to having 18 years with the institution, knowing people, being known in the marketplace, and sitting on boards. Managers are willing to call on you if you are known as in investor in the field. To be an investor, you have to be seen investigating the opportunities. You must be actively meeting with others known to the investment community."

Madding feels fortunate because of the role he has assumed in the broader industry, the places that has taken him, and the people he has met. "I'm fortunate that people will come to meet us and fortunate that I work for a foundation. Investment managers want to engage foundations and endowments because they look at us as long-term 'sticky' money."

Current Investment Themes

Madding says he is currently, "looking at the landscape broadly" and concerned that the markets are entering into a potentially low-return period that will make it more difficult for him to achieve his 11 percent target. At the same time, he believes that there are individual managers that can add alpha and will deliver the 14-15 percent return that will help him to achieve his goal.

In the global markets, Madding has observed investors chasing natural resources. Madding would rather focus on "capitalistic personalities," and he has started researching places like Vietnam, where the lack of natural resources is compensated by an entrepreneurial culture that is creating opportunities.

The rise of the global middle-class consumer, particularly in places like Brazil, India, and other emerging economies, is an important theme. China is the biggest source of potential opportunity in that idea. Concern over the rule of law has led Madding to "play" China from the outside rather than inside. This is done by investing with managers who will benefit by trading with or exporting from China.

"We looked at ways to service the Chinese economy. Their system is still somewhat opaque. My accounting background does not yet let me get comfortable with China's governance, legal structure, and reported information. One feels a bit more comfort with U.S.-based companies rather than those in emerging countries. This is changing as, internationally, companies are getting better, and in the United States we see companies like Enron blow up."

Mistakes Investors Make

Madding's early accounting training and discipline has protected him from significant mistakes.

"Knock on wood—we have been fortunate. Because we work at such a fast pace, had I not been well trained to look at the details, we might have been caught. Those that follow the crowd and forget the objectives and missions of their own organization may find themselves taking greater risks than they should. Attention to detail is critical."

He tends to see too many institutions believing in an investment opportunity and manager based on reputation and not the necessary due diligence. He cautions investors to fully understand a strategy and its potential impact on their portfolio. If they have a smaller staff, they need to recognize that they might not have enough resources to develop deep enough insight into a strategy. Extra effort is necessary to make sure they do not fall to risks that more due diligence might uncover. Follow-on monitoring is also crucial.

"I wasn't invested in Amaranth, but I can imagine a small institutional investor getting caught off guard because they relied on the firm's history and didn't adequately monitor the changes in trading activity. It's critical to conduct due diligence initially, making sure to keep an eye on the details. Sufficient monitoring must follow."

The "reams of paper" he and his team generate researching, analyzing, and documenting their due diligence ultimately form the basis of three-page recommendation reports which include:

- Manager background and experience.
- Prior results.
- Strengths/weaknesses.
- Pros and cons.
- Reasons it fits in the portfolio.
- Rationale for investing.
- Proposed amount to invest.

Even though the recommendations run only about three pages, "behind that are volumes of supporting information." Monitoring reports prepared annually are equally detailed.

Mistakes Bruce Madding Made

"I don't know if you would call it a mistake but one of the decisions I made earlier on was categorically avoiding investing with friends. It's been a costly decision. They have been among the most successful investors around." Madding no longer worries if he misses an opportunity or makes a mistake. "I don't dwell on the small ones. Where possible, I will learn in hopes of not repeating it."

Investors and managers can recover from their mistakes. "On the flip side, we have been willing to take risks on managers that are down. This has provided strong returns to the foundation. As an example, one international manager had been down 60 percent the year before we invested $20 million with him. We went in, evaluated the cause of the decline, ascertained that the missing risk controls had been introduced, and built a great relationship. Our willingness to take the risk paid off in multiples."

Thoughts on Venture Capital

As their long-time investor, neighbor, and landlord, Madding has a clear perspective on the opportunities in venture capital.

"Being located on Sand Hill Road, I believe we have an edge. Currently, venture capital is awash in investable capital, but exit strategies are more difficult. I believe it is still a home-run game. Venture funds that get a big payment from one investment will break out of the pack. We look at all the top performance numbers. Repeat successes are few and limited to a small number of organizations. It has always been a tough business, but it has gotten even more difficult. I know a successful venture capitalist that currently has stopped investing in venture. Major venture firms have an edge, a brand, connectivity to the market. They see trends and opportunities first. The sad news for investors trying to break into the asset class is that the well-known firms are usually closed to 'new' money. The good news is that experienced venture capitalists are breaking away from well-known firms and setting up new ones."

Both the venture capital industry and the Silicon Valley region experienced significant change during and after the tech boom. According to Madding, the profile of a large number of venture capitalists in the 1980s and 1990s was of a young investment banker with an MBA, while today these individuals are often executives with operating backgrounds. Industry sources estimate that in the year 2000 there were more than 8,000 venture capitalists. That figure declined to around 5,000 before rebounding. This is consistent with his thoughts that younger venture capitalists, primarily recent MBA graduates, had no experience putting together deals and left when opportunities dwindled.

As it relates to the Kaiser portfolio, Madding has pulled back on venture investing and is being more selective when he does invest. He also prefers seed investing to mezzanine and does no direct investing because he lacks the resources to perform the necessary due diligence.

Social Issues

Because the Foundation is dedicated to health care issues, including government policy, it avoids investing in health care. "If we testify in front of Congress, we want no misperceptions about where our interest lies." Kaiser also avoids investing in alcohol and tobacco.

At the urging of their board member, the late pioneering African-American congresswoman Barbara Jordan, the Kaiser Foundation created a special program to focus on South Africa. When many institutional investors divested of holdings in South Africa, she told the board to invest in the health care framework of South Africa rather than divest. This was a positive approach, but one that would not have occurred without her support. "If it had not been for her, we would have divested like most nonprofits."

Influences

Madding does not have any one particular mentor who has influenced him. He does respect a few distinguished people. "In terms of people I respect, clearly the traditional names like Warren Buffet come to mind. Arthur Rock is an interesting person to observe, his investment style and entrepreneurial approach. Don Valentine of Sequoia Capital is another. I also look at other business leaders. Bob Swanson started Genentech and created a new industry that will benefit us all."

When Madding started at Kaiser, he was fortunate that a number of investment managers helped him. "Dick Fischer of Fischer Francis Trees and Watts took the time even though we weren't a large account."

Among his fellow CIOs, he never singled one out in his mind, but he has learned from everyone. "I took a piece from everybody."

THE BOTTOM LINE

Given the many hats Bruce Madding wears at Kaiser—chief investment officer, chief financial officer, real estate developer, accountant—it makes sense that he would have learned from many different types of people. His achievements in the last 18 years—taking over an investment portfolio without any prior experience, meeting challenging performance objectives, leading investment committees and industry events, and handling daily basic investment tasks—all accomplished while overseeing finance and foundation functions, show that Bruce Madding has not only learned the many skills required of his position, but also that he has mastered the role. Bruce Madding can truly be considered a master of all trades.

CHAPTER 11

Agile Investment Engineer

Bob Boldt, CIO, Agility Funds

Bob Boldt brings a wealth of diversified skills and experiences to his latest chief investment officer (CIO) role. A partner with Perella Weinberg Partners, Boldt started and leads an asset management team that applies endowment fund management principles to manage endowment funds for small to mid-size foundations and endowments as well as high-net-worth individuals and institutions. Called "Agility," the name reflects Boldt's belief that agility differentiates foundation and endowment investors from other institutional investors.

Ever since he transitioned from engineering to investments, Boldt's career has exemplified agility. Experienced as an investor and an investment manager, he has served in the private and public sectors, run pension and endowment assets, and managed money for fundamental and quantitative investment firms. With experience as an entrepreneur, public servant, and endowment executive and skills in portfolio management and investments, Boldt personifies an agile CIO.

Prior to joining Perella Weinberg Partners, Mr. Boldt served as the CEO and CIO of the University of Texas Investment Management Company (UTIMCO) from 2002 to 2006. During Mr. Boldt's tenure at UTIMCO, he led a team of professionals who managed the organization's nearly $20 billion endowment. Previously, Mr. Boldt was a managing director at Pivotal Asset Management, and from 1996 to 2000, he served as senior investment officer for Global Public Markets Investments at California Public Employees' Retirement System (CalPERS), where he oversaw the start of a hedge fund investment program.

Mr. Boldt received a BS in engineering and an MBA from the University of Texas. Mr. Boldt earned the right to use the Chartered Financial Analyst (CFA) designation.

BACKGROUND

Bob Boldt trained in engineering as an undergraduate at the University of Texas. "I'm old enough to say that I was in the early days of computers being used in engineering. We didn't have the miracle tools that exist today and were just starting to use computers on complex projects."

His first job out of college, Boldt designed advanced scientific computers for Texas Instruments. Working on a new supercomputer, programming, and designing circuits, he loved the technical challenge but "didn't like looking at a big problem through a keyhole. Engineers often look at a very, very small part of a large problem and rarely get to look at the whole picture."

Knowing he didn't like looking at the small picture, Boldt considered his next move. "I realized it was important; I wasn't going to be happy continuing down this path."

He stepped back and thought about things he liked to do. He liked investments, but had not explored it as a vocation. "I thought I could apply my knowledge of programming and equations to investments and design a system to come up with good investment ideas."

Investment Management

Boldt returned to UT for graduate school in business, majored in finance, and joined Northern Trust when he graduated. "I got my first taste of what investments were like. Nobody trusted quantitative analysis. Mostly clients did not believe in it." Although some of his colleagues saw the merit in quantitative investing, the firm emphasized fundamental investing, so Boldt gained experience in that discipline as an analyst and portfolio manager and managed the quantitative analysis area. "I covered all the roles you have when you work your way up."

Because he has such an affinity for quantitative subjects, he went to business school to learn quantitative investing. He says, "The longer I've been in the business the more I realize how limited quantitative approaches are." While he still has an appreciation for models, he understands more about what can and cannot be modeled. "The stock market is not physics. It doesn't act according to physical principles. You can't model it very well."

Boldt makes a point to highlight an important and influential lowlight in his investment career. "I hit the market in the early 1970s, an absolutely terrible time in the markets. Probably 20 million shares traded a day. Today, when I tell people that, they ask, 'In the morning? In an hour?' The market went down every day, people lined up at gas pumps, it was during the OPEC embargo, it was a very depressing time to come into the business."

Northern Trust provided a safe haven. "I came into a very stable situation and got to live through it without getting fired. It was a very telling experience seeing what happened in that environment, to see what risk really was, how people acted when they got depressed. It was a good training period. At the time it was no fun, but in hindsight I have more pleasant memories of it, though it was brutal."

Two formative experiences early in his career developed the skills and perspectives he relies on today. "Quantitative training was one. Two, I started in the business at such a bad time; people have never seen such bad markets. It concerns me that most people investing today have never experienced bad market conditions. They may think so, but trust me—they've never seen markets like that."

Boldt became fascinated by the way people make decisions. "I thought I was a rational thinker. I would sit down with facts and make a rational decision. Many people don't work that way." Observing other people face complex problems made him want to understand how they approached decisions. Understanding decision processes helped him improve his own approach. "I like to imagine watching myself making the decision. It helps me avoid snap decisions. It's not just thinking about it twice, but thinking about how I'm making the decisions."

His early investment experiences had many dimensions and prepared him for roles that required well-rounded skills, including the ability to see the big picture. "Back then, people in the money management business came up into the business through the banks. You did your time, actually managed money, and had decisions to make. You had to deal with clients. If you screwed up, you had to explain what went wrong. I got to do research, portfolio management, and client relations." He feels his early experience "gave me a more complete early career than some people get today, because I got to do all of it." Boldt did not just narrowly invest within one asset category; he gained experience investing in a variety of asset classes and markets.

As a "recovering techie" working in a fundamentally oriented investment firm, Boldt observed the raging efficient markets theory debate instigated by colleagues with degrees from the University of Chicago. "They had it figured out, 'Markets are efficient. Trust departments are silly. There's a better way.' I would think, 'If you went to the University of Chicago Business School and believe the same things they believe, why would you go into the investment management business?'"

Still intrigued by quantitative investing, Boldt went to work at American National Bank with Rex Sinquefield, an influential proponent of efficient markets, and formed his own opinion as the debate raged on. "Some assumptions, to make efficient market theory hold true, weren't real, weren't realistic. I thought there had to be a way around efficient markets, so I went the other way."

His incongruous career moves, from the Northern Trust active management environment to the American National Bank passive management style, perplexed industry colleagues. "They thought I was crazy, but I developed an appreciation for both active and passive, but came out with a belief in active."

Boldt left the bank and started an active investing asset management firm that eventually grew to $2.5 billion in assets. "At the time that was real money." Investors were going through a period of separating the portfolio into core and noncore parts of a portfolio; Boldt and his partners focused on investing the noncore part of the portfolio. "We believed in seeking active returns, not hugging the index; it was not a closet index fund. We gave our best ideas and charged 'crazy fees,' 1 and 10 over the benchmark. They were considered such crazy fees. We were pretty close to being a hedge fund." The firm targeted more progressive institutions, managing concentrated portfolios with "big tracking error—I hated that term"—or deviation from the index.

Managing money with partners taught Boldt some unanticipated lessons. "I learned about people, especially when we hit a performance dry patch. When you run a concentrated portfolio with high tracking error, it happens." He elaborates, "You find out about people in two situations: great success or great stress. If you haven't had that experience, then you don't know your partners yet." As they achieved great success, Boldt saw a partner "go off the deep end, buying big houses and expensive antiques." In a period of great stress, "the 'big houses and antiques guy' suddenly panicked. It completely destroyed his decision making. You put yourself at risk of making dumb decisions when you are leveraged to the hilt."

Boldt ultimately benefited from the experience. "I made a lot of personal money and learned important life lessons about partners, decision making, and money management. You couldn't hide the way managers do now. Today, they get in trouble and go back and hug the index. We told people we would not do that." He realized that his business model was fragile. "If you're charging a flat fee, it doesn't make rational sense to put your business model at risk. I found out the hard way."

His experience influenced his investment manager selection criteria and process.

"Invest in money management firms when they're relatively young and not capacity constrained, when they're really focused on the business. If young managers hit a bad patch, spend time with them. It was a bad experience, but it made me better at judging whether a firm would be successful."

Boldt tells his younger staffers, "Don't look at the track record—it's not useful. Look at the people and how they make decisions." He and his staffers enjoy it when he tells them, "I can walk in, meet the principals, spend

30 minutes to an hour, and can tell whether I smell the money. I have no idea how. It's a gut feel from how the people talk, enthusiasm, and energy—the young people are committed. It comes from the experience of having managed money and faced the intersection of investment management and business management." Most of his peers have not had sole responsibility for managing money. "It's an important perspective and it had an impact."

Scudder, Stevens and Clark, "the antithesis of a small firm," hired Boldt, intending for him to run the San Francisco office and giving him his first experience at a broad money management firm. "It's a different perspective from being an owner to being a manager and an interesting perspective to go from a small fund to a large fund."

When Boldt interviewed, he asked the managing partner, "Is this a marketing firm or an investment firm? The answer was 'It's an investment firm.' The interviewer believed it, but it was an investment firm in a segment of the industry where you needed to be a marketing firm."

Unfortunately, he believes that attitude eventually led to the firm's demise. "They didn't want to be on the Charles Schwab network. How could you not be? But it was beneath them. The firm did not charge loads on their funds, yet would not position themselves to market no-load funds effectively. It was an interesting situation." When Boldt worked at TI, employees sometimes grumbled about how the firm was run by the engineers, but would be more effective run by managers. "Similarly, Scudder was run by investment nerds, rather than marketing people."

He thought highly of his colleagues, but when the firm centralized "investment intelligence" in New York City and dedicated the regional offices strictly to marketing and client service, Boldt left the firm. While he concedes that may have been a rational management structure, the role held less interest for him.

CalPERS

In 1995, Sheryl Pressler convinced Boldt to join CalPERS, his first time "on the other side of the table. I had known Sheryl a long time, from when she was a young intern at McDonnell Douglas. We had grown up together." Pressler wanted her staff to have the perspective of having managed money themselves and to incorporate it into investment decisions and manager selection. "It was a lot of fun, a very, very fun time."

Boldt went to CalPERS just as the investment landscape began a new phase of dramatic change. "The market has changed more in the last 10 to 15 years than it had in the previous 50 years. The world is so much different today, so many more financial tools and so many ways you can earn alpha. The world was changing quickly and, unlike most public pensions that are usually yawners, the CalPERS board was at the forefront and more progressive." The board's mind-set allowed them to pursue more new ideas. "They wouldn't always let us do what we proposed, but we could look at anything."

Boldt saw it as an "eye-opening experience" because he saw what many managers did, "and it was a disappointing view, I must tell you. I wasn't that impressed." Around that time, investment leader Charles Ellis had written a book "about the big getting bigger. The behemoths will inherit the world." Managers determined to grow bigger knew CalPERS "could put money to work in $1 billion chunks" and would help them achieve girth.

"Sitting on the other side of the table, I would ask, 'What's your value added?' Many answers were disappointing." Boldt would have a few young staffers attend the meetings to listen and learn. He grew so impatient with the managers, he told them, "If I hear top-down, bottom-up one more time, I am walking out of the meeting."

Invariably in response to his question about their value, Boldt would hear, "Two important parts, top-down, bottom-up. They would say how they analyzed and picked stocks." He found none of it believable. "Everybody thought they had the most unique approach, but it was all the same approach. I couldn't sit through the meetings—I couldn't take it anymore."

Money managers should "mentally sit on the other side, as an investor. They would know not to give that speech."

Boldt steered CalPERS to invest in hedge funds. "We just had a board meeting, and I convinced them to go into hedge funds. Nobody was doing it; endowments were, obviously, but not pensions." The investment received extensive press coverage, making Boldt a household name in some California households. In the midst of the commitment, a stranger called. "He wouldn't say his name and insisted it was very important. He wanted to talk about the new hedge fund initiative." Boldt agreed to take the call only to get berated for the next 10 minutes. He said, "You're going to mess up the game for all of us. We want you to rethink it. I will do everything I can with the California legislature to keep you out." Boldt never learned the identity of the self-appointed Hedge Fund Avenger and thought it might be someone at a hedge fund or at a family office. The caller expressed such hostility, "I fully expected a death threat."

Overall, his experience at CalPERS provided an excellent vantage point for seeing money managers, observing their decision-making process, and understanding their money-making process. When he joined CalPERS, they had a failing minority manager program. Instead, Boldt instituted a manager development group, hiring consulting firm Strategic Investment Group to construct a new manager seeding program. "We seeded Arrowstreet. We did it because it was the right thing to do and the CalPERS board was at the forefront."

Boldt favors investments in smaller or newer money managers, but because they require more work and resources, he believes it difficult to accomplish without hiring a specialist in emerging manager funds. "It's not just selecting the managers; it's mentoring them, introducing them to investors, and being there when they need tough love. It's time consuming and most organizations can't invest that time."

Even UTIMCO with its resources could not manage it alone and hired an outside investment firm to assist with seeding new managers. "The staff intensity per dollar invested is too high, higher than venture capital investing. It's natural for firms like Protégé Partners or AAM, because they're really specialized."

Boldt believes investment committees and pension boards like CalPERS are better equipped to make strategic asset allocation decisions rather than manager selection decisions. "That's not their relevant area of expertise." At CalPERS, he spent more time on strategic asset allocation, using an innovative questionnaire designed to elicit underlying beliefs and priorities of individual board members rather than those they articulated in a group.

Decision Factor Analysis "Decision factor analysis was useful, because one of the biggest problems in managing these organizations is the board dynamics problem. It's complicated; I've seen it firsthand and it's hard to deal with."

The CalPERS board was partly elected and partly appointed, technically a mix of unions and management. The decision analysis "took politics out of the question; we asked the members at the board level to answer questions and then presented asset allocation scenarios that fit their answers to our questions."

The process helped them come to better-informed conclusions. "Usually, a consultant comes in; we had three consultants at CalPERS—'CYA cubed.' The consultant does risk-and-return estimates and correlations, surveys the market opinion, gets Bill Sharpe to do the efficient frontier, and then says, 'Now we know the range of portfolios we can select—which one is the right one?'

"The most important thing I've learned about dealing with boards: Never ask board members a question that they're incapable of answering. When you do, no good comes of it." Boldt feels board members can understand questions of risk versus reward and make rational decisions. "But if it's a question of uncertainty, like not knowing the likelihood of bad events, everyone's aversion to uncertainty is pretty close to infinite."

As a result, if board members try to answer questions they are incapable of answering, their responses will be inappropriately risk averse, because their aversion to uncertainty is so high. When that happens, the committee chooses a portfolio or asset allocation similar to their peers. Boldt's decision factor analysis asked a number of questions that helped identify individual relative preferences and priorities, such as:

- How important is it that the CalPERS participants don't have to increase their contribution by more than 15 percent over any three-year period?
- How important is it to be in the top quartile in performance?
- How important is it to earn a return high enough not only to meet the actuarial objective but outperform it by 1 to 2 percent?

The questionnaire presented committee members with a list of important factors in a decision, and each board member was asked to rank factors in order of importance. The process generated results that could be analyzed quantitatively. Based on those results, the CalPERS staff would simulate various asset allocations and present the decision to the board.

"Given what you have told us about what's really important to you, this is the range of asset mixes you should be looking at. In every case, it was a higher risk than they would have picked, but one that was completely appropriate for a plan with a long-term orientation."

According to Boldt, this process moved the board to a point on the efficient frontier at a higher risk level, closer to where he thought the organization needed to be. By taking a quantitative approach, identifying underlying objectives, and then rolling them up into a decision, the analysis ultimately held the board to more satisfying and successful decisions, because they were derived from a more scientific and rational process.

"So if the portfolio went down 10 percent, you could point to that factor as being fourth or fifth on the list. We chose the allocation because of certain answers to questions on the list and could remind them what they said." Groups relying mostly on qualitative discussions to make decisions will pull out the minutes to show someone their exact quote. Boldt says this usually results in that person saying, "No, that's not what I meant." Ultimately, the process "helps on continuity in decision making. A new board member can look at it. There is too much room for creativity in the phrase 'what I meant then was . . .' You eliminate that creativity."

In periods of poor performance, the analysis gave Boldt and his colleagues the ability to say, "We did this to achieve objectives one and two this year. We can't achieve objectives one or two without risk. Sometimes you draw the black bean."

More important, this approach "keeps the discussion at a strategic level, focused on answering questions. It only asks questions board members are able to answer or that are appropriate for them to answer. It moves them away from questions they really shouldn't answer, like which small-cap manager should be hired, where they have very little ability to contribute."

Boldt gives an example of how the analysis changed their policies. "The CalPERS investment policy stated that CalPERS wanted to be in the top quartile of all pension funds over time in all markets. We did the decision factor analysis and we discovered that they meant, 'We don't want to be in the bottom quartile.' We rewrote the policy statements."

CalPERS provided a great experience, "a big stage, a lot of money, meaningful work. It affected the lives of a lot of people, and I got to do interesting things. The board was interested in being innovative, maybe for the wrong reasons, but they were still interested."

After CalPERS, Boldt and some friends ran a technology hedge fund. "At the toughest time in the tech space, it was another good learning experience, not such a great experience in my wallet."

Boldt then got the call from the University of Texas, his alma mater in his home state, for the UTIMCO CIO position. "It was important to me, the university and being with an organization I really cared about."

UTIMCO

When he interviewed for the CIO spot at UTIMCO, Boldt told the UTIMCO board, "If you want a caretaker, then you shouldn't hire me. If you want to be competitive in the foundation and endowment world, then I'm happy to give my very best. Don't hire me if you want a caretaker. They bought into it."

The UTIMCO overseers wanted results like Harvard Management. "In 1992 the Harvard and UTIMCO endowments were almost exactly the same size. UTIMCO was slightly larger. Ten years later, the Harvard endowment was $11 billion larger. Jack Meyer did a great job, and when you do a good job with an endowment, it's easier to raise money.

"Texans hate to lose. Harvard smoked us; it just rankled people."

Galvanized by the large discrepancy between Harvard and UTIMCO, the regents began taking the necessary steps to increase the endowment. Hiring Boldt was a step toward closing the gap.

The University of Texas had a history of being more progressive. UTIMCO was the first investment company set up by a public university in 1996. In bringing on Boldt, "the idea was to make UT a competitive organization. To the board's credit, they let me do it for a number of years."

CalPERS's $160 billion portfolio had been too large for Boldt to invest in certain assets—"too hard to move the needle." The smaller UTIMCO portfolio gave him the opportunity to invest across more categories, invest more aggressively in hedge funds and activist strategies, and pursue "high potential value-added" strategies.

Like CalPERS, UTIMCO was a public institution impacted by state politics and personalities. "Politics is politics everywhere. Texas politics is just as tough as California politics; it's easier to get caught up in politics in Texas."

A LASTING LEGACY OF CULTURAL TRANSFORMATION

UTIMCO trustees wanted to achieve another objective by hiring Boldt, changing the university bureaucracy culture to an investment management firm culture. One of the motivations behind forming UTIMCO in 1996 was that the elusive goal motivated them to install a new leader.

"We wanted to change the culture of organization. It felt more like an accounting and operations group rather than a professional investment management company. We had solid people, but the 'vibe' just wasn't right."

Management experts will say that one of the greatest challenges leaders of any organization face is changing the culture. Boldt recruited different people onto the staff as an early step, but knew he needed to act more strategically to instill an investment management culture.

Boldt established three important goals focused on revenue, reputation, and results. On the surface, the goals seem the same as any other investment management organization. When reviewed closely, it becomes clear that they conveyed a message of aspiration intended to change individual staff member behavior. Instead of setting specific cultural goals and messages (i.e., "I will think and act like an investment professional"), the goals focused the team on achieving objectives that naturally forced them, as a group and as individuals, to think and act in new ways.

The approach sounds like a reverse version of the decision factor analysis he employed with the CalPERS board. In the UTIMCO case, top-down organizational goals spurred a change in behavior, shifted individual mind-sets, and allowed cultural change to happen organically from the bottom up.

Three Goals for UTIMCO

Goal 1: Earn at least $100 million a year in value added over and above the portfolio benchmark. UTIMCO needed to clear $100 million in profit over the benchmark return by achieving good investment performance from active management of the portfolio and good manager selection. Boldt later increased the objective to $200 million.

Goal 2: Be recognized as one of the five best-managed endowment funds. An admittedly immeasurable and purposely vague goal, Boldt knew it would ultimately be measured by qualitative methods.

Goal 3: Achieve high satisfaction scores from clients inside the UT system. UTIMCO identified more than 400 constituents, including board members, deans, and the heads of the smaller endowments UTIMCO managed.

Boldt reinforced the goals and messages in a variety of ways, posting them in common areas, even programming the computer network so they displayed when employees logged on. To the extent he could measure the goals, he did. Performance was posted monthly, and he would seek regular feedback.

Boldt Achieves Impressive Results

Goal 1: In the four years he was at UTIMCO, the cumulative value added was $1.4 billion, an average of $350 million per year, $3 \frac{1}{2}$ times the original goal.

Goal 2: UTIMCO was nominated as the best large endowment by an Institutional Investor publication. Because those nominations come from reporters, peers, and other industry insiders, Boldt saw the nod as a good measure of a growing reputation. He began hearing "UTIMCO had moved up in the ranks." Being in the top five was an ambitious goal with Harvard, Yale, and Stanford among the contenders. "We weren't there, but we were very, very close."

Goal 3: Boldt conducted regular surveys using a web-based survey process. "We went out three times and, like the mayor of New York, asked 'How are we doing?' We got really good feedback."

Boldt expresses justifiable pride in the accomplishment. "It was one of the best things I did. We organized behind a set of big worthy goals and changed the tenor of the firm to be more like an investment management organization."

At CalPERS, Boldt contended with the competing politics of labor unions and a Republican-controlled executive branch, but that provided balance. The UTIMCO board consisted of five investment management professionals, including hedge fund and private equity managers, three wealthy men from the board of regents appointed by the governor, and the chancellor of the UT system, an academic. Eventually, he came up against problematic governance issues and left the organization.

"My time at UTIMCO was a great time, too. If you don't have your own firm, the second best job is to manage an endowment fund, because you can be creative."

Agility

Boldt notes that when recruiters call him, no matter the job, they all seem to want to hire the CIO of an endowment.

"Why are CIOs from endowments better equipped to handle investments? Why do endowment funds perform better than other pools of money? It comes down to one word, which you're going to hear me talk about until you're sick of hearing me talk about it, the difference is one word: *agility*."

Endowments are more agile in a variety of ways.

"Agility in thinking; I never heard we can't look at timber or weather derivatives; or it's stupid, we can't use leverage, it's not prudent. Endowment boards just don't think that way. They tend to think in ways that are open-minded and agile."

Boldt says this thinking leads endowments to invest in new asset classes "well before others see the merit" and then divest as other investors begin to invest in the asset and dilute returns.

A flattened governance structure makes endowments more agile by fostering shorter time periods for making decisions and delegating many of those decisions to the CIO. Small endowments, though, have less agility. Large endowments have more resources, skills, and manager access—advantages that allow them to grow even more and gain even greater advantages over smaller endowments.

Endowment agility stems from a number of factors. "It's not the asset allocation per se; allocations have been changing through time as opportunities presented themselves. But being more open-minded and having better governance and process helps with access. Great managers want to work with good investors. If you have resources, you can get skill; it completes the whole picture."

Boldt imagines the challenges for institutions with small asset bases.

"It must be frustrating to have $200 million and great board members, while such an organization may be well meaning and agile in thinking, it simply doesn't have the resources and staff to run it properly. The majority of people that invest in venture capital and private equity should not, and that could probably be true in hedge funds. Investing in those asset categories has become a game worth winning, but not a game worth playing for most small funds. It has got to be frustrating."

Boards of small foundations and endowments, defined by Boldt as asset bases between $50 million and $2 billion, see an increasingly complex investment environment and recognize that they cannot handle it unless they have resources and skill.

"I'm on the board of a number of foundations, and I never walked into one that the people didn't care about the foundation—they wouldn't be there otherwise. Smart, successful people that have invested, they want it to succeed. The problem is that they don't have the resources to get it done. Not just picking managers, but monitoring the portfolio, overseeing managers, and implementing risk management systems. It's expensive. You just can't do those things if you're small.

"They're trying to do the right thing and know in their heart of hearts that they can't get it done. They're never going to have the performance."

AN AGILE CIO

Boldt believes so strongly in his solution to the problems smaller institutions face that he launched an investment management firm to provide it. Teaming with the highly regarded firm of Perella Weinberg Partners, Boldt married his words to his actions and started an investment management division with the brand name "Agility."

"It will let boards do what they do best, focus on the questions that only they can answer for that organization, like strategic issues, while delegating the day-to-day management to managers that have resources and can execute. Ultimately, the solution is what some people now call *outsourcing*. I don't like that term. I think of it as joint venturing with an outside money manager that can take the will and the vision of board members and implement them in a portfolio that's efficient and agile."

Boldt compares his business model with other former CIOs that have started investment management firms focused on serving foundations and endowments. Models that force board members to choose among options presented in a consultative way violate his basic principle of never asking a board member a question they cannot answer. Other organizations provide a single fund with no customization. Agility falls in the middle of those models.

"Talk to the board at a high level, give them a set of decision factors, weigh the decision factors. Most important, tell them, 'Given what you told me, this is the portfolio that best meets the criteria. I would like you to delegate to us the decisions to build this portfolio. We're good at it and do it day by day. You will remain involved at the strategic level.'"

Boldt describes it as "a model where board members are fully engaged, but not involved in decisions that are difficult for them to make."

Consulting firms like Cambridge Associates may see Boldt's firm as competition; he disagrees. "Cambridge is a great organization with great people, but nobody's managed money. They tend to be academic and not as good at making the decisions 'down inside the Lego's' or building blocks of the portfolio." Regarding Morgan Creek, of CIO Mark Yusko (Chapter 15), he says, "I like him a lot, a very smart guy. He's adapting to the marketplace by offering a hybrid model."

With at least three different models available, he seems prepared to let the market decide.

Asset Allocation

Asked about the evolution in his approach to asset classes, Boldt says, "This is a really good question; you really hit a hot button." Boldt has given numerous speeches on the topic explaining his views of asset allocation trends.

"Look at endowment portfolios in 1980. They look like a pension fund looks today, concentrated in stocks and bonds. A category called 'alternatives' is 4 to 5 percent of portfolio. All equity investments lumped together.

"In 2000, you see a pie chart with all kinds of colors. It's broken down into very small pieces, equities into growth and value, hedge funds into absolute return and directional, private investing into venture and private equity, with set targets for each piece, 'consultants run wild.' They get to do a lot of searches. At the end of the day, you've run all the tactical opportunities out of the portfolio."

Boldt expects investors to revert back to broader asset categories:

- Global equity
- Global fixed income
- Absolute return
- Real assets
- Private equity

"Inside of those categories you will have international equities, emerging markets and U.S., directional hedge funds, alpha transport. You will have the ability to make more tactical choices without getting all caught up in regimentation."

Categories will collapse because investors have gotten too hamstrung by such narrow categories. His biggest argument at UTIMCO centered on the definition of a hedge fund.

"What is a hedge fund? According to the SEC [Securities and Exchange Commission], it's any pool that is not registered. What about so-called

130/30 funds? What about someone like Relational Investors that does not do shorting?"

Definitions that do not make much sense to him end up driving the process. Boldt consider hedge funds to be nothing more than a form of active management.

"We spent a lot of time at UTIMCO arguing about this. Board members are trained by the press to be afraid of hedge funds. It becomes an asset category because board members want to keep an eye on how much the portfolio holds in hedge funds. Our disagreement started with the board's reluctance to include hedge funds inside the domestic equity asset category. It looked like the board was going to be locked up in discussions for a long period of time. At this stage of my career, I didn't want to do that—argue whether it belongs in equity or not. It wasn't worth a year of my life."

Boldt remains adamant that hedge funds represent a form of active management and not a separate asset class. "Sounds like I'm railing against consultants, but we wrung the opportunities out of traditional active by putting managers into increasingly smaller cubbyholes. If you find a good active manager, they're rare enough that you need to give them every possible opportunity to add value. To my way of thinking, that's a multistrategy hedge fund."

Idea Generation

Boldt finds that ideas mostly come to him when others express a thought in a new or different way. "Truly original ideas are very rare. Creative ideas come from reordering a way of thinking about something. Somebody will say something I hadn't thought of that way, and it changes the groove of my thinking to a different track."

Boldt generates ideas by talking to other people, reading and observing and "jumping to a new track." Original thoughts usually come to him from another field. "My daughter is in the medical field and talking with her will trigger a completely original thought for me. An example is Alpha Transport. When I was back at CalPERS, nobody was doing it. Convertible arbitrage gave a small return, so it was not interesting, but it was a fairly certain small return. Certain return is very valuable and, in public equities, very difficult to earn. It hit me, transporting the small convertible arbitrage return, using derivatives, and suddenly we had active equity returns."

His daughter, a genetic specialist, told him about cracking the human genome. "How difficult, how amazing it was to do it. What managers are trying to do in statistical arbitrage is probably 100 times harder than what was done with the human genome, yet we have the confidence to think we can do that. Markets don't follow rules."

Looking at quantitative modeling from the human genome perspective made him rethink whether it was possible to model a really complex world.

Saying, "Not that I completely disagree with quants," Boldt thinks quantitative managers can add value by taking huge data flows, running mathematical models to refine the data and applying the results across a universe of securities. "If you have the data flow and computer power and can apply it to a large number of securities, that's an edge. It is a quantitative, very short-term edge from acting on data processing. But that's a far cry from successfully modeling financial markets."

Neural net models intrigue him—"I love the elegance"—but he is now a "recovering quant," and less likely to invest in quantitative strategies than earlier in his career. He feels less confident that sustainable models can be built.

Contrarian Investment Ideas

Boldt offers a mind game to describe *spaceship markets*, the term he uses to describe new or different investment ideas.

Spaceship Markets "You're a hedge fund guy. You've been really successful, but your edge is diminishing. You made a lot of money and start looking for the next gig. You build a spaceship and send two of your traders to fly around outer space looking for a great idea. Finally they land on Planet Z. They find a fully functioning stock market, but they don't like it there and don't want to stay. They decide, 'We're going to buy a Planet Z index fund in Z dollars.' Back on Earth, they say, 'Here it is, boss, the index fund from Planet Z.'

"Is the return from the Planet Z Index Fund alpha or beta on earth?"

Boldt corrects anyone that believes it is beta. "You overlooked one really important thing they did. They built a spaceship. That's an edge. It's alpha."

In the spaceship markets he describes, investors gain a first-mover advantage. "You don't have to be the best. Alpha is not a zero-sum game. Markets are always expanding, there's so much money to be made by going to spaceship markets."

By looking for the next market, he believes investors can earn high returns relative to the risks from assets uncorrelated to the rest of the portfolio. "You might go to 12 planets before you get to Planet Z; institutional investors have looked at stamps, art. You have got to keep looking."

In the early 1980s, hedge funds were a spaceship market and first movers had an advantage. "You didn't have to be good at picking hedge funds." As markets go from being spaceship to being fully developed, like hedge funds in the United States today, then it's hard to get an edge and skill is more important than speed.

Boldt considers carbon trading a current example of a spaceship market. Investing in music rights is another that proved profitable for a Canadian pension fund. He encourages investors, "Always have your eyes open. You're not always going to find the big ones, like hedge funds were to endowments, but you need to keep looking for the little ones. You will find managers that specialize only in spaceship markets. If you find one, it can be incredibly valuable."

At the same time, investors should not spend their time on spaceship markets for fun or ego gratification. "Guard against the *Star Trek* syndrome. Everyone wants to be Captain Kirk. You can't get carried away. It comes down to resource allocation. There are only so many good people with only so much money to spend. Focus on the highest potential value-added opportunities."

Investors need to invest at the margin because opportunities get depleted, at some level because of technology.

"I don't like BlackBerries, but they are a symbol of what we have now. Technology is so wonderful—today, the best and the brightest end up in our business in increasing numbers. Any time that happens, it makes it tougher to maintain an edge."

Multistrategy Fund Model Along with smaller endowments and foundations, pension funds will have few, if any, advantages. "The pension fund world is out of touch, really behind the times. Investments that endowments have already gotten out because of diminished opportunities, pension funds are still deciding whether or not they are too risky." On the other hand, Boldt says that foundation and endowment CIOs can be so isolated from other investors, "they think everybody's at the forefront. It's not the case."

Boldt suggests that foundations and endowments and multistrategy hedge funds have many similarities.

In the hedge fund business model, managers have the ability to use every tool at their disposal; the client will allow them to try many things and they make a great deal of money for delivering performance. New managers tend to make significant profits by identifying niche markets early.

For some firms, "maybe the answer is to stay focused, but if you want to get big, then you've got to expand. Then you have to be successful in more than one segment." As single hedge funds grow into multistrategy firms, they create more complex organizations. "Managing multistrategy firms is one of the toughest businesses around."

The best multistrategy hedge funds implement all the best tools and commit to remaining in the forefront of the industry. Viewed from that perspective, Boldt believes an endowment is like a multistrategy hedge fund. "We know that model works very well. Harvard did it."

He argues that the endowment model has advantages relative to a multistrategy hedge fund model. "Take even a great fund like Farallon; it's still a closed model. Tom goes out, hires people, and brings them under his roof. In the large endowment model, you find the best managers and invest in their strategies. It's really an open-architecture multistrategy hedge fund model."

REAL REWARDS

Boldt does not find inspiration from any particular famous investor. He tends to find it among his peers and wishes he could identify the secret sauce that brings them together.

"There's a tremendous amount of camaraderie in the endowment fund space, with some exceptions people do share ideas."

Boldt acknowledges that in such a close-knit community, groupthink can be a problem. "One of the reasons we're starting our business is that simply following the leaders doesn't get it done in the long run." Organizations with limited resources have to use caution in following others. "You can't just piggyback off other people, because you're not going to get the call when it's time to get out." Investors still have to do the job. "If you make an investment because a prominent CIO says it's good, then you have got to make that CIO promise to call you when he gets out."

Boldt identifies two additional elements that make him happy to serve as a CIO and investment adviser in the foundation and endowment world. He credits the consulting firm Cambridge Associates with fostering "such a strong cohesive force in the industry. Everybody had them as a consultant." With everyone using Cambridge, nobody gained or lost an advantage, and made their surveys and opportunities to share information more complete and valuable.

Probably the most important reason he finds being a CIO in this community so gratifying is, "Everybody feels like they're working for a worthy goal. When I interviewed at CalPERS, they asked, 'Why are you interested in doing this?' I almost didn't get the job, because I said, 'I want to save the taxpayers money.' That didn't fly. It was 'I want more money for retirees.' After CalPERS, I had to choose something that appealed more to me. At Duke, Notre Dame, Stanford, or the University of Texas, CIOs care about what they're doing. It's important."

Since his days designing components of supercomputers, Bob Boldt has traveled a career path of "spaceship experiences." Taking on new roles, exploring various types of organizations, learning new skills, and constantly seeking opportunity, Boldt is an agile engineer of investment success.

CHAPTER 12

Driven by Intellectual Curiosity

Donald W. Lindsey, CIO, George Washington University

Don Lindsey has succeeded as a chief investment officer (CIO) by diverging from the pack. Entrepreneurial, creative, articulate, dedicated, and humble, Don Lindsey embodies the characteristics he seeks in his investment staff and investment managers. Most of all, Don Lindsey distinguishes himself as a CIO by acting on innovative ideas created by unfettering his innate intellectual curiosity.

BACKGROUND

Donald W. Lindsey joined George Washington University (GW) in April 2003 as CIO responsible for management of the University's $960 million endowment. Prior to joining GW, he established the University of Toronto Asset Management Corporation (UTAM) in May 2000 and served as its first president and chief executive officer (CEO). UTAM was established to manage the University of Toronto's CAD$ 4.0 billion in endowment and pension assets. He began his career with the University of Virginia Investment Management Company in 1987, where he served initially as investment analyst and proceeded to become assistant director of investments, senior investment officer, and director.

Mr. Lindsey holds a BA in political science from Virginia Tech and an MBA from James Madison University and has earned the CFA designation. He is also a professorial lecturer of finance at GW and teaches applied portfolio management in the MBA program. He has taught in the McIntire School of Commerce at the University of Virginia and the Rotman School of Management at the University of Toronto. He is a member of the investment advisory committee of the Virginia Retirement System.

University of Virginia

Don Lindsey developed his interest in finance and economics early in his career while serving as a research assistant at the Taylor Murphy Institute, then part of the University of Virginia's Darden School of Business. He learned from supporting and producing economic studies, but felt frustrated because he had no way to measure the results of his work. As he was finishing his MBA at night, he sought a position that would allow him to measure the success or failure of his efforts. He found it in the UVA investment office and joined in 1987, intending to gain experience and then join the private sector.

A Spark Ignited   "It was a fascinating time; the endowment was growing rapidly. I relished the creativity and entrepreneurial environment and few boundaries on the job description. The sky was the limit for new ideas. I found it very exciting."

In 1988, Alice Handy, the CIO (profiled in Chapter 6) was appointed Treasurer for the State of Virginia. Everybody in the department had to take on additional responsibility. "I was enthralled with it. All of a sudden, I was managing cash and really didn't know the difference between a T-bond and an agency bond. It didn't matter because the portfolio was very conservatively constructed. It was great on-the-job training. I developed as a more sophisticated fixed-income manager, gained tremendous experience and continued to run the portfolio until I left the university."

In the early 1990s, he started a hedge fund investing program, choosing merger arbitrage because he thought it would be the strategy most acceptable to the investment committee. When merger arbitrage hit a rough patch, those managers began investing in distressed debt, leading him to learn that strategy. He found it a tremendous opportunity due to much inefficiency in the market, but rather than invest with an evolving former merger arbitrage manager, he believed in selecting experienced managers with more focused expertise in distressed debt. He continues to take that approach today. In the mid-1990s, he began investing in long/short equity funds and later moved into investing in more specialized funds and sector-specific hedge funds such as the Pequot health care and technology funds. By the time he left the university, he had constructed a fairly extensive hedge fund portfolio and had gained substantial investment experience, despite the fact that he had started as an investment analyst in charge of mortgage lending.

His fixed-income management experience in particular taught him the importance of being active in the market and being able to understand the psychology of the market.

"A lot of people think the market's efficient, but it's not because it's made up of human players, and human emotion is really a key component of market activity and market noise." For instance, unfavorable economic reports often spurred selling that created buying opportunities for him.

"During the first Gulf War, we didn't have a television in the office, but there was one in the office next door. James Baker met with the Iraqi foreign minister Tariq Aziz to negotiate withdrawal of Iraqi troops from Kuwait. The meeting had gone on for several hours and there had been no news. The bond market thought this was favorable; 'it must be coming to a resolution because it was taking so long.' I read on Telerate [a precursor system to the Bloomberg terminal] that Baker was about to make an announcement. I went to the office with the television. Secretary Baker's first words were, 'I regret to inform you.' That's all I heard. I rushed back to my office. Oil shot from $28 a barrel to $40 a barrel, 5- and 10-year Treasury notes were falling. I called my broker and he said, 'There's no bid, no buyers.' I replied, 'I don't care. Get me whatever, get them wherever you can. I don't care.' I told him as long as they keep falling, I'll keep giving you orders. I kept piling on the orders as the notes fell 5 to 10 points in a matter of seconds. The market recovered within 24 hours, and I unloaded our bonds at a huge profit.

"You learn to take advantage of the psychological impact of market activity. Noise can be a good thing. Opportunities arise as other investors react irrationally to news. But you also learn to ignore noise, looking for what really matters, such as long-term trends. I think there's a tremendous amount of selling out of fear, which creates opportunities. This understanding helps you interview managers and really get a sense of their confidence in their strategy and the likelihood they will stick to it in the face of adversity."

University of Toronto

Still at UVA and approaching his 40th birthday, Lindsey contemplated the next important step in his career and decided he wanted to become a CIO. He interviewed for a number of positions and accepted a position at the University of Toronto. That situation was a complete start-up, a separate investment company where he was responsible for managing not only endowment investments but all facets of the organization.

Feet to the Fire "What I learned in three years, I don't think I could learn in any MBA program. I learned quickly to identify what you're very good at and what you're not and hire people that are very good at the things you

STILL TUNING OUT MARKET NOISE

Years later, Lindsey continues to apply the lessons learned in his early days at UVA.

"At George Washington University, we overweighted energy late in 2003. I had spent three years in Canada (at the University of Toronto), and was one of the first investors along with Ontario Teachers to invest in the Canadian Oil sands. Working with a private equity firm, I got a tremendous appreciation for the demand for oil from Asian countries, particularly China, and started building up exposure to energy. In the summer of 2006, energy fell out of favor after oil hit a price of $78 per barrel, causing leveraged energy trades to unwind. All of a sudden, it was the sector everyone hated. I thought the long-term thesis was very much intact and had no desire to sell or reduce the position based on what was taking place. I saw that as noise. That's tough to do when you have portfolios that are down anywhere from 5 to 10 percent in one month. That's a tremendous amount of volatility. You have to have confidence in the strategy. We reexamine it all the time. We looked at publicly traded stocks valuations; long-term trends were still in place. It helped me to maintain the course, knowing this is a long-term play and we're going to stick to it."

don't do well. That's a critical part of running the organization. In many human resources reviews, people become concerned with the skills they can improve. My philosophy is if I hire someone to be good at something, I don't want them to waste their time learning how to be good at something else. Many CEOs make that mistake. It's important to have the right balance of people with different personalities and different skill sets. That's what makes the organization run smoothly and will help you out in the end. When you're bad at something, give someone complete charge of it."

Toronto had $4 billion in assets—$1.5 billion in the endowment, the rest in pension. In the space of three years, among other things, he learned Canadian pension law and built a staff of 14 people. "The chief operating officer would bring me investment agreements to sign and then she'd say something like, 'By the way, here are the carpet samples for the new office.' That was the range of issues I would have to deal with in the course of two minutes. It was more like running a company, not really running the money. I had a lot of influence in asset allocation and manager decisions, but was one step removed relative to today.

"It was a difficult process, complete culture shock. I came from an environment where endowments were expected to be cutting edge. They said they wanted that, but still had overwhelming fear because this endowment and pension fund was structured significantly different from any of the other endowments and pensions in Canada. There was a tremendous amount of curiosity about what we were doing. The national newspaper, the *Globe and Mail*, wrote about it, and I appeared on 'Report on Business Television,' the Canadian equivalent of CNBC, to talk about it. I felt like I was living in a fish bowl, everything I did was being examined. My own board at the management company, the university board, and a number of governing bodies were scrutinizing everything. I learned to focus in the face of adversity. It was a tremendous lesson and made me a better investor today.

"I was fortunate to have hired fabulous people who worked hard. They were very supportive and aligned with the mission. You learn that your strength is based on the people that are working for you. There's no question."

George Washington University

While he had no intention of staying in Canada permanently, he had anticipated being there for at least five years. The George Washington University opportunity came along sooner than he expected.

"I thought, 'What if I want to come back in a few years and the only opening is somewhere I don't want to go?' Washington was just perfect. It's near where I grew up, the center of power of the universe, and the best of all possible worlds. I decided the timing was right.

"George Washington University is a different experience. It's a smaller pool of assets and a smaller staff, but I liked that because it was taking me back to hands-on investment management. I knew we would build over time and it would be a slow process."

BEING CHIEF INVESTMENT OFFICER

Lindsey takes a broader view of asset allocation than many of his peers and agrees with the suggestion that his approach is more akin to "theme allocation" rather than "asset allocation."

Asset Allocation

"The approach has evolved over the last six years. Often, people want to be unconventional to be provocative. CIOs spend a lot of time thinking about what our colleagues and peers are doing and looking at our performance relative to theirs. The more you can tune that out, the better off you are. You must really understand the individual attributes of your institution, what makes it different and how to custom tailor a plan to your fund.

"I try not to think about how much I should have in each asset class. I am taking a much broader view and seeking the best sources of growing cash flows over the next decade or longer. You start by removing yourself from the investment universe and thinking about world politics, key trends changing the world today, and those making it significantly different 10 years from now. You have to step back from thinking about what manager to hire and really delve into studying economic and demographic changes. Have a global view, meaning really understanding globalization and making certain that you are just as familiar with what is going on in other countries as you are with the United States. Once you identify big themes from this process, then you want to determine whether these themes create executable investment ideas that will produce growing cash flows.

"A demand/supply curve will exist in equilibrium for a long period and themes will dramatically shift it up or down. You have to look at whether something is mispriced for the moment or because a long-term secular shift is taking place. Energy is a good example."

Once he believes he has found an investment opportunity, Lindsey finds the best way to implement the idea, generally by finding expert investors. He is indifferent to whether he invests through private equity, public equity, or other structures. If he finds the right manager and the manger executes in a long/short equity fund, he will choose that approach rather than deciding he has to execute in a certain asset class.

Although the university still has asset allocation guidelines, he expects tracking error and is not concerned about it.

"Even though we have target allocations, we'll probably never be allocated based on those targets. They are an anchor to say, 'If I didn't do anything else, this is probably what I would do.' We want to look back after 5, 10 years and ask how we did relative to this anchor. If we did significantly better, then I did my job; if we didn't, then I know we might have been better off not being so creative. You must look at it over a really long time period. Communicate with the investment committee frequently and let them know there will be significant outperformance in one period and significant underperformance in other periods. We can't be worried about that if we believe that we are allocating the best way we can for the long term."

Any theme implemented has a five-year time frame. It must be long term in nature and outside the trading mentality. "Engrossing yourself and becoming more knowledgeable about a theme and industry also helps generate other themes." Themes can have time horizons longer than five years, and some will have larger allocations than others. In certain cases, he might not be able to allocate to a current theme. The decision will depend on risk management parameters.

"Themes don't really change; new ones just evolve, and they may take a number of years to implement. We think it is okay to research something that may take a year or longer to implement. You want to be early and implement before anyone else recognizes the opportunity."

A Living Theme   A current theme evolved from the energy theme, a potential investment in farmland. "It's highly underinvested by institutional investors, where timberland was 10 to 15 years ago. Most people think of a field of wheat with mom and pop on a tractor. It's an industry with significant changes taking place because of global trends and demand for energy. We have this intersection between ethanol and energy and nobody knows how that will play out between the need for crops and the need for energy.

"Looking at farmland then led us to look at water investing, because it's crucial for agriculture. I spent a lot of time looking at water infrastructure; just in the United States it's over 100 years old. There's going to be huge demand; over the next 10 years, it will require billions of dollars to make sure people continue to get water. But where is the money for it? It's not coming from another federal trust fund. Look at Social Security and Medicare. Local governments can't pay for it. The logical solution is private-sector investing. People think 'Invest in water?' Water is free, it falls from the sky. Abundant or not, getting it from the reservoir to your house costs money. This theme will play out over the next several years."

Portfolio Construction and Management

Managing the assets of an endowment or a foundation requires not only portfolio and investment management skills, but also character assessment, people management, and diplomatic skills. Lindsey often employs both sets of skills at once since leading a team, selecting investment managers, and interacting with an investment committee all factor into constructing the portfolio.

On Characteristics of His Staff
"It's important to have people that are very confident in their own abilities, know what they're good at, what they're not good at, and are not afraid to make mistakes or try new things. They find good ideas by trying to be unconventional in their thinking. They are so excited about their job they don't view it as a job, but as a

lifestyle. They're home all weekend working and delving into new ideas. That may seem excessive, but that's the personality you have to have. You need to be driven by it and cannot see it as a job centered on a certain number of hours in the day. You tend to have people that have a tough time balancing their personal life with their professional life, but unfortunately that's an important attribute—lack of balance and excessive drive.

"Another really key attribute is humility. As soon as they believe they have all the answers they're dangerous. You need people that can say I screwed up or I really don't know how to do that. It's important."

On Governance Standards

"For governance to work there must be a clear delineation of duties. The CIO and staff should have responsibilities that everyone accepts as their responsibilities and the board should have their responsibilities. Board members taking on the role of staff is very dangerous. While the CIO has to make many decisions, there are decisions that ultimately belong to the board or committee. To make it work, the board or governing body has to be relatively small, because it forces them to be more accountable and buy into the process. When you have a very large group of 10 or more, it's hard to get a consensus and decisions tend to be compromises that are suboptimal.

"The CIO should have a lot of input into the asset allocation process, but approving the allocation and any deviation from it remains the board's decision. The board has to set the parameters, but the CIO should have complete responsibility for implementation. Timely decisions cannot be made if they have to go to the board. It's not fair to ask new board members to vote on things they know nothing about. Especially when the staff is doing all the work, the idea of giving someone inadequate information—a four-page write-up and a half-hour presentation—and asking for a decision is bad governance. To do it right, they would have to go along on all the meetings and that can't be done.

"This may be a political sore spot, but I think it is wrong for the CIO to rely on consultants for investment decisions. It's okay for special projects like finding a better risk management system, but to rely on an investment consultant to make decisions is wrong. You are a fiduciary, you were hired to do the job, you have to stand firm behind your decisions and if you have to rely on a consultant then you shouldn't be in the job."

Similar to what he looks for in staff, he prefers creative managers that try new ideas, but also have a strong sense of humility.

On Manager Selection

"Humility, if it's not most important, then it's in the top three. Investment managers can become wealthy and money tends to change people, frequently for the worse. You want to be cognizant of their reasons for going to work every day. They've got to be doing it because they love it, not because of the money.

"Honesty is very important. You want a manager that would rather overcommunicate than undercommunicate. I have had managers call me over the weekend even on little things that have gone wrong. There's nothing more disconcerting than having a voicemail message at home on a Saturday afternoon at 3:00 PM and hearing, "Don, this is so and so, call me as soon as possible." That can give you heart palpitations, but when it does happen I know there's a good culture. I'd rather they tell me right away rather than not at all. Even though it might be small and might not impact the relationship, I'm still glad they took the time to call me."

He tends to avoid highly leveraged strategies because he thinks a greater downside than upside is likely. He likes managers that have been through adversity. Even though many highly intelligent managers with good track records come from proprietary trading desks or platforms, he views those managers cautiously because they had the support of the platform and have not faced adversity on their own.

On Risk Management

"The key to risk management is to think about and anticipate the worst-case scenario, anticipate unexpected events. It's knowing what is the worse thing that could happen, what could cause it to happen, and how you will survive. You want to stay alive to play another day.

"The key is to allocate heavily to your best ideas and make certain you have other aspects of the portfolio that are going to act significantly different over time. In periods of extreme events everything tends to act the same. It all goes down. Recognize what will go down in price the most and what will go down the least and then come up with a balanced allocation to all these strategies. Most people think of it has highly quantitative. I think it's much more subjective and highly qualitative. Most of the data you get is so limited it's a big mistake to rely on it too heavily."

LESSONS, OBSERVATIONS, AND ADVICE

Throughout his career, Don Lindsey has shown a willingness to express opinions and give advice. He shared his thoughts on a serious of topics related to managing investments, pursuing this career, and foreseeing the future.

Communication

Lindsey says he has learned to communicate as much as possible with the investment committee and never takes for granted that they think all is going smoothly. He constantly reminds himself to call individual committee members or send a memo to the group. Even though he finds it tough and time consuming, he believes it is crucial.

Investment Mistakes

"A huge mistake is being made now. A lot of institutions in general have a very shallow and inadequate view of asset classes and rely too heavily on the balance between them. There is too much emphasis on what is the right amount in each asset class. They're announcing they're going from 5 percent private equity to 10 percent private equity, 5 percent hedge funds to 10 percent. What's the decision? There's nothing magic about a specific allocation to private equity. It should be based on the available opportunities. If there are none, then having a target to fill is a huge mistake.

"There is an inadequate process for monitoring the relationship with managers. After six months of underperformance, they put the manager on the 'watch list,' and after another 6 months terminate. There's too much emphasis on underperformance compared to a benchmark over a period of time. I am comfortable with managers that underperform relative to other parts of the portfolio. Then when the parts that are doing great start to do badly, I think I have a chance for the underperformers to do well.

"In evaluating managers, there should be less focus on performance and more focus on the culture and dynamics of the investment management firm. You want a strong culture of responsibility and due diligence, where they feel they are a fiduciary for outside money and try to always do the right thing. If you have that and the manager underperforms, then you should look at why the style isn't working and in what environment it would likely do better."

Overcrowded Investment Strategies

"People are too willing to overpay for perceived reduction in volatility and are naïve about their return expectations for a strategy that charges a 2 percent management fee and 20 percent performance fee. Too many investors are lulled into thinking they can get 'great returns with little downside.' That's the number one mistake. Another is believing they should have a significant portion of their portfolio reducing volatility. When it comes down to it, volatility should not be an issue as long as you understand liquidity requirements. The only way to make money is to take on risk as defined by volatility. When there is volatility, usually the instrument is mispriced. This creates opportunities for investors that recognize it. Rather than take on that opportunity, many investors walk away.

"The flood of money into hedge funds was precipitated by the performance meltdown of 2000–2002. People realized, 'Oh my gosh, I can be down 20 percent!' It seemed that investors took the viewpoint, 'I'll do whatever it takes to avoid having that happen again, I have to have all this hedged exposure.' That was the time to starting to take on risk again, because we just had a big drop and it might not happen for another 10 years. I think people will learn at the end of this decade that they overpaid for a very low return and could have paid considerably less to get a slightly higher return. I don't have great expectations for the S&P, but in the end, investors probably will have come out ahead if they just held the S&P rather than portfolios of funds with very high fees and fee hurdles too hard to overcome to generate attractive returns."

Separation of Alpha and Beta

"I could care less about alpha versus beta. I think it is highly overrated, oversold, and quite frankly, preposterous. What's my best estimate of the discounted cash flows of the strategy? Are those cash flows going to grow over time and by how much? Whether it comes from beta or alpha or gamma or sigma, who cares? I mean it's just irrelevant to the process of making money."

Monitoring Investment Managers Effectively

"Formal meetings are important. What's more important are more frequent communications for a few minutes. If I hear from someone once every 6 weeks for 10 minutes, that will tell me a lot more than a one-hour annual meeting. It's not only me calling them, but I will also have managers call me. Sometimes they call when they're underperforming and want to hear what you're thinking, but I also like when they have had a really good run and call to tell me why. I am lucky to have really good managers that do call me."

Investment Influences

When asked about investors that influenced him, Lindsey said, "I don't think a lot about investors. We all know the great investors. One of the first books I read was Peter Lynch, and I thought he was a fabulous investor with great insights.

"I spend more time reading trade journals, *Water World*, oil and gas, grain and feed journals. People look at me incredulously and seem to think, 'What do you do for a living?' But I want to know what the people in the industry are doing and thinking. I spend more time focusing on people in an industry where we have investments rather than people that are also investing in that industry. I was the only endowment manager at a recent feed and grain conference. Everybody looked at me like I was crazy. I don't care whether the people I talk to know a stock from a bond—I want to know what they think about their business."

Advice for Investment Managers

"Managers should have the discipline of putting their thoughts in writing. That's time consuming, but I think it's important. An example is Howard Marks of Oak Tree. He's a fabulous communicator in the written form. I think it's a skill managers should focus on. Too many managers talk about the latest GDP [gross domestic product] and CPI [consumer price index] reports, what the dollar and Dow did, and how the portfolio reacted. While it's important to know what happened in the portfolio, managers should spend more time writing about their thoughts for the future, how they execute their process, how things are changing and how those changes are affecting their thought process.

"Another thing that's somewhat esoteric is the conflict and dichotomy between running an investment management firm and managing money. Running a business is about growth and marketing and that's in direct competition with good ideas and making money. Less than 50 percent understand that inherent conflict and can focus on making money. Managers need to balance the two."

Endowment and Foundation Management Issues

"The biggest culture clash is trying to create professional organizations within the confines of an academic institution. You have to give incentives to investment people, yet incentive compensation is in direct conflict with the culture of an academic institution. We will probably see more CIO and staff turnover than in the past. It's rare to see the person that's been a CIO for 20 years now." He expects this debate to continue and more organizations will outsource the CIO function to avoid the political problems.

INQUISITIVE, INNOVATIVE, INTELLIGENT

Absorbed in his work; fascinated by politics, economics, and markets; and enthused about new ideas and creative opportunities, Don Lindsey not only gives this advice, he lives it.

"You have to be really hungry and devote your whole life. You don't have much of a life in the early stages. It's so competitive, that's what it's going to take.

"Become a good communicator, both written and verbal. Be able to talk to people and communicate, 'This is what I think and why.' Too often, I see people that are brilliant but inarticulate."

He recommends credentials. "CFA accreditation shows you are serious, willing to go through the pain and making the commitment. Study economics, finance, and accounting. Your undergraduate major is far less important. Enjoy learning for the sake of learning. If you are too focused on your grades and the next exam, you don't enjoy the process of learning. In the investment business you have to enjoy the process of learning and looking at things you never would have looked at before. You have to be curious—that's an important attribute."

CHAPTER 13

The CIO as CEO

Jonathan Hook, CIO, Baylor University

M ost chief investment officers (CIOs) manage a small to mid-size endowment in an increasingly challenging investment climate that rewards size. Over the course of the next several years, if fiduciaries choose not to outsource asset management, industry observers expect more such organizations to hire a CIO for the first time. Jonathan D. Hook at Baylor University represents this new breed of CIO.

Named the university's first CIO in February 2001, Jon Hook has successfully handled the career challenge of defining a role that had not existed, doing so without previous investment management experience. *Foundation and Endowment Money Management* magazine honored him in 2005 as the "Endowment Officer of the Year" for the endowment's investment performance in 2003–2004. As the first-time manager of a mid-size endowment, his experiences and approach to the role provide a good model for first-time CIOs and managers of mid-sized endowments and foundations.

BACKGROUND

Baylor University is the largest Baptist-affiliated university, enrolling approximately 14,000 students at its campus in Waco, Texas, with an endowment worth just over $1 billion. Hook joined the University after spending 20 years in the corporate and investment banking fields. Immediately prior to joining Baylor, he was a senior vice president with First Union Securities in Atlanta, Georgia, focusing on origination in the business services sector. Responsibilities included origination and delivery of public debt and equity offerings, private placements, syndicated lending, derivatives products, and capital management services. During his banking career, Hook also spent

8 years specializing in the energy and utility industries throughout the western and southwestern states.

An active fund raiser for many charitable and civic organizations including United Way, Boys and Girls Clubs, the Metro Atlanta Chamber of Commerce, and the Baylor Bear Foundation, Hook graduated from Willamette University with a BS in economics and sociology in 1978 and from Baylor University in 1981 with his MBA in finance. He and his wife, Karen, have two children, Kendall and Connor.

Investment Banking and Relationship Management

After receiving an MBA from Baylor University in 1981, Jonathan Hook had a 20-year career in both corporate and investment banking, before returning to Baylor in 2001 as CIO. Becoming CIO without having direct portfolio management experience, Hook applies many of the same skills and leverages the knowledge of companies, industries, and finance he developed in the corporate arena. Spending half his corporate career covering companies in energy, oil, gas and utilities has helped because, "In Texas you have to have oil and gas in the portfolio."

He finds most of the process in the CIO role is similar, down to contracts like limited partnership agreements mirroring loan agreements in the corporate banking world.

"I'm used to being the one with the pitch book. I learned how to present ideas and make the case although I think some of those tricks were easy to see through. The sales process and communication with the other party, whichever side of the table you're on, some of the same characteristics apply and are very similar to what I'd done. What wasn't similar was people throwing around jargon like 'Sortino Ratio'; I thought I better figure that out."

Much of what Hook does now and throughout his career has to do with people, "Figuring out whom you want to do business with and whom you want to do business with for an extended period of time. You may have lockups and be joined at the hip for long periods. It's not much of a difference, not much of a stretch from a fundamental standpoint."

Being at a Christian school perhaps influences his philosophy, but even if he worked somewhere else, he says, "Boil down the relationship to the Golden Rule and treat people the way you want to be treated. If you do, you end up with a much better situation.

"Everybody understands each other's pressures; everyone has their own set of issues, so when things come up then you can have a discussion. 'Let's reprioritize, readjust.' If honest and straight, if there's mutual respect and good communication, you can have a good relationship, even if it doesn't lead to a piece of business. I am not sure there's enough of that in the business. Hearing stories from other people, I'm not sure it's followed in the same way. I would suspect most of the good folks are like that."

Hook's education and corporate experience influenced his investment philosophy.

"I'm somewhat of a contrarian and probably always leaned toward being a value-ish person. I didn't get the tech bubble, although I participated in it in my personal portfolio on the way up and on the way down." Chuckling, he continues.

"Trying to buy things below market prices seems to be a good fundamental approach rather than trying to buy the sizzle. We structured the portfolio heavy on the value side, and over the long run I think we'll end up in good shape. There are always periods where one outperforms the other, but what I've seen over any 10-year period the value side always ends up winning."

Contrarian and value biases factor into selecting investment managers and allocating capital.

"We like niche-y things. We like managers that have either figured out a way to find a space without that much capital in it—of course, that's getting more difficult—or one that has found a different way to play in a space."

Hook credits his undergraduate education in sociology with shaping his view. "I look through a lens of behavioral finance and try to overlay a value or contrarian type of idea. I don't spend a lot of time thinking about how efficient markets are, and they're not all going to be orderly. People do act irrationally at times, so behavioral finance does make more sense to me."

Baylor University: Becoming CIO

When Hook started talking to Baylor, the portfolio already included its first alternative investment from the 1999–2000 period when hedge funds began gaining broader acceptance among institutions. Even though some thought it was "icky" given the investment climate at the time, Baylor invested in distressed debt and, as it added to the alternatives portfolio, overweighted distressed relative to other categories. Fortunately, they had chosen good managers with good returns that got them through the period when the tech bubble burst. Hearing about that experience gave him the sense that the fiduciaries were value investors and in sync with his thinking and made joining as CIO an easier decision.

"Philosophically, it matched up well. The board and investment committee seemed to be more that bent. It helped decisions and helped on timing, when to bring things to the board, when to push for changes, and when to let go."

Hook approaches his role as if he manages a business, not just an investment fund—another example of how his corporate experience shaped him.

"Trying to read the group, understand the dynamics, who is making decisions and why. This case it's an inside sale, easier to get at individual motivation. Instead of thinking about what some corporate CFO is going to do, getting people on your side is easier because you don't have a corporate veil to go through."

Hook applies his corporate presentation and relationship management skills to working with the board and investment committee to educate them and win their approval for new investments. Surprisingly, given that many investment managers covet institutional investors, Hook needed to apply his sales skills to attract investment managers to want Baylor as a client.

When he joined Baylor as their first CIO, he found that the market had no knowledge of Baylor as an investing institution. The endowment had been handled by a third party, so the school had no name recognition and the market had limited awareness that Baylor had been an investor in any particular manager.

"One thing that was easy to see at the onset: If I was going to be successful, I had to get Baylor out there. Get out there and market, let people know that Baylor has institutional capital and is ready to invest. One way to do that is to use conferences and talk to peers and managers, to get the name out in a concentrated dose. The other way that I found out the hard way is to get yourself published in a periodical saying that you are planning to invest."

On Getting the Word Out

"After I had been at Baylor for about 6 weeks, I went to the Commonfund annual meeting, thinking it was a good chance to network with people at other schools.

"The first morning, I come down to breakfast, into a room with hundreds of round eight-seat tables so you can have a conversation. The guy next to me had a bunch of questions—he's asking, I'm answering. Finally I say, 'I didn't catch your name, who are you with? He replied, 'I'm so-and-so and I'm a reporter.' My skin tone went white and I immediately thought, 'This was the shortest job I ever had!' I had no idea how it would come out in print and was very concerned, but two or three weeks later nothing had been printed.

"Four weeks later I get a call from a business school contact, the head of client service at an investment firm. 'Have you seen this article? I'm going to fax it to you because you're about to get 5,000 phone calls.' 'Before you do that,' I said, 'is it really bad?' He said,

" 'That depends. It doesn't sound bad, but it's going to make a lot of people call you.' Then he faxed it.

"In huge font, the headline said, '**Baylor Looking for Hedge Funds**'

"That was a Friday morning. By 9:00 AM on Monday I had gotten 150 to 200 phone calls. With people trying to leave messages, my voicemail box filled up and rolled over to other offices, even the university president's offices. I got calls from all over the university. 'Are you not answering the phone?'

"It was a nightmare, although it got Baylor out there. We had the phenomenon of the pig going through the snake, so it was painful in the short run. But it opened people's eyes that there was at least one pool of capital between Dallas and Austin and that it might be worth stopping by on their travels.

"We started working hand-in-hand with managers. As time passed—it never hurts to have decent returns—people hear about you, you build on the success.

"It's probably an easier sell if you have a larger pool of capital, a $2 to $5 billion endowment. That might be a little more interesting to some managers, but that's not anything we can control, at least at the outset. Hopefully, we'll grow into those numbers.

"It's made it interesting to use some of the marketing ideas or, if you want, call it corporate tactics. It was a job where we needed to do some selling. I don't think we needed to do as much as that."

Managing the Endowment

Hook became the first CIO at Baylor University in 2001 after the university had taken control of endowment assets that had been managed as part of a related larger foundation. Lowery Asset Consulting, a Chicago-based firm, was already in place, advising solely on alternatives investments. Since he had no other staff at the time, it made sense to use consultants for support.

"We did not have a full-service consultant, and I think the board had a bit of trepidation about what they were about to do and thought having another set of eyes on the portfolio made sense. We hired Hammond Associates, a firm based in St. Louis."

Baylor continues to employ both consulting organizations. Each has their area of responsibility, although Hook says there aren't sharp delineations. He discusses the entire portfolio with each organization to have another perspective and compensates them accordingly.

"It's still a good decision from a cost-benefit analysis. If we hired a couple of extra people, I'm not sure we would get the same horsepower. It seems to work for the board, so it's best to leave as is, though it puts more of a burden on the investment office to coordinate. They don't overlap, and it casts a wider net for us when they're out looking for managers."

Early Success

Three years after he took over the Baylor University endowment, the portfolio returned over 25 percent for 2004, making Baylor the top-performing endowment that year as measured by the annual NACUBO study.

"You have an understanding of where you are; you never quite know where anyone else is. I'd say, 'We're doing okay, up 19 percent, up 21 percent.' I had the view, throw in Harvard or Yale (at the top), and it will be a good year for everybody. I was surprised when I got the call saying we had outperformed. I thought Harvard and Yale would beat us. I wasn't thinking along those lines—I was just hoping we wouldn't stumble. You'd always like to be there, but never really think about coming in at that level."

As a result, Hook received the "Endowment Officer of the Year" awarded by *Foundation and Endowment Money Management* magazine.

"I got one call telling me about being nominated. About six weeks later, I was at home, doing due diligence on a manager, sitting at the computer and googling through the universe. A link led me to the magazine's web site and I see 'Baylor CIO wins award.' I thought, 'Oh, I guess I won.' I couldn't access the story online and it was midnight on Friday. On Monday when I got to the office, three or four people had contacted me, but nobody from the magazine called until 2:00 PM. They were nice and sent me five copies; I think they are still in a drawer. I'm not sure what it meant; I just had my Andy Warhol 15 minutes of fame. It was one of those years, a 'career year.'"

Despite—or perhaps because of—that experience, Hook remains conscious of competition against other endowments.

"Two thirds of the way through last year, I thought, 'I know we're doing well; I wonder how we compare?' I had to think, 'Don't worry about that, you can't control it. Just focus on doing the right things for Baylor, and it will all take care of itself.'

"I think there's a big danger to compensation tied to comparisons against peers. Everyone's portfolio is different. Everyone's investment committee is different. You earn a bonus or you don't earn a bonus because you did this well against this peer group of 10 other schools. I'm not sure that's a good way to judge anyone.

"It does make me wonder about CIOs being compared to the top 25 endowments and having compensation impacted by that. A large part of that group is comprised of private universities and Ivy League schools and many have probably been in alternatives longer. The world is a much better place for a private university CIO."

BEING CHIEF INVESTMENT OFFICER

Since Hook and the investment committee work together closely, the governance structure of the endowment serves an important role in its management.

The Office of Investments reports to an investment committee of seven individuals from three different subgroups. Three members work for the school including Baylor's CFO, the committee chair, the dean of the business school, and Hook, who is a voting member. The board of regents (trustees) has two members on the committee, and a special alumni group called the Baylor Foundation has two members.

Because of Baylor's historical ties to the Baptist church, all members of the board of regents are members of the church, a requirement that has been in the bylaws from the beginning. Although there have been discussions from time to time about updating the rules, it has not been an issue.

The Baylor Foundation consists of alumni unaffiliated with the Baptist church who serve as advisers. Started by the head of development to help with fund raising and encourage involvement with the school, members include successful, experienced financial and business professionals: entrepreneurs, a venture capitalist, a hedge fund manager. When he joined Baylor, Hook thought the group had been underutilized and helped transform it into an investment advisory board. Most other schools do not have such an arrangement.

"The foundation meets twice a year. I tell them, 'Here's what we're thinking about.' Because many of them are in alternative investments, I could call and get good ideas before investing. It means two additional board meetings, each lasting something like four hours, each year, but it turned into something that works quite well. I virtually never take something to the regents for final approval unless we have vetted it through them. The Baylor Foundation has no authority, no capital—it's just advisory. But if they're signed on to it, it's much easier to get the board of regents to give final approval."

Presenting Investments for Approval

Hook is currently required to get approval on every investment. The committee has thought about changing, many of his peers can make all investment decisions or decisions up to a certain dollar limit.

"There would be some advantage and nicety to say, 'Let's approve it and move on.' On the flip side, I'm still comfortable that it gives us cover to anything that goes wrong. Fingers can be pointed, and you know the final finger will come back to our office. It hasn't caused us to miss out on an investment because of timing. If we're looking for a new manager, then just the investment committee gets involved, not further up the chain."

The board of regents gets involved in asset allocation. Anything going to the board for approval, Hook definitely brings to the Baylor Foundation first. If a decision can be handled through the committee, he will inform the foundation rather than ask. Since the group also helps the development office, he wants them to understand his approach.

"Not everyone is going to agree, but you have to account for that. It's an easier process than that of some other people in the industry.

"If the process is working perfectly, I send out a monthly communication by email, telling them what we're thinking about and looking at and asking if they have any ideas. I am just trying to make sure they're on the same wavelength."

When he wants a new manager or investment to be approved, he can accomplish that by memo and e-mail. A recent example involved investing in the follow-on funds of two existing managers.

"We wanted to re-up. I put the memo in place, spoke to consultants, and gave them 2 weeks to review. We can usually get something approved within 10 days to 2 weeks. Even approving a new manager would be on the same timetable."

If Hook wants to pursue a new asset class, he takes the time to educate the committee and lay the groundwork.

"The monthly missive to the committee is a good place to bring it out. I write it up, say we're looking at it and talking to managers, that we like what it does in terms of risk and return. It gives them the information and encourages feedback, basically, asking do you like this or not?"

Hook cites his first investment in timber as a good example.

"Previously, all the assets had been handled by the outside foundation with no alternatives. The school had independently invested 2 percent in alternatives, but that had been established prior to my arrival. When I suggested timber, the first words were, 'Trees, you want to buy trees?' So I wrote four to five pages, laid out the parameters for timber. I got the point across that there would not be private equity type returns, just a decent, steady return relative to the S&P 500 with less volatility. I started getting phone calls within two hours saying, 'I never knew this.' That's the way we worked it into the portfolio."

Winning approval for a proposed portable alpha program took a bit more firepower.

"The portable alpha project, I had the same mind-set, then realized people didn't pick up on it as quickly. It's a harder topic for people to get their hands around, so we took it to a special investment committee meeting, made it an agenda item, and presented it formally. We spent 1 1/2 hours talking about portable alpha."

Hook sees good communication among committee members, the administration, and himself. "I probably talk to the CFO a couple of times a day. With investment committee members, it's very easy to pick up the phone and talk to those folks."

To encapsulate his approach to working with the investment committee, Hook says, "You can't communicate too much, keeping them informed about what you're thinking. On the flip side, a lesson I learned in the corporate world is 'Don't surprise the boss.' Let them know early and get input.

"Don't surprise your boss and think of the committee as your boss."

Asset Allocation

Until early 2007, the endowment had an asset allocation broadly divided between 60 percent in traditional investments and 40 percent in alternatives. That included 27 percent in domestic equities and 23 percent in international holdings with 10 percent in fixed income. The alternative categories had 10.5 percent in private equities, 17 percent in real assets, and 12.5 percent in absolute return strategies. That allocation represented quite a change since Hook came on board.

"We have not left the asset allocation alone for more than 12 months. When I joined the endowment had virtually 100 percent in traditional assets with a 2 percent stub that had been committed to alternatives. At the first board meeting, we bumped the alternatives allocation up to 12.5 percent, a pretty big move. I had been there three weeks and thought maybe I really had a job!"

Hook began to see that he needed to pick up the pace.

"Understanding where the market was moving, the market being asset allocations by sophisticated investors, 12.5 percent wasn't going to get us there. With the board just getting into it, I wanted to be cautious and bring them up to speed. The best way to do it was not to go from 2 percent to 50 percent in one swing, so with the board's tacit understanding the allocation developed over time.

"We would fill up the bucket and keep going back to increase the bucket. Each year we added somewhere between 5 percent and 10 percent in alternative capacity, taking it up gradually, but steadily. We kept the foot on the pedal, didn't go too fast, changing steadily until we got to 40 percent."

At that point Hook decided it would be a good year to stop.

"Let's get the target and the actual allocation closer together. Let's take the pressure off the board and let them breathe, which they did. The board had gotten used to me asking for more of an allocation, so when I told them 'I am not going to do it,' I looked around and could see the big sigh of relief. We never had the request turned down, but it was a good year not to raise the bar again but to take a different tack. We have used the theory, 'If you're leaving things the same, then maybe you're falling behind.' When things are good people tend to do that. Because of the macro and micro events that happen around us, I am not sure we want to keep it the same for that long, although I say that knowing there's a risk of too much tinkering."

Conscious of the organization's risk tolerance, Hook wanted to grow the alternatives allocation to a reasonable percentage of the portfolio while also having it be representative of an institutional portfolio. "Combine good returns with a hopefully lower volatility and a comfort level of allowing the board to sleep at night."

Outside the Boxes Allocation Policy

Working with the board through 2006 and into 2007, Hook moved the asset allocation approach away from allocating to "style boxes" more toward allocating to themes defined by the role an asset plays in the portfolio. It separates alpha and beta somewhat and tries to combine similar styles, volatilities, and risk/return profiles. The portfolio now consists of four broad categories titled "Market Exposure," "Risk Reducers," "Return Enhancers," and "Inflation Hedges."

"The move is based on the environment and the strategies that would fit—it wasn't radical.

"We lump all long-only managers, both U.S. and international, long biased and long/short managers into the beta (market exposures) bucket. Risk Reducers groups lower volatility strategies including low-volume hedge funds and fixed income. These assets have different return patterns, but we think by and large they will have fairly consistent return streams."

Return Enhancers mirrors Risk Reducers and includes private equity and emerging-markets instruments.

"If you have volatility north of the S&P 500, that's fine. This is a holding pen for those assets. We are willing to do strategies that maybe have higher volatility and a bit more risk, hopefully commensurate with more return. We can move allocations in this bucket up and down based on environment."

An additional inflation hedge bucket includes Treasury inflation-protected securities (TIPS), real assets. "Not that dissimilar from other folks, maybe in nomenclature, real estate, infrastructure, commodities, and energy. Over time, the biggest risk to the endowment is the negative effects of inflation. I'm comfortable with exposure in these strategies should inflation pick up."

The previous asset allocation had a hard ceiling with specific percentages for asset classes and strategies. The new approach has broader definitions and ranges:

- Market Exposures or Beta: 40 to 50 percent
- Risk Reducers: 15 to 25 percent
- Return Enhancers: 15 to 25 percent
- Inflation Hedges: 15 to 25 percent

"It's a fair bit of room. Over time, I would like to widen the ranges on some and would leave others pretty much where they are. I am in the camp that would be comfortable reducing long-only domestic equity exposure. I have been able to increase long-only international, and that has been a positive provider to returns. We have got a lot of sublimits baked within these ranges. The investment committee will pay attention to those things."

There are some boundaries built into the thinking.

"Looking at the broad numbers, you could say, 'If you took the beta bucket to 40 percent, then you could have 60 percent in alternatives.' You really can't. Realistically, the most would be 50 percent in alternatives; we're essentially in line with all those buckets. We have 35 percent in alternatives, about as low as we could go to be in compliance, and we've got quite a bit of room on the upside. It gives us latitude to push up or down certain strategies."

This approach puts the onus on the investment committee to be doing their jobs and providing oversight to his office. "It's appropriate; they should be asking questions, following along with what the university should be doing."

Not Too Far Outside the Box

While Hook has more latitude for allocating to certain types of investments, he does not have the ability to run overlays or establish a hedge if a manager underperforms.

"Tweaking is not something we could do. We don't have the approval at this point. The board recently approved portable alpha and rejected overlays. We thought, 'Isn't portable alpha the harder of the two to get your hands around?' My number two, Scott Pittman, presented portable alpha and I presented overlays. Maybe that had something to do with it."

He laughs and gives the real reason for the decision. "One member was concerned about our buying and selling swaps and options in our office. He's not sure that's the mandate and was concerned about shorting stocks. He didn't get the concept of shorting the index rather than shorting specific stocks. We decided to back burner the idea and get the portable alpha going. We will let it work, see that it does what it should do, get some comfort that it's not crazy, weird stuff. It's a defined size, a pilot program, and we will revisit it in 12 months to see what's been good, what's been bad."

Some of these programs are difficult to implement even with the approval of the committee. "One of the hardest things I've ever done is get an ISDA [International Swaps and Derivatives Association] document approved. I had worked with them many times in my prior life and didn't appreciate some of the nuances at the university. Corporations are used to hedging risk like oil prices and have a better handle on the documents. We got the approval to implement the program using options or swaps. We got the options part done and started with that. The people helping us structure the program told us the critical path was going to be the ISDA document. They were exactly right; it's a longer process than we thought. It's just a different animal, from the university side."

He doubts he would seek or receive approval to invest directly. "I don't think we would ever have the mandate to do emerging markets fixed income from Waco. It wouldn't match up. Going direct would be confined to core assets. If expectations are low for fixed income, 5 to 7 percent, is investing direct the best use of our time? I don't think the equation works today or even if we were twice our size. I am more than happy to let outside managers have that space."

The investment committee has given him access to a small amount of capital to deploy in case he needs to make a quick decision or wants to coinvest.

"They set up a guidance line of a couple million dollars to allow us to coinvest when opportunities came up. It's not for specific managers, just a bucket to pull from. Some opportunities come up that have short time fuses, a short time to do due diligence if you want to play. This gives us dry powder to invest and report back to committee."

In the six years he's been at Baylor, they made one such investment and he expects it to turn out well because of the near-term sale of the asset.

"It has not been a place where we have sought to do direct or coinvesting. It's a manpower issue, because you want to spend time on it, so I'm using it sparingly. With one investment paid off, we went back for approval and asked for the line to be increased and reestablished at zero. It will be a good piece of feedback whether we get it approved. The committee has different opinions—is it where we should spend time or use capital?" (The line was approved after Hook's interview.)

Hook has overseen one direct investment in a company in the oil and gas business. "They had built their predecessor company to a certain size, sold it, and started another company to do the same thing. We invested last year, after watching the new firm get started and work through one round of capital raising. We're comfortable with the team, know where they're exploring, know the fields, people on our board know it, so we had a good comparative advantage to make that investment. We may get a seat on the board and will see how that plays out. We're well within the information loop with good access to the senior management.

"We should and need to have some capital available for opportunistic situations, within reason. Philosophically, it's good to be able to do some interesting things. You need to know why and explain it to committee members. It's a bit different than picking managers."

Direct investing requires a significantly larger time commitment than other investments. Hook says, "We won't get that big into it, but having a little bit of powder makes sense for when you see opportunities to get a nice multiple. It could be pretty valuable."

Portfolio Construction and Management

Establishing an asset allocation policy and accelerating from 2 percent alternatives to almost 40 percent in five years could challenge the most experienced CIOs. Hook accomplished that task while working with a new investment committee unaccustomed to institutional capital risks and learning his job. He then engineered an asset allocation policy revamp that much larger institutions had yet to implement. Managing endowment funds requires more than setting policy. Hook executes.

Finding and Selecting Investment Managers   Even though he got the word out about Baylor's readiness to invest, the process of identifying strategies and picking the right managers requires more effort than checking your inbox. The best ideas don't always come knocking at the door, and those that do knock at your door may not be the best ideas for the portfolio. Like his peers, Hook still needs to source ideas and search for what he needs, always refining the process.

"I wish I had the perfect answer. We all probably get the same things, e-mails from managers you have never even talked to sharing how well they've done. All these different things coming at you, it does get to be information overload. Aside from hitting the delete button, we keep asking, 'What do we need? What are we missing?' and make sure we think we're still on the right path.

"If we can keep focused, it lets some of these more distracting ideas fall by the wayside. By discounting certain strategies and saying we're not interested in something, you can just carve it out quickly and keep focused on what is more interesting to the portfolio."

Hook stays on top of his priorities and objectives by remaining conscious of the views of the board and investment committee.

"To some degree I think the more you know what the board does and doesn't like can also help you define your task. If you know that you've got a board or investment committee member that will not stand X strategy, it's not worth fighting that fight—just let it go. We've tried to add diversity and be as diversified as we can be for a portfolio of our size, but we know we're not going to be in every asset class. We try to figure out where not to spend time and where not to burn up too many calories for a meager or nonreturn. Some of that probably does go back to the communication angle, if you're in good communication with the committee members then hopefully you will know their hot buttons, what they like, what they don't."

Like many of his colleagues, Hook finds investment managers using a variety of tactics, least of all the calls and e-mails that come in over the transom.

"Combination of methods, some of it going out and finding managers, some from consultants, some from events like the NMS Management small group conference on hedge funds. We hired three managers we got to know there. I am not opposed or ashamed to use any means necessary for finding folks or figuring out whether there is a manager we can work with that would like to work with us."

Hook taps into the consulting firms advising the endowment.

"This is where we use the consultants fairly well. We like to run in parallel with them; we won't cede the decision. We want to do our due diligence and come to our conclusion. Hopefully, they will have done their process and come to the same conclusion. We put our heads together and see if everything matches up, but that's not always the case. We can butt heads and arm wrestle and hopefully come to an agreement."

Sometimes arguing with consultants can identify information one or the other missed or can lead to a better conclusion.

"After combining all the data, we probably bake in all three opinions. We try not to worry about who found the idea. Just is it a good fit in the portfolio?"

If he knows he will never invest in a certain investment strategy or fund, he addresses it directly. "I will tell the manager we're just not going to do something. Treat people the way you want to be treated. In this business, time is money, and it doesn't make sense to me to string a manager along. If you come to the conclusion it's not going to work, there's no point wasting time. Being up front, saying I like you, but the answer is not going to be yes and here's why. You owe it to the person to tell them why. If it's an issue tied to the committee or board members, those people can change. Sometimes it's no for now, but if it's no forever, nobody has the time for that."

Manager Selection Criteria   When selecting managers, Hook considers several factors, ranging from personal characteristics to investment style and temperament.

"A couple of characteristics that come to mind fall into the honesty and integrity camp. I want a manager to be very square with us, similar to how I want to communicate with the board. If something is going wrong or not going as expected, it makes a lot of sense to communicate that to the investors. Bad news you can deal with as long as I know about it. I'd much rather know about it and not get the surprise three months down the road or after the write-off. Good to keep up the dialogue; it gives us an opportunity to manage up within our organizations."

Hook assesses a manager's mind-set when they meet. "Sitting down, looking the manager in the eye and talking to the guy, you get a sense of many things. They're not going to tell you everything, but you get an understanding of how they will react in certain situations, not just personally but also in investment styles."

Hook finds value in networking with his peers and hearing their criteria and evaluations of various managers. He would like to see more of it. "Networking among foundation and endowment CIOs and staffs, I think, is still probably underutilized. We could all probably use our personal networks better than we do. It does help if you have certain peers at certain schools, from whom you can get their thoughts on certain managers. You're going to uncover things they might not, and vice versa; comparing notes can be very important in the process."

A consultant took Hook and another endowment CIO client on a trip to meet managers, an experience Hook found valuable. "Three of us saw another six or seven managers on the trip. Having another point of view opened up the dialogue and added color to the discussions."

The characteristics of managers they want boil down to character. "At the end of the day, we are looking at firms we think are principled, I don't want to say strong moral fiber, but folks we think have a high degree of integrity. We seek firms we think can manage in dismal markets or have a high degree of ability to navigate while managing risk. A lot can do well when the market does well, but when the market goes south, that's when they distinguish themselves. To the extent we can get a good bit of comfort on that front, that helps us decide as well."

Constructing the Portfolio   Baylor has structured the portfolio with an eye toward managing risk and earning returns from meaningfully sized positions. To mitigate "firm risk," they limit all investment managers to a certain total percentage in the portfolio. Alternative investments generally have a position size of 1 percent.

"Rounding the numbers, that 1 percent gets you a $10 million position. Some managers in the early days, we had $1 million here, $2 million there, but you do the same work whether you do $1 million or $10. I told the committee, '$5 million or nothing—if we're not comfortable with that amount, then we should not be comfortable with any amount.' A minimum of 5 to 10 million is a good round number, a good comfort zone. We have not taken a view that we want to be in say distressed so let's put everything with one manager."

The Baylor portfolio holds three to four distressed-debt mangers, including the first fund they invested in from 1999. "The fund that keeps on giving, after we get distributions, revaluations have kept us at the same level for quite some time." Hook believes having a number of different managers in a space such as distressed or venture capital has been a good decision for them.

In leveraged buyouts, Hook has largely avoided mega-cap buyout funds and has concentrated more in mid to small buyout size funds. "Whether that's good or not, time will tell. From my corporate days, I remembered the saga of RJR Nabisco; such big funds chasing such big deals concerns me, the exit strategy, other issues. They may do well; shame on us if we're not there, but I feel more comfortable staying away from those funds."

Baylor has significantly reduced its long only allocation since Hook moved to Baylor, concentrating a higher percentage of assets in fewer funds, ranging from 3 to 6 percent of exposure. They tend to have at least two managers in every space that they are in and have not devoted any allocations to just one manager in any particular asset class.

"I'm not sure having a manager in every box makes sense in an institutional portfolio. You also may have two managers doing different things in the same space, like a fundamental manager and a quant. We have 10 or 11 traditional or long-only managers and 45 alternative asset managers. It's the old 80/20 rule, with more managers holding smaller positions in alternatives. It makes sense from a risk standpoint. If there's a blowup with any one alternative strategy and you lose 1 percent of a portfolio, it might be painful but you can live with that."

From his banking days Hook recalls an analogy lending officers would use to evaluate the "blow-up risk" of a loan. "We called it 'the burn it on the lawn scenario.' If you lent $2 billion to a multinational, well-capitalized company and it just wasted all the money, would it kill the deal? You wouldn't be as profitable if it happened, but most of the time it did not kill the deal or ruin the company's financial position. If you minimize what you have at risk, if the worst case happens, it's not the end of the world."

Risk Management   At a broad level, the Baylor portfolio has been structured to guard against a year of negative return.

"We have built a portfolio that if markets don't do well, we believe we can still have a good year, one that can work in all seasons. I do not give a lot of credence to saying our portfolio has a volatility of X therefore our risk is Y. Correlations can all move to one when certain events happen. We're trying to build and manage a portfolio that can withstand shocks, that is not going to be hit excessively hard by one certain shock or one certain event, hopefully, even parts of it would be going up."

Hook strives to minimize damage if or when those events happen. "We all know you can't tell when that event is going to happen or what type of event it is going to be. Whether on the order of global terrorism, decline of the dollar, or bird flu, they are all different and all would affect the portfolio to some degree. If those risks did happen, it would not just affect the portfolio, but operations of the university, including attracting new students."

Hook and the committee think strategically about portfolio risk constantly, asking, "Have we missed anything? What have we missed? What could come around the corner and blindside us?"

He analyzes it qualitatively. "We say, 'We think we got this right, but do we really?' When you get to a point that you seem comfortable, that's when something is going to come from left field and bite you, so try not to get too comfortable. We are persistent worriers; consultants are persistent worriers. They need to worry on top of our worries. A never-ending battle, always be aware and always be thinking about it. As we know, things can happen quickly and happen on the other side of the world; a chain reaction happens, and then the unexpected happens."

Goals and Direction   To supplement their efforts, Hook and Pittman started an investment intern program similar to an investment bank "up and out" training program tied to Baylor's business school. Pittman, an adjunct business professor, identifies candidates from among his students. Although a relatively new program, Hook seems pleased with early results. For the first project, "one you only reserve for interns, no full-time employees want to do this," the intern analyzed documents and contracts buried deep in the files to identify certain legacy endowment assets. "It's been an issue for years and years, but wasn't something anybody wanted to spend time on." Given the likely benefit to the endowment, having this intern resource should add value to the portfolio.

Baylor University targeted a $2 billion endowment by 2012 in a program the administration announced early in Hook's tenure. Fortunately for Hook, the school did not expect the existing endowment to deliver all the desired growth. The initiative budgeted for major gifts, so he is not under additional pressure.

Baylor "started with $600 million in 2001 and we have just surpassed $1 billion. In 2001–2002 we dropped into the 500s. It's unlikely that we'll double it in 5 years, but it could happen, if we get the gifts we had anticipated. If we don't get to $2 billion by 2012, I won't look at it as a failure. We earned a real return, in excess of spending, and have real endowment growth. 2001–2002 when the campaign started were tough years to grow. Post-9/11, the tech bubble, it was not the best time to start a campaign. It's a 10-year goal. One always hopes big gifts are around the corner, and we'll start a new capital campaign soon. Without any major gifts, performance has grown the endowment to just over $1 billion."

Hook and one other staff member handle other investment-related tasks such as campus real estate acquisition or divesture. Since having an accessible pool of endowment capital is a relatively recent phenomenon, he continues to educate colleagues on the purpose and use of endowment capital. As he puts it, "fight the 'piggy bank' perception of the endowment."

Even with those concerns, Hook asserts, "Nowhere in there is the desire to put up an excessive amount of risk, just to hit a number. People are much happier with consistent good returns over the long run. It should mean you're doing just fine."

LESSONS, OBSERVATIONS, AND ADVICE

Jonathan Hook offered his thoughts on investments and advice for both institutional and individual investors.

"Diversification may be the only free lunch you get. Institution or individual, make sure you have a fair bit of diversification. Individuals are more likely to be undiversified, but can get there without a whole lot of work and protect themselves, which is critical."

Hook expresses concern about investors getting hung up on fads. "When styles get hot and money rushes in, is that when you want to be there? If you're following too much money, it's probably not the right time."

Attending an investor conference a few years ago, he heard the speaker tell the crowd, "You're stupid if you're in this asset class," and strongly recommend another investment. "I turned to the guy next to and me and said, 'Isn't this the time to be going in the other direction?' Returns bore that out."

To fellow CIOs, Hook repeats his message to get to know the board and the investment committee you serve. "Try to understand, the best you can, their tolerances, what they and you are willing to do and not willing to do. You as CIO can be focused and make sure you're working in the right vein for your organization.

"Making sure your board understands what you're trying to do and why, keeping negative surprises away from them—positive surprises, fine—helps toward longevity. At the same time you have to do what you think is right. Take a position, have the conviction, but knowing the context of the governing group, you can guide the process."

Investment Mistakes

Hook spends more time and effort preventing his own mistakes rather than observing others' mistakes. "We're always concerned that we have made a mistake, before there's any hard data to prove that we did or that we didn't. After a commitment we go through a post mortem, have a session and ask, 'Do we have buyer's remorse? Is there something we missed?' We try to check ourselves; maybe we didn't see something and after the fact it's a glaring error. Nothing has bitten us—not to say one won't happen."

Hook identifies getting into investments at the wrong time in their life cycle as a major problem for investors. Before he arrived, Baylor made that mistake in March 2000, choosing a technology and telecom long/short fund as one of their first equity hedge funds investments, at the peak of the tech bubble.

"Somehow the manager forgot to short. The single worst fund the school has had in its short history. The portfolio manager came out of a good shop, an analyst that became a portfolio manager. The Peter Principle kicked in the same time the environment turned into literally the worst ever, a bad situation. Baylor got out with 30 percent of its capital, but it was a tiny position, it didn't hurt that much. I am not blaming the previous managers of the assets. Maybe if I had been there at the time we might have done the same thing, so I don't want to kick sand on anyone. A lot of people were running around with unrealistic expectations."

The institution learned a lesson.

"Those were good times, 'blow and go,' everything running up 40 percent a year, until it didn't. Those are the kinds of things we want to watch. The level of experience of the manager was not what we'd want to see in a new manager going forward. A good analyst decided to do something different, the skill set didn't transfer."

Fortunately, they have not repeated the experience, and Hook aims to keep it that way.

"Knock on wood—we have not been burned at this point and would love to say it will never happen. If you're in it long enough, it will happen. It's more about the need to keep your guard up, keep the vigil and don't shortcut. That's probably when people get caught, they shortcut the process. That's what bites them in the rear a year or two down the road, and it's why we keep asking if we missed something to make sure we didn't."

Issues and Concerns

Hook views the collateralized loan obligation (CLO)/collateralized debt obligation (CDO) market as a concern and says, "It could be scary, seeing something pop there and having ripple effects; it certainly is possible. Not too concerned about too many hedge fund strategies, although certain managers should not hang out the shingle. We pick hedge funds by manager as opposed to the strategy. So it's not a factor." Basically, Baylor chooses a hedge fund manager because they believe in the manager's skill and ability to produce returns under any market condition, including overcrowding.

Hook reiterates his concern about the large-cap buyout market since it has attracted a tremendous amount of capital.

"I do wonder about any events that may suck liquidity out of the system. We know there's a lot of liquidity in the market, rates are reasonably low, financing terms are easy. Who's left holding the bag? I have not figured out the answer, and it is something we're concerned about."

RETURN ON LEADERSHIP

Jonathan Hook represents the advent of the next generation of foundation and endowment CIOs. Although approximately the same age as many of his peers, he has relatively less portfolio management experience, making his transition from banking to successful CIO in just over five years a remarkable achievement. Lacking traditional investment experience has not hurt him; it has helped. Approaching the role from the perspective of a CEO has served him well. For CIOs managing mid-sized endowments now or in the future, Hook provides a good model for performing the role. Hook's practical, successful approach suggests that in addition to investment skills, future CIOs will need to develop leadership, managerial, and marketing skills. Jonathan D. Hook represents a harbinger and model of the hybrid CIO/CEO to come.

CHAPTER 14

Navigating New Investment Waters

Daniel J. Kingston, Managing Director, Portfolio Management, Vulcan Capital

Dan Kingston oversees the investment portfolio for Vulcan Capital, the investment arm of entrepreneur Paul Allen's family office. Earning an MBA at the Wharton School after a brief military career, until joining Vulcan, Kingston spent his entire investment career in nonprofit and endowed institutions, most of the time at Stanford Management Company. Having gained experience at a leading endowment management company, learned from such talented colleagues, and managed the assets of a leading foundation, Kingston has the historical knowledge and the progressive vision to lead the foundation and endowment investment community into an uncertain future and represents a new breed of investment officer.

Navigating ships on the water as an officer in the Coast Guard, Kingston explored his interest in adventure and developed leadership and management skills. His skills and interests have given him an affinity for entrepreneurial people, causes, and thinking and the ability to navigate the investment environment in new ways. As part of an entrepreneurial family office, Kingston will be well positioned to understand and manage the next wave of foundation wealth creation.

In addition to developing strategic and tactical asset allocation, he is responsible for Vulcan's investments with external managers. He has direct experience in public equity, private equity, venture capital, real assets, alternative investments, and fixed-income areas. Additionally, Kingston serves on a number of investment advisory boards and several nonprofit boards. He is currently chairman of the Kauffman Scholars, Inc. board.

Previously, Mr. Kingston was chief investment officer (CIO) at the Kauffman Foundation, where he was responsible for managing the foundation's investment function. Prior to the Kauffman Foundation, Mr. Kingston was a managing director at the Stanford Management Company. In that post, he was responsible for the development and management of internal investment strategies for Stanford University's investment portfolio. He first joined Stanford in 1990 after having spent time as a financial analyst with Hewlett Packard Corporation's investment department. Before starting a career in investments, Mr. Kingston spent five years as an officer on active duty with the U.S. Coast Guard.

Mr. Kingston holds a bachelor's degree in science from the U.S. Coast Guard Academy and an MBA from the Wharton School of the University of Pennsylvania. In addition, he is a current charter holder of the Chartered Financial Analyst (CFA) designation.

BACKGROUND

Like many of his colleagues, as a youngster Dan Kingston did not have his heart set on becoming a CIO. Instead, like a lot of boys growing up in the Apollo era of the 1960s, perhaps watching *I Dream of Jeannie*, he wanted to become an astronaut. Learning that many astronauts had attended a military service academy like West Point or Annapolis, he pursued that educational and professional path.

"Unfortunately, I learned during the process that my eyes weren't good enough to fly. My career as an astronaut ended at the ripe old age of 17 years." Kingston's father, a career Coast Guard officer, encouraged him to apply to the Coast Guard Academy instead. "Even with glasses, the Coast Guard lets you drive ships." He accepted a commission, assuming he would follow family tradition and make the Coast Guard his career.

The Coast Guard sent Kingston to Hawaii after graduation for his first assignment as a gunnery officer on board one of the Coast Guard's largest cutters. Later he became the ship's training officer. "It was a line officer position, with nine people reporting to me. It was a tremendous challenge and incredibly rewarding." Both jobs required heavy interaction with the U.S. Navy, experience that positioned him for the next assignment, working in the Readiness Division at the 14th District Headquarters in Honolulu.

Readiness is unofficial Coast Guard code for the defense planning function and required Kingston to coordinate with the other branches of the armed services, particularly the U.S. Navy. "Eventually, I was coassigned to a naval defense command. That experience gave me a chance to look at the world from a more strategic standpoint, and I discovered I really enjoyed working on the bigger picture rather than line activity." Taking classes at the University of Hawaii, he began to envision a life beyond the military. "I realized I wouldn't be able to do the things that I wanted to do if I stayed in the Coast Guard." Since he had studied management and engineering at the academy, returning to graduate school for an MBA seemed like a logical step. "In any case, it would give me a year or two to figure out what I wanted to be when I grew up." He soon moved from the "sunny shores of Hawaii to the historic banks of the Schuylkill River" to attend the Wharton School at the University of Pennsylvania.

"Not knowing exactly what I wanted to do, I went to a lot of presentations—investment banking, investment management, strategy consulting. It was a great way to learn all the possibilities and get dinner at the same time. Five years of triathlons and surfing in Hawaii hadn't prepared me for the real world."

The Wharton School

During his first year of business school, Kingston took part in a contest that helped him set sail on the next phase of his career. Contestants in the Merrill Lynch Investment Challenge receive a hypothetical $100,000 to invest. "My friend Sam Lee and I realized we weren't going win by making conservative investments. The limited time horizon and structure of the game encouraged risk taking. Sam took the pessimistic route, and I took the optimistic path; between the two of us, we figured that we would win." Remembering "the January Effect"—the tendency for stocks to perform well in January—from class, Kingston took advantage of it to turn the hypothetical portfolio of $100,000 into about $300,000 and won the contest.

"It was, of course, complete luck," he says. "It taught me the importance of luck in investing. Having good performance isn't proof of anything. It's having repeated performance under various environments that counts." The lesson still resonates with him. "Too many investors chase yesterday's returns when they ought to be looking at the conditions that led to that performance."

Kingston decided to pursue a career in investment management, thinking it made the best use of his mathematical skills and affinity for strategic thinking. Luck, in the form of his sister, played a role in finding him the right summer job. "My sister helped me get an internship at Hewlett Packard in their Investment Division. It was a terrific assignment and allowed me to look at investment strategy and asset allocation from the vantage point of a plan sponsor."

A specific assignment taught him important investment analysis skills and gave him experience evaluating new asset types. "Because of my engineering background, I was assigned the project of reviewing and analyzing the collateralized mortgage obligation [CMO] portfolio. At that point in time, 1989, CMOs were relatively obscure investment vehicles. I was able to understand how value could be created by parsing risk, so that each investor gets the amount of risk that they wanted."

Stanford Management Company

Hewlett Packard's location in beautiful northern California enhanced the good experience. Having grown up in the area, upon graduating from Wharton, he returned there just as Stanford University was forming the Stanford Management Company (SMC). Similar to the formation of the Harvard Management Company, Stanford recognized it needed a professional investment management organization with a different culture than a university to manage its endowment most effectively.

Four hundred people applied for the assistant portfolio manager position that Kingston eventually accepted. Most university assets were managed by external managers, but roughly 25 percent were managed internally in the "Internally Managed Funds" area. He joined that unit, reporting to Charles Froland and working with David Russ (now the CIO of Dartmouth College).

"Both Charles and David are extraordinary individuals. Charles got me incredibly excited about the SMC opportunity. He was remarkably articulate and had an amazing sense of perspective. At the same time, David is one of the most intellectually curious people that I know. I learned an immeasurable amount from both of them. Charles Froland taught me the difference between strategic and tactical investing. David taught me a good deal of what I know about the fixed-income markets and trading dynamics."

Stanford Management worked closely with the renowned Stanford finance faculty to convert investment theories into pragmatic investment strategies. Kingston says that many common strategies, like meaningful venture allocations, portable alpha, and style analysis, were initially implemented at SMC in the early 1990s.

"Bill Sharpe had a consulting practice, and limited himself to only 10 clients. Fortunately, the school where he was a professor, Stanford University, was privileged to be one of those few clients. Having an academic mind-set and being willing to explore new areas is an incredible advantage in the investment markets."

During the first few years, Kingston developed tactical asset allocation models, traded derivatives, and managed a real estate investment trust and equity and fixed-income portfolios. He thought it was perfect training for understanding risk taking and managing assets, because it helped during his first exposure to a bear market in 1994.

"After seeing the fixed-income market get to an unsustainable place in 1993, we saw the reversal in 1994. We managed to achieve a respectable return that year in fixed income, but only if measured on a relative basis. Being the tallest midget was poor consolation."

Five years later, that bear market experience benefited him when the equity markets had their own period of overextension. Within that period, Russ and Froland left SMC and Laurie Hoagland, then president of SMC and now CIO of the Hewlett Foundation, named him the director, and subsequently managing director, of internally managed funds, responsible for internally managed investments in all of the asset classes.

"The strategy effectively meant we did whatever investments we thought we could do as well or cheaper than external managers, or strategies where we wanted direct control. The former included fixed-income, private equity distributions, and commodities management. The latter included a series of future overlays and equity hedges. Those hedges mitigated a great deal of the exposure during the technology bubble and helped Stanford weather that storm."

Kingston gained broad investment experience and developed a wide array of skills during his time at SMC. The most critical and invaluable experience he gained was direct investing. "That experience cannot be gotten through a textbook. It is incredibly helpful to understand what it's like to be in the shoes of a manager that you're hiring." It helps him analyze how the manager views risk and recognize how that might change during up and down cycles. Although investors can probably glean that information from talking and interacting with managers, "there are few substitutes for having held a bad position overnight and recognizing when it's time to cut losses. You understand that analyzing investment managers is not about performance, it's about their process."

The Kauffman Foundation

After a dozen years at Stanford, Kingston joined the Kauffman Foundation in 2003. With 12 years of trading experience, he had several job offers from hedge funds.

"While those opportunities would have likely been financially more rewarding, there wouldn't be the same emotional satisfaction. The Kauffman Foundation's mission supported not only education, a cause that I believe in passionately, but also entrepreneurialism, the creation of value in our society. It's an extraordinary place."

Kingston shares a thoughtful perspective on the true value of foundations. "Most people tend to measure the importance of a foundation based on the size of its asset base. That's a bit like judging the quality of a company from its stock price. It's not the size of the assets that is important; it's what's being done with them that is critical. Having a large base of assets enables some foundations to do tremendous projects. However, ultimately the success of those projects should be really measured by the second-order effects. Does the grant really facilitate permanent change?"

At the Kauffman Foundation, Kingston observed an interesting set of dynamics. Its educational mission tends to attract personnel with more liberal political leanings while the entrepreneurial side tends to bring in more conservative viewpoints. "Election season can be quite fun with lunchroom debates that can become incredibly animated. In addition, being in the center of the country, in Kansas City, gives it a perspective that is frequently lost on either coast."

Unlike most foundations, Kauffman's entrepreneurial mission applied directly to investments. "The experience gave me tremendous insights into the importance of innovation on society, and how that innovation can ultimately be monetized." Kingston interacted frequently with the Kauffman Fellows, a program that had been spun off the foundation several years prior to Kingston's arrival. "Started in 1995, its goal was to bring technical professionals into venture capital, and ultimately expand the scale of venture capital activity. Though other factors contributed to the boom in venture capital in the late 1990s, the program succeeded perhaps too well."

Kingston found the investment portfolio in relatively good shape, well diversified with a number of outstanding managers, when he joined Kauffman. He focused on a key issue initially that he describes as "a return driven asset allocation process."

Kingston elaborates. "The perverse implication of that approach is that as expected return goes down, that suggests taking more risk to make up the difference. The risk of the portfolio swings with the market opportunity. When expected returns are high, you don't have to take as much risk to achieve your target, while the opposite is true when opportunities fall.

"Risk taking should not be dependent on the market; it should instead be focused on the institution's capacity to take risk. I prefer the term *risk capacity* to *risk tolerance* because to me the latter implies more subjectivity. Institutional risk capacity needs to be measured, and while it clearly has some subjective features, it must be systematically assessed. Using a historic risk tolerance or peer evaluation is only part of the analyses. Instead, you really need to know the institutional needs.

"Foundations often have the ability over time to scale their grants up and down based on their assets. The adjustment process isn't easy, particularly when extreme events suddenly occur. Still, losing funds is particularly challenging for a foundation. Unlike a university with a development office, if you lose the money, it's very difficult to make up for it." With assets and investments providing the primary revenue stream, losing money in the portfolio has a more pronounced effect on foundations.

During his tenure, the Kauffmann investment committee approved a degree of discretion for the CIO for the first time. While that may seem like a significant step for many organizations, in many respects it was less important for the Kauffman Foundation. "The governance structure worked especially well there. It was a small, knowledgeable investment committee that was able to move fast when market opportunities occurred." He rarely experienced having insufficient time for the committee to get involved in important matters, but knowing that organizations change over time, he thought it important to establish more lasting structure.

Vulcan Capital

In many ways, the Kauffman Foundation and Vulcan, Inc. were established with similar organizational missions: to be catalysts for change. The foundation explicitly will only fund any one project for just a few years, during the most risky stages, believing that a successful program will eventually receive other sources of funding. If the foundation's funding ends and other grant makers do not recognize the program's value by funding it, the foundation will concur with the market view that it should probably cease to exist. Likewise, Vulcan, Inc. is an organization that is dedicated to changing the world. Named after the Roman god of fire, Vulcan, its goal is to transform great ideas into reality.

"Coming to Vulcan Capital was an extraordinary opportunity to start a team from the ground up, to put a new structure in place, and scale it up appropriately. Paul Allen is clearly a visionary and will leave a lasting legacy on our society. In addition to his seminal work at Microsoft, his family office is involved in projects like space travel, energy efficiency, wireless world and breakthrough brain research. The organization looks at what's happening in the world and asks where can we add a little bit of knowledge and a little bit of capital to produce dramatic change?"

Kingston brings a top-down view to all the investments to ensure portfolio cohesion. To accomplish that objective, he needs to understand the existing investments, the prospective internal opportunities, and the potential external opportunities. "Our external strategy in many respects is a completion portfolio. We want to have the best opportunities populate our portfolio. In some cases, we're in the best position to execute those strategies, but in others it will be an external team or organization."

Addressing unfamiliar tax issues provides a new challenge for Kingston at Vulcan Capital, requiring him to evaluate manager performance net of fees and net of estimated taxes. "It has profound implications on how you would structure a portfolio. The typical endowment structure doesn't translate perfectly; consequently, the structure needs to be tailored specifically to Vulcan's needs."

Vulcan receives an enormous amount of flexibility as a positive trade-off for paying taxes. Its internal private equity capability gives it the ability to capture "extraordinary" market opportunities. "While Vulcan Capital clearly wants a diversified base, it also wants, consistent with its dynamic culture, to take meaningful positions when warranted. That kind of operational control is impossible within the current endowment and foundation structure."

BEING CHIEF INVESTMENT OFFICER

Kingston thinks of his own ability to add value when he thinks about his investment philosophy. "Each of us must be willing to ask of ourselves the same question we ask managers we hire, 'What's our edge?' Aside from institutional advantages, it ultimately probably comes down to our discipline, knowledge, and relationships. Most of those are competitive advantages are hard to defend. That means producing sustainable outperformance is always going to be difficult, and to achieve it you have to focus on the issues that will ultimately move the needle."

Chief Information Officer

When he first became a CIO, he frequently received mail addressed to the chief information officer, the title frequently abbreviated "CIO" in a typical corporation.

"It got me thinking that perhaps the title wasn't so far off. In a real way, my job was to absorb, process, and manage information to make good investment decisions. I realized that investment management was really, in effect, information management. Obviously, having a monopoly on a piece of information can be incredibly valuable, but equally valuable is the ability to understand what to do with the massive amount of information around all of us. Most people recognize that the challenge today is less about getting the information, and more about making sense of it."

To get that information Kingston taps into all the sources he can: books, publications, managers, analysts. "Many participants see the investment process as a direct competition; however, there is enormous room for cooperation. Much of the work many of us do is redundant, and there's still enormous room for creating communities for sharing information. Some of that's occurring now informally, but it could be more pervasive and more structured."

In processing information, some investors take a top-down approach, while others prefer bottom-up. However, Kingston believes they don't have to be mutually exclusive. "Bottom-up analyses tend to work better for shorter time horizons, while top-down approaches work best longer term. I try to have a process that covers all the different time periods. When I was in Hawaii, like a lot of people, I learned to surf." Smiling, he explains, "While that might seem like the farthest thing from alphas and betas I deal with today, I took a few valuable lessons from my surfing days. Not every wave is worth riding, and when the better waves come around, you had better be able to recognize them and be ready to take off."

Kingston believes the only way to process the endless amount of information is to parse the responsibilities among different groups of individuals. "The managers typically focus on individual security opportunities, the asset manager focuses on asset opportunities, CIOs look at those opportunities in the context of the long-term strategy, and the investment committee protects the integrity of the long-term strategy. The CIO is responsible for managing the flow of information, but throughout this value chain there is decision making and oversight."

Asset Allocation and Portfolio Management

Asset allocation provides the crucial framework for evaluating investments, but only if used actively. "A number of institutions go through the process in a rote fashion, and do not genuinely understand the implicit trade-offs. If you believe that asset allocation is one of the most important decisions in the investment process, and if you believe the world is not static, then you should recognize that changes in the asset allocation are essential." Determining how to make those changes under uncertain conditions and with limited control, the typical situation for most investors, creates a challenge.

"History is filled with anecdotes of asset allocation failures. As a result, many institutions naturally have an aversion to market timing. Making up the missed return can take a long time. The fact of the matter, though, is that investments return is measured by change per unit of time. Therefore, if you don't consider timing, you've missed an important part of the objective. Institutions clearly need to be concerned with capricious changes to their allocations, but that doesn't imply rigid adherence."

Kingston encourages institutions to adopt flexible allocation mandates, an approach that provides necessary structure without forcing an allocation in overvalued markets. "The goal is to constantly search for the best trade-off of return and risk. Even at the height of the tech bubble in 2000, substantial opportunities existed in other parts of the markets. Reallocating from growth to value equities would have eliminated much of the pain of the reversal." He thinks that the best risk mitigation is strong accessible cash flow, and that flow need not come from just bonds.

He gives an example of an asset allocation framework and what instruments it would include:

- *Value creation.* Growth equity, activist, and private equity segmented by sector/geographic/liquidity factors.
- *Subordinated cash flows.* High-yield bonds and value equity.
- *Relative value.* Hedge funds that identify and profit from disparities in valuation.
- *Priority cash flows.* Either deflationary with nominal bonds, or inflationary with inflation-linked bonds and core real estate.

Generating Ideas   "The more you understand how the market functions, the more you can see the many investment opportunities that exist every day." Unfortunately, large institutions cannot capitalize on many opportunities, either because the vehicles are too small to absorb large amounts of capital or they have too short a window for most institutions to act. These conditions lead institutions to hire managers that can take advantage of these short-term opportunities. "From time to time, though, opportunities that fall in the purview of endowment and foundations will occur. That was the case in high-yield bonds in 1989 and 2002."

Before acting on an idea, Kingston says investors need to understand the type of risk that they're taking on, particularly as it relates to their current portfolio. "They should ask themselves what they are seeing that thousands of other intelligent people are missing." To reinforce his point, Kingston refers to a favorite quote by George Santayana, "Skepticism is the chastity of the intellect, and it is shameful to surrender it too soon." He recommends that investors consider why the opportunity exists, how long it will last, and how the market will respond. "In 2000, it was easy to foresee the proliferation of hedge funds. It was a natural response by many institutions, which were concerned about volatility. The question today is whether investors are getting what they really expected."

Having great ideas is not enough. Investors have to be willing to implement them. "Historically, endowments and foundations have shown a greater willingness to try new ideas and sources. Unlike many corporate cultures, innovation has been the currency of the endowment world. Many institutions are concerned with what others are doing, while the endowment and foundations world have been advancing by incrementally implementing what they see as the right approach."

Contrarian Thinking   When looking for investment ideas, Kingston strives to find situations where there is more opportunity than capital. "Look for places where you receive above average return for the dollars invested. One way of doing this is by being a contrarian—going where the capital's not."

Being contrarian is not as easy as just doing the opposite of everyone else. Investors need to understand the conventional wisdom in the market so they know what they're being contrarian about. To diverge from the pack confidently and successfully, investors need to have enough good insight into a situation to conclude that most other investors are incorrect and must have the conviction to act.

"We all know the old saying about succeeding unconventionally: It's often second best. Some academicians have suggested that the return that you get for being a contrarian is a risk premium—for the risk of potentially losing your job."

Contrarian investors usually have history on their side against the current pervasive sentiment. "We've been trained to be cautious about claims that 'it's different this time.' However, sometimes the circumstances really are different, so I try to make room for ideas and thoughts that contradict my own." Investors naturally want to hear support for their opinion and it takes "enormous discipline and intellectual honesty" to admit that you could be wrong. Kingston urges investors to listen and understand contradictory opinions. "You have to make sure you are your own devil's advocate."

Greatest Worries Kingston worries about "what most CIO's worry about": tail risks and the fact that unlikely events actually occur quite frequently. "We have statistical methods for managing normal return distributions. However, second-order effects can cause a chain reaction. That was the case in 1987, 1989, 1991, 1994, 1998, and 2000–2003. We've been privileged not to have faced another shock since then. By 2003 though, risk premiums had adjusted to reasonable levels." Low risk premiums can be dangerous because investors don't price in appropriate risks, so when an unexpected event happens, "as it usually does," they realize too late that they're not getting rewarded for the risk, and panic. That panic leads to other surprises and other panics.

For that reason, he generally tries to understand not only his rationale for investing, but also that of other participants. "Such situations can create unusual investment opportunities for those institutions with the right fortitude and time horizons. In each of the dislocations that occurred in the years I mentioned, there were investors that benefited greatly."

Selecting Managers Kingston describes two fundamental approaches to hiring managers. The first is an outsourced model replicating what would otherwise be accomplished in-house, but presumably for lower costs. "That model is largely a matter of scale. They can provide attentive service at a lower cost by sharing the overhead of other mandates."

The other approach is finding talented managers and letting them employ their skills freely. Due to opportunity and risk management, though, this type of manager cannot scale. "Typically, size is the enemy of performance. Interestingly, though, at the start of an opportunity, size can be the friend of performance. In that case, a large capital base allows for better infrastructure and helps the firm recruit the best talent. The other drawback to giving an investment manager free reign is that moving a significant portion of an institution's assets, say, one day from value equity to another day in capital structure arbitrage, ends up fundamentally undermining the importance of the strategic asset allocation process."

Governance

Governance structure should change as the size and complexity of an investment program changes.

"In early stages, having a set of volunteer investment committee members managing the assets may practically be the best option." As assets grow the benefits of employing full-time professionals begin to outweigh the costs. Hiring a CIO allows the investment committee to fulfill its main purpose: oversight.

"Management of the assets needs to be separated from the oversight of those assets. You want to see the people in the best position to make decisions, making those decisions. Have a second group evaluate how well those decisions are being made."

Kingston believes most boards lack the specialized knowledge needed to oversee investments and should delegate responsibility for governing the CIO to the investment committee. "Just as it does little good for a CIO to second-guess the stock selection of a manager, it does little good for an investment committee to second-guess individual manager selections a CIO makes. Instead, the committee should focus on developing reasonable reporting mechanisms to ensure the program is being carried out as they want, and in an efficient and prudent manner."

His ideal investment committee includes mostly individuals with multi-asset class experience, such as other CIOs. "Having an investment specialist, such as a venture capitalist or public-equity manager may not provide enough perspective. It's similar to having a divisional manager for a large corporation providing counsel to a small company. The advice is often good, but may not include the full perspective of the needs of the entire organization."

Hiring and Managing Staff   Kingston hires people that match the culture and mission of the organization. "For the organization to be successful over the long run, you have to have people in the investment area match the ethos of the organization. At Stanford, people were intellectually curious. To retain them, I purposely found projects that would allow them to grow and Stanford to benefit from that growth."

At the Kauffman Foundation he primarily screened for people that seemed genuinely dedicated to the mission and suited to the intellectually bright culture. "It's important for those investing to see the fruits of their efforts, and where appropriate, have a voice in how that capital is used."

Vulcan is a particularly dynamic organization. "Having players that can change with this organization as it changes is important. They'll need to have a broad set of skills and the flexibility to move quickly on opportunities."

As portfolios become increasingly complicated, organizations need larger investment staffs to monitor existing investments and research new opportunities. Kingston recognizes that smaller foundations will have trouble establishing depth in its investment management team. Even if they can make the economic case for devoting more resources to the investment area, they cannot make a human resources case for adding a disproportionate number of employees. "As a result, foundations can be particularly susceptible to the outsourced CIO models. It makes quite a bit of sense for smaller organizations to pool resources and share headcount."

LESSONS, OBSERVATIONS, AND ADVICE

Kingston avoids giving general investment advice saying, "Free advice is worth what you pay for it." On a more serious note, since different investors have different needs, he believes generic advice is not that helpful. Nonetheless, he shares experiences and lessons learned.

Investment Advice

"Aside from the commonly touted principle of diversification, I would encourage individuals and institutions to really consider the amount of risk that they're taking. In some cases they're taking too much of it, but more often than not, they're not taking enough of it." Participants in 401(k)s or other self-managed retirement accounts in particular tend to have much higher allocations to bonds and cash than suitable for long investment horizons.

"The British Special Forces have a motto, 'Who dares wins.' Over the long run, you have to take risk to get return. Some call it taking equity risk, but it's just taking really incrementally higher risk, whether in the form of equity risk, credit risk, or liquidity. The job of any investor is to get appropriately compensated for that risk, and when possible, more than appropriately compensated."

How Investors Succeed or Fail

Kingston expresses novel reasons for his concerns about groupthink. "It's easy for all of us to fall into the comfort zone of groupthink. However, if each investor is not making independent judgments, the basic premise of efficient markets can breakdown. Markets only act efficient in the aggregate when individual mistakes wash out, not when a systematic bias invades the process. It's incumbent upon everyone to contribute to that efficient market.

"While many investors look for sages of wisdom, there's really no shortcut to understanding how a business, how the economy, and how the markets works."

Kingston finds that investors often miss great investment opportunities, because they fail to reevaluate their investment thesis after periods of change. "Facts behind long-accepted notions can change, but mental inertia doesn't allow most to recognize it."

He offers Dell Computers as an example. The stock once sold at a price-to-earnings (P/E) ratio ranging between 5 and 10. Many investors considered it a cyclical, and therefore risky, stock. "In the late 1990s, we saw a secular shift in the purchase of computers. Those who saw that shift did very well."

Experience living in Kansas City convinced Kingston that people have not properly evaluated the trade-offs between the Midwest and the coasts. "Quality of life for many people in coastal cities is being eroded by high costs and population growth, while the quality of life in Kansas City and other parts of the Midwest has only improved with time."

Anticipating likely counterarguments, Kingston says, "Saving several hundreds of thousands of dollars on your home cost greatly affords a significant amount of travel around the world. People prefer to look at the world with old glasses, rather than getting a new prescription."

Learning by Example

Kingston learned through painful experience that one of the hardest parts of investing is getting the timing right.

"Opportunities can stay that way for years, and bubbles can get even larger. At Stanford, we believed that the equity markets were overvalued in the late 1990s and moved to mitigate some of the risk exposure in the portfolio. Initially at least, it was a classic failure—a good idea at the wrong time. The market eventually turned in 2000, but not without going through months of painful returns."

He advises investors making such moves to have the knowledge and ability to deal with being early or wrong. "If you can't plan for that possibility, then perhaps you shouldn't make the investment."

Future Challenges for Foundations and Endowments

Kingston identifies two factors that benefited endowed institutions over the past 20 years. "First, a secular fall in interest rates caused falling discount rates and rising asset values. This was a one-time event. Second, led by a few key institutions, they were at the forefront of an expanding investment horizon. For the incremental risk of being pioneers, the organizations that were first to expand into asset classes beyond cash, bonds, and stocks generally got rewarded an incremental return premium. Until now, it's been a relatively easy strategy; go where others are not and collect the premium for investing capital in undercapitalized markets."

Today, asset classes like international markets, private equity, emerging markets, venture capital, and hedge funds all belong to the mainstream. Before, institutions had only three asset classes: cash, bonds, and domestic stocks. "However, the marginal value of an incremental asset class is not going to be substantial beyond seven or eight in the mix."

For those reasons, he thinks replicating the returns of the past 20 years will be very difficult. "The challenge now is to perform better, because you no longer have the wind at your back and it will be difficult to be materially different from your peers."

Kingston predicts endowments and foundations will contend with huge capital flows from other institutions attracted by past performance of these assets. "Presumably, they don't recognize that the environment that produced those returns is very different today. Many of the opportunities are not scalable and will not withstand the enormous flow of capital.

"The merger arbitrage segment of the hedge fund market provides a vivid example. Fifteen years ago it had a historic return of 16 percent with only 8 percent volatility, and therefore a very attractive Sharpe ratio." Kingston quotes the economist Joseph Schumpeter: "However, as Schumpeter suggested, 'success breeds the seeds of it own destruction.' More capital flowed into the segment, managers began to commoditize that risk, and gradually it became a cost-of-capital business."

Because he believes that proliferating hedge funds are attacking much of the market inefficiencies, Kingston thinks investment managers now need to focus on incenting the creation of value in the economy.

"Will Rogers once said, 'Buy land, they ain't making any more of it.' When I lived in Hawaii and Mauna Kea would erupt, I saw new land being created. Now that we investors have largely explored the world, our next challenge is to create new land."

In his view, the urge to create value partially explains the substantial growth in private equity and activist funds. "Institutions recognize that governance issues at corporations often don't lead to the best results. Passive investment management is not sufficient for extracting full value."

Career Advice

Individuals starting a career in investments should resist specialization and gain experience in a variety of asset classes. "Because the environment has gotten more complicated, investment professionals have been getting "silo-ed" into single-asset-class specialties, often to our detriment." As a result, Kingston adds, "people tend to view the world through their narrow venture capital or hedge fund prism."

Individuals should develop deep understanding of specific assets, but if an individual hopes to manage large pools of capital, it is critical for the person to get exposure to different asset classes. "Corporations learned this a long time ago, and intentionally rotate their rising stars among various roles and divisions, so they get a more complete picture of the enterprise."

Important Influences

Grateful for the opportunity, mentoring, and education, Kingston says, "I owe a lot to the wisdom that I received from my colleagues at Stanford. Charles Froland, David Russ, Anne Cascells, and Laurie Hoagland have all taught me a tremendous amount.

"However, I would be remiss if I didn't mention Rod Adams. Even though he passed away shortly before I arrived at Stanford, his work was etched indelibly on the Stanford investment landscape. In more ways than most people can appreciate, his work pervades the entire endowment community."

DISCOVERING NEW INVESTMENT WORLDS

Combining his love of adventure and the unknown with his leadership and analytical skills has served Kingston well. He has developed an enviable record of investment experience, a strong body of investment knowledge, and innovative ways of thinking about investing. For a relatively young CIO, he has a solid grounding in the past and his hands firmly on the wheel of the future. Dan Kingston stands ready to navigate portfolios to vast, unexplored waters.

CHAPTER 15

Invest without Emotion, Act with Conviction

Mark W. Yusko, Chief Investment Officer, Morgan Creek Capital Management

O ne of the youngest and most prominent chief investment officers (CIOs), Mark Yusko of Morgan Creek Capital Management, has accomplished more in his 14-year career in the foundation and endowment investment world than many people accomplish in a lifetime.

After a few years in the private sector, he joined Notre Dame as an investment officer and then became the CIO of University of North Carolina. At UNC, he led the transformation of the investment office into a management company, taking in assets from other schools and gaining a reputation as an expert proponent of alternative investments. Yusko has suffered hardship along the way, particularly the untimely death of the visionary leader that recruited him to UNC.

Mentored and supported by leading investors and board members, Yusko envisioned and promoted the outsourced CIO model before founding an asset management company to provide it and other endowment-style investment services to investors. Yusko runs Morgan Creek Capital Management and serves as the CIO, overseeing over $4 billion in assets.

Some question his motives and while it takes savvy career management and self-confidence to become an investment management entrepreneur, it also takes strong investment philosophies and performance. Having those qualities, Yusko represents a relevant CIO for today and tomorrow.

Yusko is the president and CIO of Morgan Creek Capital Management, LLC, a firm he founded in July 2004 to offer investment services utilizing the university endowment management model, including an "outsourced CIO" service.

Prior to forming Morgan Creek, Yusko served as the CIO for the University of North Carolina at Chapel Hill (UNC) from 1998 to 2004 and founded the UNC Management Company (UNCMC) in July of 2002 to manage the UNC endowment and other endowment assets within the UNC system. Total assets under management were $1.5 billion. Prior to joining UNC, he was the senior investment director for the University of Notre Dame investment office, an organization he joined in October 1993.

Yusko received his BS with honors in biology and chemistry from the University of Notre Dame in 1985 and an MBA in accounting and finance from the University of Chicago in 1987. He serves on several investment partnership advisory boards and on the boards of the MCNC Endowment, the Weaver Foundation, and Carolina Meadows.

BACKGROUND

Mark Yusko grew up in an "investment agnostic" family. He went to Notre Dame planning to be an architect, decided against it, switched to pre-med, and graduated with a degree in biology and chemistry. After ruling out medical school, he planned to join Arthur Andersen in consulting, but since he lacked business experience, an Andersen partner urged Yusko to apply to business school. He attended the University of Chicago and started learning about investments, but felt no special affinity for it at the time.

Upon graduation, he joined MMI, an Illinois insurance company. "If I were a resume inflator, I'd say I was an M&A analyst, but I was a business analyst for the CFO as we were purchasing smaller insurance companies. My life has been a series of happy accidents. A few months after I joined, the portfolio manager for the company retired, my boss and I took over the portfolio, and I handled fixed-income investing."

Yusko then joined Disciplined Investment Advisors, an Evanston, Illinois, firm led by two professors from Northwestern University. "It was the first time finance professors had launched an investment firm where they had full-time jobs as professors and were consulting on the side." That arrangement foreshadowed the progression of his career. Their motto, emblazoned on brown "collector's item" coffee mugs, was "Invest without Emotion." Applying quantitative tools developed on Northwestern's large computer systems to investing, they indoctrinated Yusko in the value investing style.

"I might have stayed forever but for another happy accident. There's a story about the football coach Lou Holtz. He had a lifetime contract at the University of Minnesota unless Notre Dame called." Similarly, Yusko got the call from Notre Dame. "I was meeting with the CIO, Scott Malpass, and he asked if I wanted to come there. Absolutely, I signed up."

The shift to managing endowment assets from managing portfolios led Yusko to one of his first career "aha moments." "I really thought I'd miss markets. I'd been a bond manager, a stock picker. What I learned early on at Notre Dame was that security selection has little to do with portfolio performance. It's all about asset allocation. I got interested in really perfecting a model of asset allocation, strategic versus tactical, portfolio construction, and manager selection."

Harvard's Jack Meyer became a mentor. "He took me under his wing, and after a time, started to nudge me out of the nest. I would get calls about CIO jobs. Jack would give them my name, saying he thought Mark should be a CIO somewhere." Yusko refused to budge, "I'm perfectly happy to be the number two at Notre Dame, my alma mater; I don't want to leave."

About five years into his tenure at Notre Dame, he considered an opportunity at University of Chicago, his other alma mater. The hiring committee told him, "We love you, but we love Bill Spitz better. You're the number two choice." They asked Yusko to wait while they pursued Spitz. When the phone did finally ring, the University of North Carolina at Chapel Hill wanted to talk to him about an opportunity. When he told his wife about the job, she said, "Take it, I think I'd like to live in North Carolina," so Yusko agreed to meet.

"I met with Michael Hooker, the chancellor, and Max Chapman, the chairman of the board. Michael Hooker had a vision that really changed my life. He said, 'Why do all small schools try to build a Yale-like portfolio? They can't do it. They don't have Yale resources, Yale people, Yale assets. There's no chance that they're going to build that portfolio. What about rolling up all the smaller schools and pooling all these assets together? You could build a better team, and ultimately a better a portfolio. You could create a Carolina Asset Management Company within the university.' I was hooked. I called Chicago, said 'I'm not coming,' and moved to North Carolina. When Chicago called a week later and said, 'Bill Spitz changed his mind, do you want the job, I had to reply, "Sorry guys, I've got my dream job.'"

University of North Carolina at Chapel Hill   Yusko and Hooker began to work on the management company. "Michael Hooker was a visionary leader, he saw the opportunity. I embraced it and we started down the path. Eighteen months later, we were getting ready to go on a trip and he wasn't feeling well. He was diagnosed with lymphoma within days, and died within six months."

Hooker had the credibility to champion an idea unpopular with the local investment community. Yusko was not sure what to do. He received an offer to run Blackstone Alternative Asset Management. "In hindsight, it was a bad economic decision not to do it. It was $1.4 billion in assets then, $18 billion now." His wife wanted to keep the family in North Carolina and he did not want to commute to New York.

"I decided to stick it out and try to make it work and stayed for another four years; I really pressed on. About one year in, it was not going as quickly as I hoped, and Texas came calling. I was scheduled to interview there on September 12, 2001. I didn't make it because no one was flying that day. Two days later, we got the board approval for the asset management company (UNCMC), or I probably would have gone to Texas."

Over the next three years, UNCMC brought in outside assets, but Yusko felt a constant pall. With Hooker's death came turnover in the board, a new board chair, and diverging visions.

Yusko knew that his friend Lou Moelchert at the University of Richmond had been recruited by two families to manage their money. Rather than lose Moelchert, Richmond asked him to stay on and allowed him to manage the families' assets on the side. Yusko pursued a similar arrangement.

"I had told Michael Hooker I would like the opportunity to consult on the side. He said, 'You are like any other person on staff, and are entitled to a day a week. However, if you use that day, I'll fire you.' So we joked about the 'sixth-day activities,' and I had a couple of wealthy families I advised on the side."

Yusko reconnected with his friend from Notre Dame Andrew Linbeck of Salient Partners and along with his partner, Haag Sherman, they founded the Endowment Fund. Targeted to individual investors, the fund replicates a university endowment portfolio, resembling the UNC portfolio. It had $40 million in assets in April 2003. Today, it has $1.6 billion, but was just starting to grow back in 2004. "The new board chair of the management company told me, 'We would really prefer you spend all your time on UNC.' No time as an outside consultant? You can't do that seven years into the game."

Unwilling to accept the "new rules," Yusko resigned from UNCMC in spring of 2004 to form Morgan Creek Capital Management.

Outsourced CIO Leads to Morgan Creek

Although clearly influenced by Hooker's vision, his own experiences and observations convinced Yusko of the need for outsourced CIO services, leading him to start Morgan Creek Capital Management. He sees his approach as further progress in a historical series of endowment management models.

Models of Endowment Management

1. *Passive management.* The board approves consultant recommendations. Yusko says this behavior results in more traditional portfolios.
2. *Active management.* Could also be called the Yale model. Internal staff makes decisions, diversifies the portfolio to outside managers, and builds a better portfolio. This model or an attempt to implement this model is prevalent in the top endowments today.
3. *Direct management.* "The pioneering Harvard model, driven by size. Once you reach a certain size, say somewhere between $18 and $20 billion, you have to start doing things a little bit differently. They had to do direct investing."
4. *Hybrid asset management.* Model has elements of active investing, allocating to outside managers and direct investing using overlays and coinvesting tactics. So the new Morgan Creek model is essentially a hybrid of the active and direct management models.

Yusko envisions Morgan Creek as this next model of endowment management. "We don't view ourselves as a fund-of-funds, a consultant, or an adviser. We view ourselves as investors. We manage capital in concert with the client to build this better model that includes coinvesting and overweighing certain managers."

Outsourced CIO From the day he met Hooker, Yusko has championed the outsourced CIO concept practically before it had its name.

"Obviously, I staked part of my career on the outsourced CIO idea. I absolutely believe it's a durable model, because it alleviates some of the tension between the academic side of the house and the business side of the house. Whether we like it or not, universities are becoming very large businesses. Historically, they have not been very profitable, but they have been made quite profitable by the huge benefaction of donors."

Yusko uses his experience at UNC as an example, explaining how UNC had recently announced receiving a total of $2 billion in gifts for the latest capital campaign. Yusko believes that as universities become wealthier, they must show they can manage the gifts better. "If you don't, you don't raise as much money." When he started in 1998, he saw the school struggling to complete a capital campaign; today, UNC has a top endowment with excellent investment performance. "Strong investment performance helps attract billions in gifts, because people feel the university will be good stewards of their capital."

The growing demand for CIO talent may make hiring a dedicated CIO too costly for many organizations.

ON THE HARVARD MODEL AND THE CHRISTMAS HAM

"Given the recent departure of much of the Harvard Management Company team, perhaps the Harvard model cannot exist in the bureaucratic world of endowments. The reason might be found in the Christmas ham story:

"A mother, daughter, and grandmother are celebrating Christmas. The daughter begins to prepare the dinner. She cuts off a third of the Christmas ham, throws it in the trash, and puts the rest of the ham in the pan. The horrified mother asks, 'Why did you do that?' The daughter says, 'You always did it that way, why?' The mother replies, 'My mother always did it that way.' So they went out on the porch, found the grandmother in the rocking chair, and asked her, 'Why did you always chop off a third of the ham?' She replies matter-of-factly, 'because my pan was too small.'

"People do things the same way for so long nobody ever thinks to question why it's done that way. I use this word cautiously, but I actually believe it, there is a near, *near* socialistic view of the world within the world of academia. Everybody should be the same, office sizes the same square feet, titles the same, assistant professor, associate professor, full professor. Compensation has to be the same; professors can't make more than the dean; the dean can't make more than the chancellor; and the chancellor can't make more than the chancellor of the system, regardless of value added.

"They make exceptions for athletics, and they do make exceptions occasionally for superstar professors, world-beating professors, usually at the behest of a donor who endows a chair and allows them to do that. Within the rest of the organization there's so much of this near socialism, the construct of somebody being paid in excess of what other people are being paid just doesn't work.

"In the Harvard model, they paid their managers, the internal managers, roughly 4 percent of profits. When they left and started their own firms, Harvard paid 20 percent of profits and a management fee. They're spending five times as much! Jeremy Grantham is a Harvard graduate; he calculated that over the next 20 years the decision to dismantle Jack Meyer's group could cost Harvard $500 million a year. That's a pretty staggering number.

"I think there will be natural evolution over time, but I think it will be slow. Unfortunately, in my mind, bureaucratic institutions aren't truly capable of thinking like for-profit management companies. It's a shame, because that could change the nature of business."

"Today, for a small to mid-level endowment that wants to hire a CIO, the stakes have changed, higher compensation, high turnover. To get an adequate candidate, let alone a great candidate, you have to pay $1 million. For $1 million, firms like Morgan Creek and Investure give you access to a full team, decades of established relationships, access to talented managers and ideas that a single person cannot replicate. For the price of a single person, you can share a team across a lot of schools."

Yusko reiterates, "I do think the model has legs, but I think it will take a while to catch on completely. The biggest 'aha' moment hasn't happened yet. Universities have to go from thinking about their investment office as a cost center to thinking of it as a profit center."

UNC experiences illuminate the point.

"In 2002, we spun out and took in outside assets from a number of other schools in the system and a couple of other related North Carolina organizations. UNC is still managing those assets today. The growth of those outside assets was restricted to other schools within the system, even though we had inquiries from outside schools. I still get business from inquiries made to UNC."

Yusko believes that offering the services of an in-house investment group to other institutions is no different than selling any products based on intellectual property developed at the university. Examples include dry-cleaning chemicals invented by a chemistry professor, branded sports merchandise related to the athletics department, and stents developed by researchers in the medical school.

"If the school has built intellectual property in investing, why not capitalize on that? The fear, the irrational fear, is you will dilute the return to the school if you share. People don't understand that as you grow from a small base to a mid-size base, you'll get better. You can extract lower fees, have more clout in the market, can do more interesting things.

"Here's the real key: You can attract and retain better people if you have better resources and income from asset management fees. The team at Morgan Creek is two or three times bigger than my team at UNC. Most of the team I have today wouldn't have come to work at UNC because of the compensation structure. I can afford them now because of real-world fees. That's how Harvard was able to attract and retain the most talented individuals when they had the management company."

Yusko confronts his critics on the compensation issue. "It has nothing to do with money. My partners and I started Morgan Creek because we want to make what we know is a superior way to manage capital available to a broader population of individuals and smaller endowments. We know the model works. The best investors in the world are the top 40 endowments.

We decided that we could do this for some other groups of people, and it would be of great benefit to them.

"Do I get paid as much? My wife asked me once when my W2 was going to get better. I pay 30 people and invest in travel and technology. We are investing in our future. It's about the mission more than the dollars, contrary to popular belief."

BEING CHIEF INVESTMENT OFFICER

Yusko obviously cares deeply about asset management policies within endowed institutions to develop such firm and comprehensive opinions. As the CIO of Morgan Creek Capital Management, he devotes himself, with an even greater level of thoroughness and conviction, to implementing his investment process. "Conviction is what differentiates investors. If you don't have it, it is difficult to develop into a great investor."

Investment Philosophy

Yusko could not be more definitive about his philosophy. "The most important element of investment philosophy is that asset allocation drives returns. Full stop."

He presents a secondary corollary: Manager access is critically important. "Groucho Marx had a saying, 'I would never join a club that would have me as a member.' We don't want to give money to people that want our money. We want to give it to people that don't want it. We have built relationships with dozens of managers that won't take money from others but that will take it from us. We have been there since day one."

That leads to a third corollary: "In my mind, you have to be early."

He continues, "You have to be invested with people. People manage money, not institutions. It's the biggest differentiating characteristic. I don't care about the name on the door; I care about the person. It's not the name of the team; it's the name on the jersey."

For example, Yusko followed prominent investment managers such as David Diamond from the Boston Company to High Rock Capital and Lee Ainslie from Tiger to Maverick.

"You have to be early, because the best of the best won't take your money if you wait for a track record to prove that they're actually really good. If you wait too long, then you're out in the cold."

Yusko focuses on a simple set of investment guidelines:

1. *Implement a strategic investment policy.* Yusko has adopted a modernized variation of the Markowitz model "Markowitz was right and

our core philosophy is based on the framework that combining risky individual assets in one portfolio reduces the risk of the whole portfolio. Reducing risk leads us to rule number two."

2. *Remember the Roy Neuberger rule.* Others may claim credit for this rule. Yusko attributes it to legendary investor Roy Neuberger. "Rule number one, don't lose money. Rule number two, don't lose money. Rule number three, don't forget the first two rules."

3. *Aim to generate return with lower volatility.* "If equities return 11 percent historically with volatility of 16 percent, I don't have to do better than 11 percent in return. I just have to do 11 percent with less than 16 percent volatility and I will earn a greater compound return. The math is elegant, simple, and robust."

4. *Gear all activity beyond asset allocation toward managing and reducing risk and volatility in the portfolio.* "We are not so much return chasers and return enhancers as we are risk managers and volatility reducers."

5. *Focus on portfolio construction.* Yusko establishes a strategic target allocation for each asset class. He believes it even more important to establish a tactical range around each asset class, allowing them to do two things.

   a. Express a view of the asset class: Underweight or overweight the target, depending on valuation and attractiveness of the asset class.

   b. Set upper and lower limits: "Forces us to do the opposite of what human beings do. Humans buy what they wish they would have bought. Discipline off a tactical range forces you to sell into strength and buy into weakness, a simple recipe for success."

During the technology market bubble period, Yusko went through an experience that permanently convinced him of the need for upper and lower bounds.

"Everyone else was buying stock in 2000 because stocks were up so high and everyone was chasing returns. In February, we went to the board and explained that the upper range for equity was 35 percent and in the fourth quarter of 1999 we had been long and strong the market, so the portfolio exposure got close to 40 percent." When Yusko told the board it was time to sell, they wanted to know why and did not like hearing that it was the recently adopted investment policy. The board resisted and insisted on changing *policy* to *guideline*. In May 2000, Yusko convinced the board to reduce the allocation to the top range of the new guideline. At the September meeting, the board finally said, "Okay, sell everything down to the target and change *guideline* back to *policy*."

Yusko says, "It wasn't that I knew that the market was overvalued, I wasn't smarter, I wasn't a good market timer. It's the discipline that we must sell. Having that discipline is so important. I go back to my first job 'invest without emotion.'

"If you let your emotion and ego side of investing take over, you get crushed. Be unemotional and use discipline. As Yogi Berra said, 'If you don't know where you're going, you'll end up somewhere else.'

"You have to have a plan that is hard coded, that gives you flexibility to wander off the path, pick flowers along the way and then get back on the path. You can't allow yourself to wander off, get lost in the woods, and never be found again."

Asset Allocation

At the top level Yusko encourages investors to think global not local when they consider asset class valuations and attractiveness.

"There is a home market myopia that grips the bulk of investors. As if where they live is where they should invest capital. In the United Kingdom investors have more assets in U.K.-based investments, U.S. investors in U.S. assets, the same in Japan. It makes no sense, that just because you live in the United States you should have the bulk of your wealth in U.S. stocks and bonds. Absolutely insane, because you should have the bulk of assets invested where there's the best risk and return *prospectively*. You can't buy historical returns, you can only buy prospective returns.

"Where's growth today and more importantly tomorrow? It's global. Where are cheap prices? India, China, why have I been to all these places? I travel all over the world looking for investment ideas. You can't afford to be home market myopic. Where's the growth? Where's the value and where's the biggest margin of safety?"

In determining the attractiveness of asset classes, Yusko considers the source and the magnitude of the anticipated payoff and identifies three ways investors make money:

- Yield
- Earnings growth
- Multiple expansion

Because fixed income investments only deliver yield, he allocates very little to the asset class, usually about 5 percent long duration high quality bonds. He considers them a deflationary hedge, in the portfolio for disaster protection. Otherwise, he considers bonds, "certificates of confiscation."

Equity, not just stocks, but broadly defined to include real estate, commodities, public or private equity and energy, makes up the bulk of the allocation.

Yusko says, "Probably my most well-known biggest philosophical difference with contemporaries is that I don't believe alternatives such as hedge funds, private equity, real estate, are asset classes, I believe there are four asset classes:

1. Equity
2. Fixed income
3. Currencies
4. Commodities

"You have equity securities in real estate, debt securities in real estate, similarly in private equity or hedge funds. We look at a manager and ask, 'What do they do?' UNC never had an allocation to hedge funds. When I got there they had actually banned hedge funds after reading an article about 'The Death of Tiger' in 1996. Except for a small allocation to the fund led by the 'Second wealthiest living alum, Julian Robertson,' they had gotten out of most hedge funds."

So even though UNC had "no hedge funds," they did allocate assets to certain investment strategies with amazingly similar descriptions:

- Long/short equity
- Absolute return
- Opportunistic equity
- Enhanced fixed income

"When I presented it, the chancellor said to me, 'that's just nomenclature right?' I said, 'yeah' and he said, 'Good, as long as we're clear.' By the time I left we had 60 percent of assets in those four categories, but no 'hedge funds.'"

Basically, Yusko believes in integrating investment strategies into asset classes and sees no difference between alternatives and traditional. If he wants equity in the portfolio, he does not care if a good manager is long only or a hedged fund.

"If Lee Ainslie called his product 'an enhanced index fund,' he might have $50 billion instead of $12 billion. He has returned S&P + 700 basis points with half the volatility. If you buy the index you have S&P returns minus 10 basis points. He simply buys and sells stocks long and short, it's just different implementation."

All equity investments give him the same exposures whether public or private. Either way the investor legally owns common stock, preferred stock, or convertible bonds, only the liquidity differs.

Reduce Liquidity   Liquidity is overrated.

"The beautiful thing about endowments is liquidity. They don't need it. Most endowments actually have excess liquidity from bringing in more money in gifts than they spend. Foundations have to fund their 5 percent requirement annually. Some families need cash flow, some do not.

"Dollars are fungible. Whether it comes in from a gift or a distribution doesn't matter. You can move it around accounting-wise and never disrupt the underlying portfolio."

Since most endowment assets begin as a restricted gift for a specific purpose, the objective is to preserve the purchasing power of the asset by leaving the principal untouched and earning investment return greater than the inflation rate. Yusko and his team "have done the math. You are never going to be close to touching most of the assets, 90 percent you never ever touch. The endowment lasts forever. Why do you need so much of the fund in liquid investments? I don't understand."

People overestimate their liquidity needs. "If you know you're going to spend 5 percent then it's 5 percent. The chancellor's not going to come in and say it's going to be 10 percent this year. That doesn't happen. In fact, it's usually an average of the trailing three years and actual spending is more like 3.5 to 4 percent.

"One of the dirty little secrets that I hate is that institutions don't spend as much as they say, instead building big monuments to ego and bragging about the size of the endowment. The purpose of the endowment is to maximize the spending on the programs the endowment was gifted for, not to grow a large pool so you can be number 6 in the ranking rather than number 8."

Increase Illiquidity with Private Investments   Even for individual and family clients, Yusko advocates for less liquid private investments over more liquid public investments.

"We do have a higher percentage of private investments and hybrid semi-liquid investments. I joke that in a perfect world, I'd have half the money in private investments and half in a levered absolute return portfolio and I'd play a lot of golf."

Private investments outperform. "Private beats public by about 430 basis points compounded per year historically."

Endowments and individual multigenerational families should have a significant portion of assets allocated to private investments.

"The difference in endowment performance versus individual performance is the difference in liquidity. In just the last two years many schools enjoyed 200 and 400 basis points of extra returns from one stock, Google, a single venture-capital deal. The biggest difference is that illiquid investments can have huge paydays, you just don't know when, how, which one, so you need to put lots of oars in the water."

His oars today include 120 private partnerships in various stages in their lifecycle and in multiple geographic areas. Yusko disagrees with one wag who called it "di-worse-ification," and finds "the most unlikely places created the greatest return, even with lots of write-offs along the way."

He explains, "People think private investing is too risky, but most of their experience is deal by deal. 'Invest in my brother-in-law's bookstores' or a restaurant. When you're in 2,000 of them, the bad ones, like the restaurant and bookstore, go to zero and the good ones may return 200 times over."

Since endowments and wealthy families "live forever" they can take advantage of the illiquidity premium to add return. Most investors have a "finite life" and need more liquidity.

Even so, Yusko suggests individuals consider hybrid investments that are not fully private or fully public, such as private investment in public entities (PIPEs), small business investment company (SBIC) deals and other investments with longer lockups.

"You get extra return and most important, extra return per unit of risk. The risk of a diversified portfolio is very low. Any single deal is very high risk. The risk of a diversified portfolio of deals across geographies is actually quite low."

Yusko thinks coinvesting is a critically important investment tactic that will become more common over time as endowment management models evolve.

"We started that process at UNC. It was one of our most successful portfolios, very important but seemingly radical at the time. It's not radical, it's a logical extension of the work you have done to put a manager team in place. It's a way to lever up the work you have done and lever down the costs."

Start with Long-Term Themes   Yusko diverges somewhat from other CIOs by determining long-term themes and using them as the starting point for allocating assets in the portfolio. He identifies the themes driving his investment process:

- *Energy and natural resources.* Yusko bases this theme on the industrialization of China and India, noting that historically the industrialization of large regions has driven up demand and prices for commodities, energy and other resources.

- *Wealth shift from developed world to developing world.* "Similar to the shift from Europe to the United States when we were an emerging market in 1860 to 1920. Capital is in one place, cheap labor is in another." U.S. consumer spending on products made in India and China shifts wealth to those nations of savers.
- *The growth of the Asian consumer.* The bull market from 1982 to 1999 was driven by 80 million adult Baby Boomers in the United States. Yusko estimates 500 million budding middle class Asian consumers and predicts "an incredible consumptive boom, leading to world changing growth."
- *Japanese and German reflating economies.* These countries produce the tools needed in developing nations and are slowly reflating their economies after decades of stagnation.
- *Health care.* The rate of spending on health care is growing globally. In the developed world spending is on medical technology to make individual lives better. In the developing world, spending is on basic health care services and pharmaceuticals to improve the overall quality of life.
- *Defense! Defense!.* Using the "6th man" concept from basketball, the sixth of the five themes is, "Time to play defense. Every measure of risk is flashing warning, warning so it is time to get hedged and focus on absolute returns."

Yusko voices some concerns about proliferating hedge funds, but worries more about economic cycles. "Not to get too overly doomsday, but 2007 to 2010 is an interesting period, the overlap of three downward cycles, the 100-year cycle, 60-year cycle and 30-year cycle. All three hit a trough between 2007 and 2010. Our response is to try to preserve capital in what may become a very challenging environment."

Invest Directly   Morgan Creek plays defense by overweighting short-biased managers, monitoring positions and implementing overlay strategies to control exposures. "We're not trying to be a market timer, but if net exposure starts to creep up and we don't want to disrupt managers, we can take that net exposure back to where we want it."

Repeating a quote attributed to Yale's David Swensen, "Rebalancing is moving back to a target, speculation is getting away from the target," Yusko endorses overlay tactics as, "less disruptive and more cost effective way of rebalancing, it preserves relationships with managers and is less time sensitive. You don't have to wait for a committee meeting and redemption period; by then the issue may have passed."

Having the ability to implement overlay strategies and coinvest connects directly to the Morgan Creek Endowment management model. "This combination of overlay strategies and coinvesting is the next generation of asset management. We have this flexibility to be a little more proactive and actively manage the portfolio."

Idea Generation Generating ideas and finding talented managers permeates all his daily activities wherever he may be at the time.

"Your life is the investment business. You're doing it all the time, whether you're observing something at the mall with your kids, reading in a hammock, sitting at your desk. It's all feeding into your view of the world. When I travel to India and China and see the physical changes or walk through an apartment complex we helped build and see that 60 percent unlevered internal rates of return are not only possible but at the low end, you really appreciate the globalization of capital markets."

He travels extensively, considers it essential to success. "You cannot do our job from one place; you have to travel. When I started at UNC, I put travel into the budget; the CFO removed it. They never had a travel budget previously. I told him he could cut anything else, even salaries. We cannot do this business from Chapel Hill. Travel is incredibly important."

A voracious reading habit inspires ideas. "Reading everything you can get your hands on, not brokerage research reports, those are actually more contrarian, but magazines like *Popular Science* or trade magazines. I find *BusinessWeek* the best contrarian indicator with *The Economist* a close second. Lots of big picture ideas come from all over, also usually contrarian views. A headline like 'India Overheating?' makes me think they don't know what's going on over there."

Just talking to managers gets him thinking. The Morgan Creek database lists 4000 managers, they invest with 250 and count 3,000 "touches," calls, and, meetings annually. Yusko personally handles about 300 touches.

"I have the best job in the world. I get paid to talk to the smartest people in the world about investing. I have met some unbelievable people.

"Myron Scholes, Long-Term Capital Management notwithstanding, he's one of the smartest people I've ever met. Ken Griffin from Citadel is one of the top five smartest people. I had the pleasure to sit with Mr. Kim who runs Kookmin Bank, perhaps the most incredible banking manager on the planet. During the meeting, it was like talking to John Reed, the CEO of Citibank in 1996. I've been lucky to be able to use manager relationships to get in front of truly amazing people that give you great insights. Another is Hugh Sloane, one of the top five macro thinkers on the planet. He's usually 'early'(that's sometimes a euphemism for wrong), but he is always right, eventually."

Yusko and team generally find managers through referrals or from investment teams spinning out of one firm to start another. He particularly likes spinouts, because it usually means the manager has training, money, or experience from people or organizations he knows and trusts.

"Big ideas come from people we know, managers we know. We've done hundreds of spin outs, that's where you find the best ideas. We like to be early and usually are with managers for the first few years. We move on after the 'march of the Roman numerals.' Their hurdle rate and my hurdle rate diverge as they go from managing money to managing an asset management business. Managers focus on returns initially and later often realize 'I can make a lot more money gathering assets, because I have great numbers.' That becomes problematic and we tend to move on.

"We don't own a performance database. We have never screened for performance. We have never hired a manager for performance and have never fired a manager for performance. Performance is a symptom. If you have a cough, then you're already sick, you should have avoided getting sick. You can't treat the cough to get better. If you wait for the bad performance, you have already lost the money. When we work with managers, we fire for organizational change, disruption in life, big divorce, calling in rich or what I call 'Red Ferrari Syndrome.'"

Manager Selection   Yusko employs a proprietary, rigorous test to evaluate managers.

"Managers have to pass the Beer Test. If I don't want to have a beer with them after work, we'll never hire them. I don't care how smart somebody is, if they're not a good person, we won't do it."

To him, good means honest, with integrity and balance.

"I met a manager that was so busy he had to meet at the Philadelphia airport. It was the only time he could meet. About half way into the presentation he went into this long lament on his divorce. He was unhappy, sad, couldn't focus. Twenty minutes later, he said, 'but I'm always working. I have a cot in my office and sleep there three days a week.' I said, 'Maybe if you went home and spent time with your wife you wouldn't be getting divorced.' He had no balance, no idea that life wasn't just about managing his firm. I'm very big on balance."

Yusko seeks managers with competitive instincts and experience. "We want them to have been competitive at something, I don't care what, debate, violin, lacrosse, tennis, even sudoko, just to have been highly competitive at some point. Competitiveness, honesty, and integrity are killer for me."

Related to those characteristics, he says, "If people cheat on their partners, spouses or their mates, they usually cheat on their business partners, too. Perhaps not a popular thing to say, but personal life style usually enters into the equation."

Intellectual ability and pedigree also matter. Yusko relies on other organizations to identify and foster those traits and seeks managers trained by respected professionals, good judges of character or good at hiring talent. "There are so many good screening mechanisms, undergraduate schools, business school or 'Big Dog programs.' Goldman Sachs, Morgan Stanley, Bain, BCG do a great job of screening and finding the cream of the crop."

Hiring and Managing a Team Pedigree matters less when hiring team members. "It's an important difference for us. Most of the people we have hired don't have the perfect pedigree. A lot come right out of undergrad or from an investment firm."

Otherwise, Yusko values most of the same characteristics in employees that he does in managers. "Competitiveness, people that have been preselected by other good selectors of talent, we look at Morehead Scholars." Morehead is a highly coveted UNC scholarship. "I never met a Morehead that isn't incredible. They're just uniformly great. That's an easy way to screen."

A really important characteristic for all the members of the Morgan Creek team is "passion about the business. It has to be your passion, it can't just be a job, can't just be something to do. Everybody has to have a passion for making the endowment model available to other people."

Yusko purposely underpays salaries and overpays bonuses. "We run a meritocracy. The more you add the more you get. The best way to do that is a variable component on the bonus side." Employees demonstrate their commitment and drive by accepting a lower base.

"I earn a ridiculously lower base compared to my peers. I know 24-year-olds making more. I started with myself. I don't pay myself $4 million and everyone else $50,000."

He appreciates intellect, but avoids hiring academics, "They don't have the interpersonal skills and the passion for what we're doing. I hired three and all three didn't work out."

Talking about balance, Yusko tells how he picked one future superstar employee, Brad Briner, out of a pile of 200 resumes. "He was 'Greek Man of the Year'! Think about it. If a bunch of highly confident, intelligent guys voted him the best guy, how great must he have to be. Someone that can blend across multiple houses, imagine, how smart he has to be."

Yusko refers to a book entitled, *Queen Bees and Wannabes* that analyzes the social patterns of teenage girls, usually cliques dominated by one girl and "two thugs." Girls called "Transitionals" are neither. "They can play up when they have to, they can play down when they have to."

In his view every Morgan Creek employee is a "transitional" capable of bringing other people together inside and outside the organization. He values that trait because "Our job is 'Synthesizer.' It used to be, 30 years ago, that access to information was good, like Gordon Gekko. Today, information is ubiquitous. It's all about synthesis of information. You have to have broad tentacles and broad relationships and people that can talk up and talk down."

Governance   Not surprisingly, over the years Yusko has developed emphatic opinions about the best practices in foundation and endowment governance.

"Warren Buffett has it right. 'An investment committee should be an odd number and three is too many.' That's the ultimate, but you're not going to get that. What you have to have is a very strong board chair with great longevity. None of these short, two- or three-year terms. At Notre Dame the chair had been there for 18 years and when he left the new one has now been there 10 years."

Yusko believes strength and longevity of the board chair is critically important for building institutional memory. Turnover among other members of an investment committee concerns him less because it brings in fresh thinking as does generational diversity.

"Most boards are 65 year old white males. That's a shame. Best practice is to have generational diversity. There should be more members across the ages of 30 through 60 and ethnic, gender, and cultural diversity."

Contrary to standard practice, he finds investment professionals often hinder the investment process. "Boards that tend to have fewer investment professionals have done much better. Professionals are usually focused on only one area, U.S. stocks, international stocks." At one investment committee meeting, "We were looking at investing in emerging markets. A committee member that worked in U.S. equity stocks said, 'You just don't understand that everyone outside the United States is lazier than us.' How do you even respond to that?"

Board members mean well. "A lot of boards think they're doing a good job, bringing in investment professionals." In his view, doing so has led to portfolios too U.S. biased, too risk averse, and too heavy in traditional assets. "They don't have enough diversified experience in real estate or energy and tend to lean toward the classic bonds, stocks, cash portfolio."

Frequently committees view investment company employees as investment professionals. A mistake, says Yusko. "Being an administrator or an employee of a brokerage firm doesn't necessarily qualify you as an investment expert. Those experiences tend to make you too transactional and short term. One committee member worked for the stock exchange as a specialist; he would say that his idea of a long-term investment was 10 minutes." Although the specialist did not apply his professional thinking to his investment committee decisions, he thinks members with more transactional experience tend to disappoint.

On the other hand, adding certain investment professionals to the committee is a good practice. "If you bring other CIOs to the board it usually adds value. At UNC we were fortunate to have Allen Reed, the CEO of GM Asset Management. He ran all the pension money for General Motors. His son went to UNC."

Of the four steps in the investment decision-making process, Asset Allocation, Manager Selection, Portfolio Construction, and Security Selection, most endowments "outsource security selection" by hiring outside professional managers. In his Yusko's experience unfortunately, the committees use meeting time to discuss managers and securities.

"Worst practice is to spend too much time on talking about that, the best practice is to stay at the top level. Absolute best practice is to have the board focus only on asset allocation, delegate manager selection and portfolio construction to the staff, they then delegate security selection to outside managers."

He recalls participating in an investment committee meeting for a Foundation. "Four two-hour meetings a year, they basically have 8 hours a year together and oversee hundreds of millions. At one meeting they spent one hour listening to me explain my view of the world and spent the next hour debating which one of three managers to award a 3 percent mandate. What they should have been talking about is whether it should be a global mandate or emerging market. Let the consultant or staff choose the manager.

"You can't make a decision based on a pile of papers. An industry friend says, 'The only thing a board could do in 15 minutes with manager selection is make a mistake. Even if they make the right decision they will make it for wrong reason.'"

Investment Mistakes   Yusko sees investors making plenty of mistakes. Certain mistakes stand out more than others.

"The first, biggest and easiest is spending so much time on security selection and not enough time on asset allocation. Investors spend too much time on manager selection and thinking the manager is going to bail them out of a bad asset allocation."

Another investor mistake is "they always buy what they wish they would have bought. Chase the hot dot; chase performance. Because investors do not really understand where performance comes from, they tend to be backward looking."

Yusko cautions against relying on a short-term track record to decide whether to invest in a fund. Instead investors should look for managers with great long-term performance and poor short-term performance. Strategies with good short-term performance frequently soon go out of favor.

"Another common problem is thinking that you must make the money back the same way they lost it. They ride Cisco down from $100 to $8, back to $24, and think, 'If I can just get even, I'll get out.' Cisco may never go back to $100! You are better off putting the money where you'll get a good return, not waiting to validate that you made a good decision. You didn't. People won't admit to mistakes. We all make mistakes. An error is a mistake that you don't correct."

Galling him even more, "People are so addicted to sexy performance numbers, the right fad, and don't spend enough time on value investments. Investments is the only business I know that when things go on sale, everyone runs out of the store. If you can just stay in the store you can buy things really cheaply."

Most investors are wrong most of the time. "In this business if you are a legend, George Soros or Julian Robertson, you are right about 58 percent of the time. The rest aspire to be right more than 50 percent of the time. Most are right about 35 to 40 percent of the time. Historically the market averages around an 11 percent return, mutual funds average 9 percent, investors average 2 percent. If your ego can't handle being wrong or correcting mistakes, you will have lots of errors and have to live with a lot of bad performance."

LOOKING BACK AND AHEAD

Yusko respects and admires several people for educating, mentoring, inspiring and supporting him throughout his life and career. Different friends have given him advice that have helped him develop greater self-awareness that will serve him well in the next phase of his career.

Influences

"Influences, it's so easy and so awesome. I am one of the luckiest guys on the planet in that regard, absolutely incredibly lucky."

He met Jack Meyer, the former CIO of Harvard, early in his career. "He let me come up and pick his brain; has been unbelievably fantastic. I admire him very much, he meant a lot to my career."

Jeremy Grantham, the chairman of the board of investment firm GMO strongly influenced his investment philosophy. "His brilliance about simplicity of markets, how returns are derived, how value is the anchor to windward and how you have to have discipline in the approach to different markets. When I go to Boston, I can get a half hour with him, no matter what he's doing. I am very, very lucky in that regard."

Yusko appreciates the CIO network in the "college-ial" world of endowments for exchanging ideas. Others have made more personal impressions.

"My dad, a great guide and sage for me, especially because he's had some ups and downs being an entrepreneur. He's been helpful to me starting a business."

Max Chapman, the UNC board chairman instrumental in recruiting Yusko challenged and motivated him. "He believed in me. I was young, 34 years old, and he told me 'I would never hire anyone older than 35.' He was sage, tough. The relationship was like oil and water. People would ask, 'How do you get along with the hazing? All you do is fight.' He challenged me; he is a Marine. I took my kids to visit him at his Wyoming ranch, I introduced him and said, 'He was a Marine,' and he said, 'I *am* a Marine.' I had to survive the process for him to trust me and impart his wisdom."

Michael Hooker, the chancellor at UNC, profoundly influenced Yusko's life. "He taught me about the importance of vision and dedication to vision, putting it out to inspire, to follow. There's a great quote, 'the quality of the leader is measured by the quality of the followers.' Another one says, 'Look around at the four people you spend the most time with, that's which you will become.' "

Yusko adds, "How could I not include my wife? She has been my most important partner. For example, she met me after a long week of board meetings, knew I was smarting from not going to Blackstone and said, 'Just do it.' I said, 'What?' 'Just do it. I'm comfortable with the risk. Go start Morgan Creek.' She is so supportive, making it possible to be an entrepreneur."

"Little e" Entrepreneur

At UNC Yusko risked his career by questioning the authority of conformity and fighting for his Endowment management model. By forming Morgan Creek he risked his career, reputation, and livelihood to build the model he envisioned. Despite his passionate conviction about the best ways to invest, manage endowments and meet investors' needs, he never thought of himself as an entrepreneur.

"It wasn't something I viewed myself as. Other people did. An interesting self-awareness process as I transitioned from the university. I used to actually recoil when people would say, 'I'm surprised you lasted this long. You're such an entrepreneur.' I'd say, 'What do you mean? I've been in bureaucracy my whole life. How much less entrepreneurial can I be?' "

Yusko became more comfortable with the label when friends pointed out his entrepreneurial accomplishments prior to Morgan Creek like starting and growing UNCMC.

"The light bulb finally came on I was thinking of entrepreneur with a 'big E,' someone that takes a lot of technical risk. Somebody said, 'Mark, you don't understand what an entrepreneur is. Not a risk taker, an entrepreneur is a risk manager.' So I think of myself as a 'little e' entrepreneur. I take a vision and deliver products and services to people that need them. I do get that now."

He often disagreed with people that told him he was a salesman. Another friend had to sell him on being a salesman. "Somebody told me, 'Your problem is you don't understand that selling is transferring your enthusiasm to other people.' That, I can do."

Yusko understood it more when he announced his resignation from UNC. "I got an e-mail, 'Say it ain't so,' from Julian Robertson. I don't get a lot of e-mails from billionaires like Julian, so I went to see him. I thought he was going to try to talk me out of it." Yusko arrived and waited in Robertson's opulent office suite, studying a Picasso. "He comes out, puts his arm around me and says, 'I'm surprised you lasted this long and I want to work with you.' I said, you don't have to ask twice."

Robertson serves as an important mentor and inspiration to Yusko. "He had confidence in me from minute one." Robertson's support boosted his confidence in himself and convinced him that he really could build Morgan Creek. "He's been a great mentor and friend."

GETTING THE CALL

No matter what motivates him, for a man just entering mid-life, Yusko presents an outstanding career track record as an investor and entrepreneur. Like many rewarding investments, he achieved it by taking personal and professional risks and suffering losses along the way. Like Julian Robertson and other talented investors and entrepreneurs, Yusko saw a difference in the data and a need for change. He acted on that belief by starting Morgan Creek.

"One time we were in Julian's office talking about doing a deal. His assistant enters and tells him he needs to take a call. Julian picks up the phone and says, 'Yeah, yeah. Well you tell Putin that if he lets Yukos go down the tubes, there's going to be hell to pay!' He's talking to the guy in the Kremlin that's talking to Putin! I don't get those calls."

Julian Robertson retired from professional investing at age 67. Still in his early 40s, Yusko doesn't get those calls *yet*.

Summary and Analysis

Key Points on Investments, Endowment Management, and the Future

CHAPTER 16

Lessons for Investors

Investment Principles and Advice

The 12 CIO interviews relied on a consistent set of questions covering major investment topics, with flexibility to meander to related ideas and personal histories. This approach allowed us to gain insight into their personalities and intellects and to learn not just what they know about investing, but how they think about investing.

As we listened to various anecdotes on the phone, in conference rooms, even in the crowded elevator lobby of a busy midtown Manhattan hotel, we collected good, actionable, and thoughtful investment knowledge from varying perspectives of seniority, experience, interests, and personal style.

We thought it important to provide a summary of the key points for each of the main topics. The information falls into three broad categories—philosophy, governance, and specific investment themes— followed by a brief overview of future challenges and noninvestment challenges.

INVESTMENT PHILOSOPHY

The majority of the CIOs profiled share a value-oriented philosophy, including the CIO that did not have a philosophy, because "everyone wants value." Almost all follow the basic principles of an investment policy as outlined in Chapter 2. They believe in the power of a strong asset allocation policy and diversified portfolios of uncorrelated assets. Like any investor, CIOs believe in investing with quality investment managers but unlike most other investors they or their staff members spend a significant amount of time and resources conducting primary manager research. Choosing investments and finding managers involves generating ideas, networking, sourcing, and finding and forming relationships with the managers.

CIOs tend to deviate from each other in their execution of the basic principles. For instance, Don Lindsey of George Washington University (Chapter 12) and Mark Yusko of Morgan Creek Capital Management (Chapter 15) choose investments based on macro themes they develop. Others have an inclination to adopt new asset classes or ideas ahead of other investors.

Some develop ideas by taking a contrary position. In order to do this well, however, investors need to understand the current conventional wisdom and have an ability to doubt claims that "it's different this time." To successfully diverge from the herd, CIOs need a research advantage that can give them the conviction that their insights are different and better than the market's. Volatility provides contrarian investors opportunities when asset classes temporarily fall out of favor, similar to high-yield bonds in 2003.

CIOs have many different ways to differentiate themselves including their relationships with staff, investment committees and consultants and their decision-making process.

Asset Allocation

Asset allocation philosophy has evolved from being strictly top-down to being more bottom-up. The old top-down approach, characterized by feeding data on expected returns, volatilities, and correlations for each asset class into an optimizer and calculating the mean-variance optimal portfolio, has become less effective as foundations and endowments expanded their investments into alternative assets, such as hedge funds, private equity, and real assets. Optimizers struggle to handle those asset classes because the data are less reliable and the assets are less liquid. In addition, such asset classes produce such a wide return dispersion across all managers that average returns are fairly meaningless and often unattractive.

Many endowments' and foundations' allocations to alternative asset classes are affected by their abilities to execute—source, evaluate, and monitor such managers. A CIO will be unlikely to target a high allocation to an alternative asset class if he or she feels unable to hire the top managers. It is typically unattractive to have a passive allocation to most alternative asset classes.

A great example is venture capital. Many of the CIOs questioned whether venture capital was worthwhile unless they could get capacity or already were invested with one of the top handful of funds. Having an allocation based on a top-down analysis doesn't make sense with venture. If you can get an allocation to one of the top funds, you try to get as much as you can; otherwise, just say no. An allocation will be influenced by where the investment staff is finding the most and least attractive opportunities. An implication of this bottom-up approach is that smaller, more thinly staffed institutions should necessarily have smaller allocations to alternative assets.

Dynamic Asset-Class Definitions Asset-class definitions are becoming increasingly interesting and creative as investors try to better understand the risk and return characteristics shared by certain assets. While some institutions remain relatively traditional in their asset-class definitions and allocations, others are looking to break the mold by either bucketing investments differently and more aggressively from the norm or throwing out asset-class definitions altogether.

One method has been to migrate from allocating to buckets defined by their capital markets function, such as equities or fixed income, to allocating to buckets defined by underlying risk characteristics. This change is driven by a move to redefine risk away from being merely portfolio volatility. Volatility is a less useful measure of the risk for many alternative assets due to the lack of market pricing. *Risk* is better defined in terms of downside risk (allows for fat-tailed return distributions, which are often due to leverage), liquidity risk, and complexity risk for these assets.

Asset-class lines are blurring; definitions are converging. The most interesting asset-class opportunities are "tweeners": investments having characteristics of private equity, hedge funds, and real assets.

Certain CIOs take matters into their own hands and advocate adding value using tactical asset allocation, often implemented with the use of overlays. Lindsey does that another way. An asset-class agnostic, he finds managers to execute his themes and allows them to make the asset-class decision.

Manager Selection

All CIOs interviewed spend much of their time thinking about how best to source, evaluate, and monitor external investment managers. Although there are quantitative inputs, most rely on qualitative factors and their sense of pattern recognition when evaluating and selecting managers. CIOs tend to prefer managers with a focused investment strategy, concentrated portfolios, a good pedigree, and a stable team.

Personal Qualities Every CIO mentioned that the personal qualities—good values and trustworthiness—of the manager are as important as their investment abilities. Ideally, the managers function as partners, not just for investment returns but for new investment ideas. Communicative and transparent managers help a CIO spot and respond to trends. Several

CIOs mentioned traits like passion, hunger, a good culture, and energy as important in the investment management firms they hire.

Edge Managers must have an identifiable edge or advantage in their strategy that will allow them to repeat their past performance success. Edge can be defined as a distinctive ability to source ideas or identify opportunities that just aren't apparent or available to others (i.e., unique information edge or information processing edge). Alternatively, the edge might involve an ability to add value to the underlying assets (e.g., activist public equity, private equity, and real estate opportunity fund managers). What is important is that this unique ability is sustainable—that the manager recognizes his or her niche and is invested in maintaining that edge.

Transparency As noted above, transparency is important. CIOs appreciate managers who can be partners in exchanging investment ideas, but even more importantly, they realize that they are accountable for their decisions and, by definition, the investment decisions of the managers with whom they invest. Most shy away from "black-box" strategies where the return-generating process is opaque to the end investor. The CIO must understand the strategy so he or she is able to defend it during the inevitable periods of short-term underperformance.

Capacity Since many of these CIOs are looking for and hence competing to invest with some of the same investment managers, access to managers with limited capacity is an issue. This is particularly true with smaller private equity (e.g., venture capital) and hedge funds. As a result, CIOs will often spend years developing relationships with managers with whom they would like to invest. Furthermore, many consider managers they know from previous firms or managers spinning off from a larger firm a great way to invest in a familiar group while gaining capacity for being early. Accordingly, CIOs tend not to discuss their investment managers.

Performance CIOs cautioned investors to resist the urge to "chase performance" and invest in managers with recent good performance. They believe a fund on a hot streak is frequently close to having a reversal. If they have spent the time and resources to identify and hire a good investment manager, they will tend to wait out poor performance and find a way to help and advise the manager through rough periods. To do that, an institutional CIO needs to have fortitude and to be able to keep the investment committee or board comfortable with the decision.

Fees Most CIOs are sensitive to principal-agent problems inherent with external fund management structures and fees. They seek a proper alignment of incentives with their external investment funds, a desire for managers to make money only when they make money. One way to address this issue is if the manager invests a substantial portion of his or her own money alongside the endowment or foundation, so that they share in both the upside and the downside of the strategy.

However, the tactics managers employ to make money despite producing poor returns is a growing issue. For example, a 1.5 percent management fee on a $20 billion fund generates $300 million in fees to the manager before they add on any incentive or performance fee. If the $20 billion is locked up for an extended period of time (either a long-term hedge fund lockup or a private equity fund that is locked up until the private investments are liquidated), then the manager can earn this attractive management fee for a number of years, regardless of the quality of the returns.

The challenge for endowments and foundations is that the flood of capital into alternative investment strategies has given good managers leverage for setting their terms, including fees and lockups. One CIO warned strongly that the imbalance between investors and managers with egregious lockups gives the managers too much power and hurts foundations in particular because they have more liquidity needs. Any manager with a long lockup that experiences poor performance could hold endowment and foundation money hostage for a long time. The same CIO mentioned a corollary phenomenon called "fee creep." Managers that historically paid for certain expense from their general partnership are now charging those expenses back to the funds, meaning that investors can be paying a management fee, incentive fee, and expenses.

The business of an investment manager concerns CIOs, too. If the manager decides to grow their business and "gather assets," performance can suffer from dilution as well as the manager's taking their eye off the ball and focusing on growth rather than investment performance. The flip side of this problem is that small highly sought-after funds often offer allocations that are not meaningful for many investors. This has happened most frequently in venture capital, causing investors to question whether they should spend the time and effort to evaluate such investments if the payoffs are insignificant.

Internal Management

Several CIOs speak to the advantages of internal and direct investing as a complement to external investment management. Managing money in-house provides valuable benefits aside from the obvious fee savings. The opportunity to invest directly helps the investment staff stay closer to market trends and become more engaged with the external investment managers.

Internal investment management is likely to include managing fixed-income portfolios, coinvesting with private equity managers, and managing an overlay portfolio in order to quickly and inexpensively implement tactical asset allocation tilts.

GOVERNANCE

CIOs share a conviction that good governance and a professional staff-driven investment process is necessary for good investment results. The old model with an active investment committee and a consultant working together to derive an asset allocation policy and choose investment managers no longer works. Often, investment decisions are based on the investment committee's receiving a one-hour "final" presentation from an investment manager. Board members may be great investors, but their institution will struggle to perform over long periods of time unless they can muster the resources to research and monitor the institution's investments.

The best approach includes having a professional investment staff actively sourcing and evaluating investment themes and managers, perhaps requiring final approval by the investment committee. Along with having an internal investment team, a disciplined yet flexible process that allows for independent, quick decision making is instrumental. A strong professional staff led by a CIO and better governance have been shown to contribute to the higher returns of larger endowments.

Although the larger institutions have had more resources and staff, many of the CIOs worry about continuing to find and retain staff capable of managing the more complex portfolios. They struggle to compete with the financial incentives being offered by investment funds. While staff turnover among endowment and foundation investment offices is growing, the benefits of staff retention and stability are clear. It's no coincidence that some of the top performing institutions have had the same CIO and senior staff building and managing their investment programs over 10 to 20 years, including Harvard, MIT, Notre Dame, and Yale.

INVESTMENT THEMES

The most common theme being considered is the globalization of investment opportunities. Three sub-themes include the growth in Asia, growth in all emerging economies and the recovery of Japan and Germany. Everyone is aware of the tremendous opportunity presented by the 10 percent gross domestic product growth in China and India. Although this economic growth has attracted nearly everyone's attention, concern about governance and country risk has caused some investors to seek investments that capitalize on this theme indirectly, not investing in these countries. Emerging-market growth is related to another theme mentioned by several CIOs: a continuing supply/demand imbalance in energy and other natural resources.

Almost every CIO discussed his or her concern about risk and low-risk premia being offered across all asset classes. Low-risk premia inevitably lead to panics triggered by an unanticipated shock, but such situations can create investment opportunities for those with fortitude and long time horizons. No asset classes are cheap or mispriced right now. However, some CIOs mentioned that credit seems very overvalued, which could lead to opportunities to short or underweight this asset class and wait for an event that could lead to another interesting round of high-yield and distressed opportunities, similar to 2003.

FUTURE CHALLENGES

The long-term investment success of the large endowments and foundations has only made it more challenging to achieve the same results in the years ahead.

These institutions have been pioneers: over the past 30 years they were first to invest in venture capital, hedge funds, international public equity, emerging-market debt, and timber. Consistent with economists' models of a market economy, high profits attract additional capital, which leads to lower profits over the long run. Attractive returns of large endowments and foundations have motivated other investors to look for the "secret sauce," which has led to a flood of capital into alternative assets, necessarily depressing future returns.

Future investment success of endowments and foundations will require looking for the next unexploited asset class or subasset class. This will inevitably lead investors to look at ever more unusual and global opportunities. More opportunities to add value will come from finding investments that will capitalize on themes mentioned above and looking for investment managers who are either new or unknown to the institutional investment world because they are local to other countries and hence under the radar of U.S. investors.

A few CIOs question whether investing in a seventh or eighth asset class will add any real value. Industry consultants have suggested that institutional investors may be stretching too far in new asset classes or new countries to find unique investments. They argue that new asset classes are often too small to be a sizeable allocation. Therefore, even if the asset performs well, it may not have a meaningful impact on overall portfolio performance. Others suggest that the next thing that has to happen is the creation of value through entrepreneurial and activist strategies.

Despite these challenges, nobody is willing to settle for being average. Time will tell whether endowment and foundation investors will maintain their institutional investing edge.

Foundations and endowments will most likely retain their investment edge. Maintaining their institutional edge will become the challenge. After investments, having the resources to compete, find good investments, and grow the endowment occupied investors' minds. If not discussing money or resources within their own institution, they talked about the outsourced CIO and other evolving models of endowment management.

Managing an endowment successfully will be about managing the money not just in the form of the investments, but in the form of a business. Managing endowment assets has become an enterprise even when the investment office remains under the roof of a nonprofit institution. Its roof doesn't matter, what matters is that it's managed professionally. In Chapter 11, Bob Boldt tells the story of how he accomplished that at UTIMCO.

The 12 CIOs shared great ideas and insights into investing, but to understand their role completely, it will be useful to review the business issues they face that will impact their investing style and their institutions for years to come.

CHAPTER 17

The Business of Foundation and Endowment Investment Management

Impact of Comparison, Competition, and Compensation

A more complex and challenging investment environment has made managing an investment office more complicated. A number of chief investment officers (CIOs) had traveled extensively in Asia, India, and South America, among other emerging-market countries to seek out investment opportunities, and some actively discussed opening investment offices and having employees in foreign countries.

Bottom line: Just the anecdotal evidence of the international challenges proves that the future of foundation and endowment asset management lies in the bottom line. Can CIOs and institutions manage an enterprise that is having a more difficult time accomplishing its main objective, generating investment returns? Can they successfully manage assets while administering a global organization that has become more expensive to operate? In a way, the CIOs of the largest foundations and endowments have started to become de facto chief executive officers (CEOs) of global investment boutiques.

Basically, what will drive endowments going forward is the money, not just how well they manage it, but how well they deal with business issues such as rising costs, increased competition among institutions for talented managers, quality funds with capacity, and qualified staff.

Each CIO touched on at least one of the underlying business issues impacting endowment management. Comparison, competition, and compensation chase each other in a vicious circle, each element feeding the next.

COMPARISON

In Chapter 8, Bill Spitz from Vanderbilt described the point in his tenure at Vanderbilt when he asked for an incentive compensation plan. As CIOs have become savvier about their market value, similar to what happened with Spitz, boards and investment committees have structured more complicated packages with benchmarks. Many programs include a metric for performance relative to peer institutions. The majority of CIOs that spoke on the subject felt strongly that peer comparison as a benchmark of investment performance was an inappropriate and unfair measure.

COMPETITION

Being compared to peers has pushed CIOs to compete against other CIOs for good investments and has led to the individuals within the community becoming more secretive and less willing to share ideas and information. Ellen Shuman of the Carnegie Corporation (Chapter 9) noted that it had made the group less collegial (more like a business) but recognized it as a reality of incentive compensation based on peer comparison. Allan Bufferd of MIT (Chapter 5) put it another way, saying that more people getting paid to outperform each other in asset classes with diminishing returns could lead to "sharp elbows" being thrown around.

Shuman predicted this compensation structure would lead CIOs to imitate and perform in line with each other, but that it could negatively impact everyone's returns.

Institutional rivalries have also affected the competition between endowments. Endowment size has become one of many metrics used to keep score among these institutions. To compete against other institutions, investment offices want better investment performance, so they must hire talented investment staff. Qualified people have seen demand for their services rise; therefore, so has their compensation.

COMPENSATION

The current market for investment professionals is tighter than ever, making building an internal investment office more difficult. Endowments and foundations of all sizes are finding it harder to find and retain investment professionals of all experience levels, and in particular, professionals with alternative asset experience. Spitz expressed concern that a continued rise in compensation could attract Internal Revenue Service (IRS) scrutiny. Other experts have voiced worries that incentive compensation could lead CIOs to take inappropriate portfolio risks such as adding leverage.

Even though the market for investment professionals is tight, international institutions are forming investment offices and entering the competition for the harder-to-find investment opportunities. Within the space of two months in early 2007, Cambridge University and Oxford University each hired their first CIOs.

Sandra Robertson joined Oxford, an endowment worth approximately 900 million pounds, from the Wellcome Trust. A colleague at the trust, Mark Walport, was quoted in the news release as saying, "U.K. universities have lagged far behind their U.S. counterparts in the size and quality of management of their endowments. It is important that U.K. universities enhance their endowments as an additional funding source to keep them in the forefront of education, scholarship and research." Cambridge University hired Nick Cavalla, the CIO of Man Global Strategies, a leading alternative asset management firm, to run its 1.2 billion-pound endowment. Yale CIO David Swensen serves on the investment board of the university and participated in the hiring decision. Bufferd had predicted that more universities globally will prepare to compete for investment return. These high profile, prestigious hires indicate it has begun to happen.

MANAGEMENT MODELS

Many institutions have opted for or are considering outsourcing their investment office to one of several investment firms, typically run by former foundation or endowment CIOs—the concept of the "outsourced CIO." Ironically, in 1969 when McGeorge Bundy set the wheels in motion to change laws regarding the management of nonprofit institution assets, most endowments were run by a single management firm or a bank trust. When Alice Handy joined the University of Virginia in 1974, the institution was in the process of taking their $30 million endowment from one equity manager and dividing it among three managers. The outsourced CIO model, with Alice Handy's firm, Investure, being one of the first, is a leap back to the past, in which one outside investment firm manages the entire portfolio. The primary difference is the complexity of managing large allocations of alternative assets by the external organization.

For the most part the CIOs profiled see the merits of the outsourced model given the challenges that even large endowments and foundations face in sourcing, evaluating, and monitoring opportunities in distance countries or complicated alternative strategies here in the United States.

The CIOs interviewed in this book brought up issues about administering and managing endowments that will continue to impact their ability to be effective on the job and could argue for an outsourced CIO. Competing for investment talent has gotten tougher and more expensive. Rising compensation and demand for investors with alternatives experience has led to high turnover. Economies of scale makes the outsourced model a compelling idea—getting higher-caliber investment talent for the same or lower price relative to building an in-house investment team may be attractive. Even so, the advice they would give smaller foundations and endowments varied.

Can Smaller Institutions Have an Edge?

We chronicled one small institution, the Kaiser Foundation, which was smart and fortunate enough to attract and retain their CIO, Bruce Madding, for a number of years. They have generated attractive returns to support the mission of the institution. In addition to having low staff turnover and a clever approach to managing a small staff, they have capitalized on their edge of being located on Sand Hill Road in Silicon Valley, investing in local real estate and obtaining access to a number of the successful local venture capital fund. Other investors also mentioned that they use the mission of their institution as an edge in getting access to top managers, using alumni connections or finding top-tier managers that are interested in the mission of a foundation.

Investment Committee   Another edge of some institutional investors is their investment committee. A small endowment or foundation may lack the staff resources of larger institutions, but may still succeed if the investment committee has successful investment professionals who have a lot of time to devote to the institution, few members, an agile decision-making process, members with top-tier investment manager relationships and infrequent turnover. Kenyon College is a small liberal arts college in Ohio with an endowment under $200 million. They were recently highlighted in a January 31, 2007 *FundFire* article written by Jay Cooper, as being a small institution that has successfully increased their allocation to alternative assets. Their 10-year return as of June 2006 was comparable to the average returns for large endowments, being over 200 basis points above returns of similar-sized institutions. Part of their success is attributable to having a strong investment committee, which currently includes one of our interviewees, Bill Spitz, CIO of Vanderbilt University.

Tapping Younger Talent   Institutions may supplement their strong committee-driven investment process with a small, less experienced investment staff, allowing the talented but younger investment staff a chance to mentor under the experienced investment committee. Scott Malpass advocates that smaller institutions adopt this approach. He is the model of this approach working successfully, being hired as Notre Dame's CIO when he was 26 years old. By networking, the institution can slowly build up relationships and a strong portfolio, and as the institution grows, build up the internal resources slowly over time. Scott has successfully built a team of largely Notre Dame alumni, who are devoted to the mission of the school.

Outsourced CIO

Should small institutions outsource? It depends. Again, an institution must understand its edge. If the institution has no edge, then it should either outsource or implement a simple passive strategy. Many institutions have no business trying to invest in alternative assets just because the larger institutions have been successful harvesting the seeds they sowed by starting alternative asset programs in the 1980s and 1990s. Smaller institutions should implement an in-house "endowment approach to investing" profiled in this book only if they have the ability to build a strong and deep internal team or have a uniquely strong investment committee with characteristics noted above. They need to have an edge to compete with the better-endowed institutions.

Otherwise, the institution should either outsource or implement a low-cost passive approach. The passive approach would combine a long-term asset allocation across traditional asset classes (including real assets, which can be accessed through real estate investment trusts, inflation-indexed bonds, and passive commodity funds), disciplined rebalancing and investing in low-cost index funds. Outsourcing could involve partial or full outsourcing. The benefit of full outsourcing is that so many of the interesting ideas don't fit neatly in private equity or hedge funds. A total outsourcing fund's ability to construct a best-ideas fund-of-funds across all asset classes is essentially the approach undertaken by the large endowments and foundations, making it more attractive than an individual asset-class fund-of-funds (e.g., hedge fund-of-funds).

The most telling comment in support of outsourcing came from Bruce Madding of Kaiser, with $600 million in assets, who said, "If it weren't my job, I'd recommend outsourcing it." Madding noted, however, that his 18 years' experience running the foundation made him a well-known and connected investor, which added value to his organization. For a similar reason, Scott Malpass of Notre Dame argued that the outsourced model disconnected endowment management from the mission of the organization. He believes they need to remain entwined and institutions lose institutional memory and important relationships by outsourcing the CIO function.

Should small institutions outsource? Allan Bufferd argued that it depends on the institution, its goals, its mission, and the objectives for the payout from the endowment. He cautioned fiduciaries against thinking that outsourcing allows them to outsource their fiduciary duty—it does not.

THE BOTTOM LINE

In the past 40 years, endowment and foundation investment management offices have evolved from poorhouses to powerhouses. Now these organizations and their talented CIOs face the challenge of managing global enterprises in an increasingly complex investment environment. Smaller institutions are at a growing disadvantage in this environment unless they can build and retain an investment staff. Otherwise, they will be forced to choose between a less complex portfolio and introducing some element of outsourcing. Either way, CIOs and institutions will be managing organizations that are starting to look more like global investment management boutiques.

CHAPTER **18**

Real Rewards

Investing is a People Business

The investment professionals profiled in this book have contributed enormously to the financial health of their respective institutions. These accomplished individuals represented a wide range of institutions (endowments and foundations ranging from under $1 billion to over $20 billion), experience, backgrounds and personalities. In all instances, the subjects share a passionate and intellectual interest in investing, combined with a desire to serve and add value to the nonprofit sector.

This book confirmed my belief in the value of talking to and learning from other investors. I knew from my informal survey of other institutions nearly three years ago that a number of endowment and foundation chief investment officers (CIOs) had been pioneers in their approaches to investment philosophy, governance, and strategies. A collegial group, they maintain collaborative relationships by participating in industry forums such as NMS Management and Global Absolute Return Congress (ARC), and have much to offer the broader investment community. I thought that other institutional and individual investors might also be interested in and benefit from the insights of some of these great CIOs.

My first observation is that they are all likeable people. They passed the "type of person you'd want to have a beer with" test. Second, it was clear there is no set pattern or career path required to be a successful endowment or foundation CIO. Many CIOs have a background in finance, but others in liberal arts; some are quantitative and others are more intuitive in their abilities to evaluate investment opportunities. However, they all view their position as more than a job—they love investing and are dedicated to the mission of their institutions. A final observation is that all like to travel and share ideas. Everyone said that to be a successful investor, one must hit the road and meet people to develop and research investment ideas. Nobody felt they could do their job from their office and still generate attractive returns in this increasingly competitive world.

FINAL THOUGHT

When we set out to write this book, we believed the investment insights of these CIOs would prove valuable to many types of investors. We believe we were correct. But at the same time, we learned that even the same type of investors have very different needs and goals.

Institutions such as corporate and public pension plans are confronting the same issues faced by endowments and foundations, but face others that are unique to them. Like endowments and foundations, there are a number of talented pension CIOs who have long track records and interesting approaches to investing. Now that we know how much we can learn from interviewing different types of investors, we look forward to spending time next year meeting them and hearing their investment insights.

This project wouldn't have been possible without the tireless efforts of Cathleen Rittereiser, who kept it moving while we both performed our day jobs, Cathleen's being VP of marketing at Alternative Asset Managers. She was clearly the more important coauthor. I think we both learned a lot writing this book and although we often sit on "opposite sides of the table" (client versus manager), we were literally on the same page with the new insights we gained from these CIOs. We both felt lucky to hear their stories during this project and look forward to learning more from them in the future.

Notes

CHAPTER 1   The Evolution of Foundation and Endowment Investment Management

1. www.treasury.duke.edu/endowment/administration/overview.html.
2. www.hno.harvard.edu/guide/finance/index.html.
3. www.lib.duke.edu/archives/history/durhams_bid.html.
4. Dale, Harvey P. 2006. "Prudence Perverted: Politics, Perceptions and Pressures," draft. Sourced at www.tiff.org, pp. 1–11.
5. Ibid.
6. Murray, Roger F. 1996. "The Formative Years: A Founder Reflects," pp. 10–16, and Keane, George F., 1996. "A Brief History: A Dream Fulfilled," pp. 20–38, in *The Commonfund, A Common Vision: Working in Partnership for the Benefit of All*. The Twenty-fifth Anniversary of the Commonfund.
7. Yoder, J. 2004. *Endowment Management: A Practical Guide*. Washington, DC: Association of Governing Boards of Universities and Colleges, p. 8.
8. See note 6.
9. Keane, p. 26.
10. National Conference of Commissioners on Uniform State Laws, 211 E. Ontario Street, Suite 1300, Chicago, Illinois 60611, www.nccusl.org/Update/uniformact_summaries/uniformacts-s-umoifa.asp.
11. Wingred, Daniel, Lyn Hutton, James McDiarmid, Victor E. McGee, J. Peter Williamson. 1993. *Commonfund: The Growth of College Endowments, 1960–1990*. Commonfund Press, Introduction, Chapter 7, 7-1.
12. Siegel, Laurence. 2003. *Benchmarks and Investment Management*. The Research Foundation of AIMR, pp. 34–35.
13. Light, Jay O. 1996. "Five Trends that Transformed Institutional Asset Management," *The Commonfund, A Common Vision: Working in Partnership for the Benefit of All*. The Twenty-fifth Anniversary of the Commonfund, pp. 80–88.
14. Lascell, David M., 1996. "Changing Nature of Trusteeship," *The Commonfund, A Common Vision: Working in Partnership for the Benefit of All*. The Twenty-fifth Anniversary of The Commonfund, pp. 80–88.
15. Clarke, Teresa H., Rumi Malott, and Neil Mehrotra. 2005. "Critical Issues in Endowment Management," Global Markets Institute (GMI) at Goldman Sachs, University Endowment Summit Conference Proceedings; www.gs.com/gmi, January 26.
16. See note 14.
17. 2005 NACUBO Endowment Study Information; Press Announcement, January 23, 2006, www.nacubo.org/x7616.xml.

18. Foundation Center Statistics, http://foundationcenter.org/findfunders/statistics/listing01.html.
19. "The State of Foundation Giving 2006," excerpted from *Foundation Yearbook, 2006*. The Foundation Center, www.foundationcenter.org/gainknowledge/research/pdf/fy2006ch1.pdf.
20. McNamee, M. 2005. "Who Calls the Shots," NACUBO Business Officer, October , www.nacubo.org/x6789.xml.
21. See note 15.

CHAPTER 2   Foundation and Endowment Investing 101

1. Yoder, J. 2004. *Endowment Management: A Practical Guide*. Washington, DC: Association of Governing Boards of Universities and Colleges, p. 9.
2. *Prudent Investment Practices: A Handbook for Investment Fiduciaries*. Foundation for Fiduciary Studies, 2004.
3. Ibid., p. 8.
4. Giftlaw.com, Chapter 7, Section 7.2, "Classification as Private Foundation," www.giftlaw.com/glawpro.jsp?WebID = GL2004-0655.
5. Fidelity Charitable Investments. "Charitable Planning and Tools, Regulation and Compliance," www.fidelitycharitableservices.com/charity-giving-help/foundation/compliance.shtml.
6. Giftlaw.com, Chapter 7, Section 7.2.3, "Minimum and Qualifying Distributions," www.giftlaw.com/glawpro.jsp?WebID = GL2004-0655.
7. GiftLaw.com; Chapter 7, Section 7.2.7, "Tax on Net Investment Income," www.giftlaw.com/glawpro.jsp?WebID = GL2004-0655.
8. Commonfund Benchmarks Study® of Foundations, July 8, 2003, Commonfund Institute.
9. Fidelity Charitable Investments, "Charitable Planning and Tools, Regulation and Compliance," www.fidelitycharitableservices.com/charity-giving-help/foundation/compliance.shtml.
10. GiftLaw.com, Chapter 7, Section 7.2, "Classification as Private Foundation," www.giftlaw.com/glawpro.jsp?WebID = GL2004-0655.
11. Griswold, John. 2006. "Principles of Non-Profit Management." Commonfund.
12. Warner, Timothy R., "Intergenerational Inequity?" www.educause.edu/ir/library/pdf/ffl0605.pdf.
13. Tokat, Yesim PhD, "The Asset Allocation Debate: Provocative Questions, Enduring Realities" The Vanguard Group, Investment Counseling and Research Analysis. April 2005.
14. Yoder, p. 95.
15. Griswold, p. 25.
16. Yoder, p. 50.
17. Clarke, Teresa H., Rumi Malott, and Neil Mehrotra. 2005. "Critical Issues in Endowment Management," Global Markets Institute (GMI) at Goldman Sachs, University Endowment Summit Conference Proceedings, www.gs.com/gmi, January 26.

CHAPTER 3   The Investment Landscape

1. Kaplan, S., and A. Schoar. 2003. "Private Equity Performance Returns, Persistence and Capital," NBER working papers 9807. National Bureau of Economic Research, June, www.nber.org/papers/w9807.
2. Lerner, J., A. Schoar, and W. Wong. 2005. "Smart Institutions, Foolish Choices? The Limited Partner Performance Puzzle," NBER working paper 11136. National Bureau of Economic Research, February, www.nber.org/papers/w11136.

CHAPTER 9   Investment Artist with Her Own Perspective

1. "Serving the Legacy of Andrew Carnegie: Investing for the Long Term," *The Carnegie Reporter*, Spring 2006, www.carnegie.org.

Index